The Reign of the Theatrical Director

The Reign of the Theatrical Director

French Theatre: 1887-1924

by

Bettina L. Knapp

The Whitston Publishing Company
Troy, New York
1988

My thanks to the Research Foundation of the City University of New York for the grant awarded me to complete the work on *The Reign of the Theatrical Director. French Theatre 1887-1924.*

To the Bibliothèque Nationale, Département des arts du spectacle, Bibliothèque de l'Arsenal in Paris, goes my gratitude for the wealth of information on French theatre they put at my disposal. To Artists Rights Society, Inc. my appreciation for allowing me to print some of the photographs included in this volume.

To Alba Amoia, my thanksgiving for her guidance, knowledge, and friendship, so helpful in the preparation of this manuscript.

List of Illustrations

Contents

Introduction

1887: the founding of the Théâtre-Libre by André Antoine; 1893: the birth of Aurélien Lugné-Poë's Théâtre de l'Oeuvre; 1913: the coming into being of Jacques Copeau's Théâtre du Vieux-Colombier.

Three memorable dates in the history of the performing arts. Three noteworthy theatres on whose stages France and the world were to witness not only innovative theatrical performances, but also the beginnings of the *reign of the theatrical director!* There had been, to be sure, directors of all types throughout the centuries in France. Molière, for example, was the greatest of them all. But since his time few French directors had captured the attention of dramatists, performers, and the *tout Paris;* still fewer had created styles of their own, bringing fresh insights into the performance of multiple genres of international scope. Antoine enlarged the ideals, mission, and function of the theatrical director; so, too, did Lugné-Poë, and Copeau. The three were the inspirational forces and the teachers of many successful twentieth-century French directors, such as Charles Dullin, Louis Jouvet, Gaston Baty, Sacha and Ludmilla Pitoëff, Antonin Artaud, Jean-Louis Barrault, Jean Vilar, Roger Blin, Roger Planchon, and others.

The year Antoine founded the Théâtre Libre (1887) fell seventeen years after the excoriating Franco-Prussian War, which concluded with victory for the Germans and humiliation and suffering for the French. "It isn't a war alone," Zola wrote, "it is the collapse of a dynasty, the breakdown of an epoch." The military debacle did not put an end to the misfortunes hovering over France. The harrowing events suffered during the Civil War which followed aggravated an already bad situation. Riots broke out. Fighting between the Communards, the proletarian government group occupying the Hôtel de Ville, and Thiers' government, which resided at Versailles, was vicious. In May 1871 fifteen thousand people were executed. The Tuileries Palace, the City Hall, and the Cour des Comptes were burned.

Eight years later, 1878, saw dancing in the streets, festivities of all sorts—delirium—as President Mac-Mahon inaugurated the World's Fair. Paris had emerged from the nightmare of war to become the City of Lights. Steam engines, giant balloons, and phonographs, delighted a fin-de-siècle society.

France mourned the death of one of its most celebrated and beloved poets in 1885: Victor Hugo. It also marked Pasteur's cure of the shepherd Jupille. A year later, political strife was again evident: the Minister of War, General Boulanger, attempted a coup d'état which failed; his dictatorial ways frightened many Republicans.

Pessimism, however, soon gave way to singing and festivities of all sorts. The Café-Concerts were thriving. Paulus bellowed out his famous song, *Returning from the Review*; Yvette Guilbert (the celebrated diseuse with the long black gloves whom Toulouse-Lautrec immortalized in his lithographs and about whom Edmond de Goncourt had remarked, "a pot pourri of present day Parisianisms blended with that ancient mischievous Panurgian language") captured the heart of audiences. Aristide Bruant, wearing the black cape, sombrero, and red scarf made famous by Toulouse-Lautrec in his drawing of the chansonnier, opened his *Mirliton* to songs about the wretched, the sick, the pariahs of this earth.

Theatre, however, had reached a new low. Commercial, banal, bathetic dramas dominated. Nor was Antoine the first to advocate innovations in the performing arts. Years earlier, in 1822, Stendhal had attempted to usher in reforms with the publication of his pamphlet, *Racine and Shakespeare*. He condemned the drama of his day with its posed, studied, and hackneyed verses and its utter obeisance to outworn seventeenth-century classical rules that called for the alexandrin, twelve syllable verse, which he labeled humorously a *cache-sottise*. If a new and dynamic theatre is to come into being, he argued, drama should deal with vital and actual events. Victor Hugo's ground-breaking *Preface to Cromwell* (1927) called for the abolishment of the classical unities of time, place, and action. In his *Hernani* (1830) and *Marion de Lorme* (1831), inspired by Shakespeare and the German romantics, Hugo proclaimed the right of free expression on stage and the mixing of genres—ideas that were considered revolutionary for his time.

Melodrama, performed on the Boulevard du Crime—an appelation given to 'theatre row' where so many plays were performed in which villains attempted to murder young, beautiful, and virginal girls—kept audiences on the edge of their seats. Pixerécourt, "the King of Melodrama" and author of such thrillers as *Plague in Marseille* and *Earthquake in Pompeii*, was forever dramatizing the struggle between the forces of Good over those of Evil. Although the incidents in his dramas were exaggerated, the characters artificially manufactured, the acting declamatory and pompous, and pathos arbitrarily provoked, Pixerécourt was a master at evoking dread. What intrigued Antoine about his plays and melodrama in general were the complex stage machinery and sets used for their productions. Its authors, Antoine remarked, were interested in re-creating a real milieu. Unlike most commercial theatres, which paid little heed to the historical veracity of sets—whether a play took place in ancient or the contemporary times—decors were created to suit the fancy of the designers, with frequently outlandish results.

Popular, as well, during the melodramatic and romantic nineteenth-century, were the historical dramas of Alexandre Dumas: *Henri III and His Court* (1829). Emphasis was placed on creating local color. Sound effects and *coups de théâtre* were the *sine qua non* of such works: thunderclaps, fires and floods, frenetic activity. For the most part the characterizations were superficial. Dumas' *Antony* (1831), one of the most popular works of the period, set the stage for the first of a series of plays dealing with a triangle situation and the tragic death of the virtuous romantic hero.

The lot of the martyred poet struggling in vain to make a name for himself in a cruel and heartless world was the theme of Alfred de Vigny's *Chatterton* (1835). Although highly emotional, *feelings* are lived inwardly in Vigny's plays—not flamboyantly as is the case of other romantic dramatists of the time. Vigny's works revolve around social and philosophical problems in what has been alluded to as a *drama of thought*.

The greatest of the nineteenth-century playwrights was Alfred de Musset. Although a romantic by temperament, he created original and iconoclastic works, fired by his vibrant imagination and his delicate sensibilities. Inspiration and not constraint ruled his world; so he was unhampered by dramatic rules and regulations save those which suited his fancy. Understandably, then, such works as *The Caprices of Marianne* (1833), *Fantasio* (1833), and *Lorenzaccio* (1834), were ahead of their times—and were badly received. Only years later did audiences understand Musset's genius.

Tragedies of the well-worn classical vintage were also staples drawing faithful Parisian audiences: Casimir Delavigne's *Edouard's Children* (1833), Louis-Jean Népomucène Lemercier's *Frédegonde and Brunehaut* (1821).

Eugène Scribe was perhaps the most popular dramatist of his day and probably one of the greatest theatrical technicians. His witty, clever, and complicated plots with their artificial characters and their manipulated scenes based usually on a true or apocryphal event, were spell-binders. His *Glass of Water* (1840) is considered the ultimate example of the "the well-made play." Improviser, master craftsman, Scribe knew exactly how to concoct a dramatization which included the right dosage of anachronisms, historical errors, multiple actions and surprises—all of which touched and amused a generation of theatre-goers. Sarcey, the critic of *Le Temps* and Antoine's sometime friend, had suggested that young playwrights study Scribe: "the rules of the well-made play are the rules of the theatre because they are the rules of logic."[1]

Scribe was the inspirational force for Emile Augier (*Olympia's Marriage*, 1855) and Dumas fils (*The Lady of the Camelias*, 1852). The former, with his *common sense* dramas, divested the courtesan of all romance, exposing this evil type to the scourges of society. Dumas's *thesis plays* attempted to persuade spectators to alter the laws and hearts of his contemporaries. His was sentimental *preaching theatre*, the stage having been reduced to a function, to a moralizing agent. Each of his plays featured a "good" hero-type, with whom spectators could identify.

Imitators and descendents of Scribe were many, including Eugène Labiche, the creator of such delightful farces as *An Italian Straw Hat* (1851) and *Mr. Perrichon's Trip* (1860), which enjoyed such favor with the bourgeoisie. Unsentimental, ironic, and satiric, Labiche went to almost any length to draw laughter from his audiences. So, too, was Victorien Sardou influenced by Scribe. His *A Scrap of Paper* (1860), a comedy of intrigue, focused on the mysterious contents of a love letter, and other trivial entities of incidents. Sardou's melodramatic works were sensational vehicles for such actresses as Sarah Bernhardt, whose *Fédora* (1882), and *Théodora* (1884) earned her international favor. *Madame Devil-May-Care* (1893), composed with Emile Moreau, for the celebrated Gabrielle Réjane, also played to packed houses.

Édouard Pailleron, author of *The World In Which One Is Bored* (1881), wrote comedies of manners: gentle and bantering satires, elegantly and carefully written. Although his plots are artificially constructed, based on surprises, intrigues, and mis-understandings, Pailleron's knowledge of human nature, and his wit and characterizations lend interest to his stage pieces.

Despite the success of Boulevard plays, melodramas, farces of all types, and old-time tragedies, a renewal of the birth of a pio-neering theatre was in order. A different trend, significantly, was ushered in with Balzac's *Mercadet*, a comedy written in 1832, but produced only in 1851, and reworked by Adolphe Den-nery. Realistic, it focused on such details as business matters, debts, and absconding partners. These themes not only attracted the attention of the bourgeois, who were so deeply involved in commercial matters, but also the admiration of later dramatists and directors, including Antoine. Balzac's approach to theatre was true to life, real and natural, Antoine suggested. There was nothing artificial, pretentious or baroque about Balzac's hand-ling of mundane situations.

Innovative views, new blood, and a revisioning of theatre in general was in order. "We have come to the birth of truth," wrote Émile Zola in his preface to his dramatized version of *Thérèse Raquin* (1873). Although the play was a failure—and the critics tore it to shreds, savagely and violently—Zola was a forceful spokesman for the *natural way* and to a great extent his words led to the unseating of Augier's and Dumas's dominance in theatre. Zola and his friends rejected the stylish redundant melodramas and the superficial well-made plays. "A work must be based on the real . . . on nature," Zola stated in "Naturalism in the Theatre" (1880). A playwright must observe facts, minutely and with exactitude. No more abstract characters in dramas, no more invented formulas. Zola wanted to put an end to such lies. Real characters must walk the planks; real stories must be dramatized, based on documentation, without having recourse to some idealistic fantasy. The dramatist must take his cue from the scientist. Zola's Naturalism is defined as a return to nature; it is this kind of operation which scientists undertook the day they based their studies on direct examination of bodies and phenomena and experiences, proceeding via analysis. In his *Experimental Novel*, Zola further stated:

> Naturalism in the domain of letters is also a return to nature and to man, direct observation, exact anatomy, the accepting and painting of what is. The writer and the scientist perform the same task.[2]

Realism and Naturalism were in the air. Antoine was caught up in its message and intent upon seeing it and other vigorous and innovative ideas infiltrate the theatre. His noncommercial Théâtre-Libre, he was convinced, would be instrumental in unseating the ruling powers: the abuses, hypocrisies, and fustian approaches which flooded the popular stages of his day. Incredible as it may seem, he accomplished his goal, and virtually singlehandedly!

PART I

André Antoine

The Théâtre Libre

1887-1893

Chapter 1

André Antoine (1856-1943)

March 30, 1887 was a memorable date in French theatre. It marked the opening performance of Antoine's newly founded Théâtre Libre. On that momentous night, Antoine offered spectators a new brand of realism/naturalism: a *slice of life* production that brought audiences face to face with themselves and with their environment. Decors followed the patterns of reality. A revolutionary acting technique was also instituted on that night: actors and actresses no longer declaimed in stiff and studied ways, as was the style in state-subsidized and Boulevard theatres. They walked and talked, comported themselves on stage as they did in shops, on the streets, and in their homes. They mirrored life with fidelity; a smudged mirror perhaps, but recognizable all the same, offering audiences the pleasure of recognition. Nor did the performers upstage each other. Antoine had abolished the star system. His company worked as a unit—a cohesive whole.

Not exclusively one-sided, Antoine's tastes were eclectic. He invited Parnassians, Symbolists, Decadents, and Humorists to contribute their dramas to his creative enterprise. One cardinal rule prevailed, at least at the outset of the Théâtre Libre: the works of mostly untried and unpublished authors would be staged, thereby giving a creative and motivated young person a chance in life. Broadminded in every way and an internationalist, Antoine was the first French director to produce plays by foreign authors, for the most part Slavic, Scandinavian, and German.

Fed by a fertile imagination and a will of iron, Antoine had sufficient energy to overcome the nearly insurmountable obstacles facing a person who went counter to the trends of his day. Commercial theatre, Antoine remarked numerous times, was vapid, arid, and sterile—it wallowed in mediocrity. He would change all this and create a theatre which would be meaningful to his audiences, stir and perhaps even shock them into a new state of awareness.

*

André Antoine, born in the Limousin, moved to Paris in 1869 with his parents and siblings. Because his father, an employee of the PTT, earned very little, the family was forced to move frequently, always seeking cheaper lodgings. Despite many difficulties, Antoine's mother, a dynamic and energetic woman, found time on Sundays to take her son to the theatre which she knew he loved: the Théâtre Beaumarchais, or the Théâtre Saint-Antoine on boulevard Richard-Lenoir. The young Antoine sat enthralled as he watched the harrowing plights of heroines and heroes always struggling with villains: *Atar Gull, The Lady from St. Tropez, La Voisin the Poisoner.* The joys experienced in the realm of fantasy and the arts perhaps in part offset the miseries he experienced in another domain: in 1871 he won a scholarship to the very fine Lycée Charlemagne, but his parents, ostensibly for financial reasons, did not allow him to accept it—a severe blow to the lad, who had a passion for reading and study. He was sent to the École Turgot where he remained for six months, after which his father informed him he had to look for a job.

Antoine was employed by multiple firms: as a clerk in a business; at Firmin-Didot, which he preferred, because its offices were located on 56 Rue Jacob, near the book stalls on the quays and the art shops. It was here that Antoine spent his free time reading and his spare sous buying books. He devoured the novels of Alexandre Dumas, Eugène Sue, and Georges Sand—voraciously, skipping lunch frequently, his imagination feeding on the written word. When he had the time, he walked to the Quay Malaquais, near the École des Beaux-Arts. There, he attended his first Manet exhibit and was fascinated by the colors, shapes, and luminosities which played havoc on his soul and psyche. The Louvre, with its classical tableaux and sculptures was another port of call. Antoine's curiosity seemed insatiable. No matter how arduous was his work by day, at night he had energy enough to fill a profound intellectual need: he attended the classes of Hippolyte Taine (1828-1893) on the "History of Art."

A scientific determinist with regard to literature and his-

tory, one of Taine's most famous doctrines was based on the notion of *race, milieu, and moment*, which he considered the three
most important factors in determining man's life.   In his *History
of English Literature* Taine suggested that historical documents
are the means by which individuals may be understood and
their lives reconstructed; that a human being's actions, his demeanor, his physical portrait are outside manifestations of an
inner being.   History, then, becomes a "physiological/mechanical
problem."   Indeed, it was Taine who so influenced Zola by writing that *"VICE AND VIRTUE ARE PRODUCTS AS ARE
VITRIOL AND SUGAR."*

Theatre—above all else—was Antoine's passion.   At the
state-subsidized Comédie-Française, founded in the seventeenth
century, he was able to observe the famous matinee idols in all
of their glory: Mounet-Sully, Gôt, the Coquelins, and others.
Antoine was "conquered," "overwhelmed," "dazzled," "mesmerized" by these experiences.   Coincidentally, he met a strange character with a "miraculous voice"—Marius Laisne.   When they
saw each other again, Laisne asked Antoine to recite Cléante's
speech to Orgon in Act I of Molière's *Tartuffe*.   He did so, and
brilliantly.   Laisne invited the young man to enroll in his evening class of recitation and diction—"Le Gymnase de la
parole"—and he accepted.

Life for Antoine, however, was far from easy.   His father
was outraged when he heard that his son had been fired from
several jobs for lateness—his heart being in the arts and not on
his work.   When he began castigating his son for returning
home at night at ungodly hours, Antoine understood that he
and his father were at odds as to his future.   For Antoine, there
was only *one way*: to realize his dream.   Father and son severed
relations.

Although leaving home answered one of Antoine's pressing problems, it gave rise to another: extreme economic distress.
There were days when he went without food and nights without a place to call his own, sleeping in some corner of the Halles.
His passion for theatre sustained him; it remained undimin-
ished.   It was time for him, he thought, to dialogue with the
greats of his profession and benefit from their vast learning concerning the performing arts.   He was intrigued by Denis
Diderot's famous *Paradoxe of the Comédien* (1773-78), which
states that an actor can arouse emotion in his audiences without
feeling anything himself.   He decided to write to the celebrated

matinee idol, François Gôt, on the subject. Much to his surprise
Gôt answered him:

> The actor, like the singer, the instrumentalist, the orator, like all
> those whose mission is to act directly on a crowd, the actor must be
> double, or not be at all; that is to say, at the same time the artist
> executes and experiences his role, a kind of reasonable being must re-
> main standing besides him, observing both the active being and the
> spectators at the same time, and always capable of new combina-
> tions, new resources and nuances—a moderator in one word, as one
> says in the trade.[1]

Antoine lived, breathed, theatre. When he could scrape
up enough sous, he attended as many performances as possible—mostly at the Comédie-Française. He learned quickly—fer-
vently. In Laisne's class, he became friendly with another budding actor, Auguste Marie Wisteaux, the future Mevisto.

Antoine was growing in knowledge and courage; he was
also becoming restless and somewhat dissatisfied. Laisne should
no longer limit himself to teaching recitation and performing
only excerpts from popular plays. He should produce complete
works like those given at the Comédie-Française: for example,
the popular *Friend Fritz* by Émile Erkmann and Alexandre
Chatrian. Who will direct this complicated drama? Laisne questioned, after Antoine broached the subject. Antoine volun-
teered. He would also play the difficult role of Sichel. Laisne
agreed. He even allowed him to use his furniture as part of the
stage sets. Opening night was an exciting affair, particularly for
the budding director. And the neighborhood audiences applauded with gusto.

Antoine was determined—more than ever now—to de-
vote his life to the theatre. Actor? Director? He wasn't certain
as yet. Mevisto introduced him to friends at the Comédie-Française where both young men had gotten jobs as extras—earning
40 sous. A dream fulfilled for Antoine. No longer would he
have to pay to attend performances; he would not only be paid,
but would be in a position to study firsthand the gestures, intonations, stances and demeanor of the great stars of the day. A
year later, in 1875, Antoine and Mevisto were engaged as part of
the *claque*.

Mevisto was also a good and kind friend to Antoine. It
was he who saw to it that father and son became reconciled.
Antoine's father got him a job with the Gas Company: it con-

sisted in copying hundreds of bills daily. Once again, however, Antoine reverted to his old habits: he came to work late and left early. The result was predictable. He was fired. Mevisto did not give up. He found a job for his friend at the Hachette publishing company. The ambiance at Hachette thrilled him: books abounded here and he could read to his heart's content.

Antoine, who entertained thoughts of becoming an actor at this period, decided to try out for the Conservatoire—the prestigious acting school which so many of the great matinee idols had attended and where some of them now taught. Antoine chose for his examination a role made famous by Gôt (Noel in *Joy Frightens*). So startlingly accurate was his imitation of Gôt, that the judges—and Gôt himself who was present—were struck by the precision of the young lad's performance. Yet, he was unsuccessful in passing, even though the judges—Ambroise Thomas, the opera composer; Dumas fils; Henri de Régnier, the poet; and Delaunay, the actor—all commented on Antoine's perseverance and talent. They mentioned the fact that his voice lacked amplitude and depth: he spoke in a kind of whisper. Nor did he declaim, as the actors at the Comédie-Française were trained to do.

After his audition, Antoine, a realist as well as a dreamer, decided to give up all thought of pursuing an acting career. Directing would be his goal. His inclinations at this juncture inspired him to read the writings of Émile Zola, a fervent admirer of the scientist Claude Bernard and his theories as set forth in *Introduction to the Study of Experimental Medicine* (1865). Hypotheses and observations must be carried on with an open mind in the laboratory, Dr. Bernard stated, and are not to be considered valid until such time as they are verified through experimentation. It is not the "why" of living phenomena which science attempts to explicate—this is the realm of the metaphysician—it is the "how." The determining conditions which produce certain types must be investigated and experimented upon: "observation *shows* and experimentation instructs." A scientist must remain objective. Truth can only become a certainty once all aspects of the discovery have been proven correct and even then such an achievement is only temporary and may be proven false with future experimentation.[2]

Zola followed Bernard's speculations. His study was transmuted into a laboratory; his work table into a dissecting area. In his series of novels—*Les Rougon-Macquart* (1871-1893)—Zola took the necessary scientific precautions, which for him meant remaining at an objective distance from his protagonists, and depicting them as brutal, cruel, or loving. Language reflected the backgrounds of his characters and therefore might be scatalogical, common, or elegant, depending upon the person, the profession, class and the métier of the individual. A novel—or dramatic piece—must, therefore, be infused with *real* life and energy.

Naturalism, in Zola's view, must be distinguished from Realism. The latter was a term used around 1855 to indicate a literature that attempted to depict life as it was, without glorifying or idealizing it with moral or didactic connotations. Realism flourished in England, with such novelists as Defoe, Fielding, and Smollett; after which it passed into France in the nineteenth century and became visible in the works of Stendhal, Balzac, Flaubert, and Maupassant.

Naturalism, in Zola's words, dealt "with the human problem studied in the framework of reality." A "slice of life" should be depicted in a novel or on stage, using nonidealized raw material without the introduction of heart or soul to mar objectivity. Industry, poverty, problems of all types should be singled out for analysis with heredity, environment, and the period under observation as the determining factors. A scientific attitude and approach to the creative work is necessary, he stated, despite the fact that such writings may encourage a pessimistic attitude toward life. To face facts squarely, Zola suggested, is to help individuals better their lives by dealing with their problems directly, and remedying them as best they can. Naturalism rejected romanticism; it proscribed a metaphysical approach to life and did away with those "idyllic" and idealistic heroes in vogue. Instead, it proclaimed social reform by the depiction of life *as it is lived;* it prophesied a future based on scientific discoveries able to improve man's earthly lot.

Antoine's theatrical ventures came to a sudden halt when he was drafted into the army in 1879. Neither his new environs or métier prevented him from reading as much as possible or dreaming up new plans for the future. Shortly after completing his army tour of duty, which took him to Tunisia and to various areas in France, he married Marie Rambour in 1883. That he was more strongly committed to theatre than ever perhaps may account for his divorce after the birth of their son, a year later. He could not play the role of a bourgeois husband, work thirteen or fourteen hours a day at the Gas Company (they had given him back his job after serving in the army) and indulge his theatrical bent. Antoine was not one to harness himself with restriction, be it on the part of his parents or his wife. He had to be free. Although Antoine made the following remark years later, he knew at this time that "the battle, already won in the novel by the naturalists, in painting by the impressionists," had to be fought in the theatrical domain.[3] He felt ready to draw swords. No obstacle would stand in his way, he remarked, not even money, for without the theatre Antoine felt *empty*.

Two important events, which occurred fortuitously, were instrumental in encouraging Antoine to forge ahead: meeting Pauline Verdavoine, an aspiring actress who worked in the telegraphic service and later became the love of his life; and joining with the *Cercle Gaulois*, an amateur theatrical group where people met at night, after a hard day's work, to rehearse plays. It had been founded in 1885 by a retired army officer who loved theatre: his friends called him Father Krauss. Antoine was fascinated by the production he put on in Montmartre—at 37 Passage de l'Elysée-des-Beaux-Arts. Although the monthly dues of eight francs were high for Antoine, he considered it more than worthwhile since, as a member, he could participate in their dramatic events.

After some months, Antoine's enthusiasm diminished. Father Krauss was not sufficiently ambitious. Antoine suggested to him that he stop producing old-time plays by such old fashioned writers as Scribe, Augier, Sardou, Dumas and focus on new works: *The Marquis de Villemer* by Sand, or those of Naturalist writers. Father Krauss was amenable at the outset, particularly after Antoine's portrayal of the Duke d'Aléria in Sand's play which had made such a strong impression on both the members of the troupe and their audiences. Antoine had offered them something unheard of: not the usual declamation of lines, the style of the actors at the Comédie-Française and commercial theatres. His natural and unaffected speech coupled with his simple and authentic gestures aroused a sense of excitement in the audience. Paul Alexis, one of Zola's devotees, writing under the name of Trublot in the newspaper, *Le Cri du Peuple*, singled out Antoine's acting for praise:

> No sooner does he come on stage, than the entire scene stands out in stark relief, taking on a special life of its own. His voice, though not strong, is clear and marvelously biting. In addition to his perfect diction, his silences reach out into the entire theatre.[4]

Father Krauss, however, was not in accord with Antoine's view of theatre nor with Alexis' review. A fervent admirer of Scribe and the old-guard dramatists, he refused to go along with Antoine's "revolutionary" projects. Although meeting with rebuff, Antoine remained undaunted. He knew what he wanted: artistic renewal on *his* terms, and not a theatre dominated by money or by bad taste.

The reign of the banal and the mediocre—the commercial theatre—had to come to an end. Other factors were also at stake: the powerful censorship which reigned in France in the world of the arts had to be abolished. Such narrow vision on the part of the powerful ultra-moralists not only plagued artistic creation, it limited all sense of freedom, forcing authors to conform to well-worn plots and characterizations, to repeat their wares indefinitely by adhering to so-called sacrosanct rules.

To put his plan into practice required aggressive action on Antoine's part. He had to look for new authors, unpublished plays. State-subsidized theatres, such as the Comédie-Française and the Odéon, or commercial houses, could not afford to invite young and unknown dramatists to their stages. Because they were always under great economic pressure to fill their houses, they had to draw on the tried and true.

When Paul Alexis heard of Antoine's plans to create a Théâtre Libre—a kind of *experimental laboratory*—and produce unpublished plays, he gave him his one-act comic farce, *Miss Apple*, based on a work by the Naturalist writer, Edmond Duranty (1833-1880). Three other one-act plays were offered him: *Jacques Damour*, by Léon Hennique, drawn from Zola's short story; *The Prefect* by Arthur Byl, and *The Vain One* (Cocarde) by Jules Vidal. The indefatigable Antoine now had sufficient material to open his Théâtre Libre.

First and foremost, however, he had to find a building that would permit him to produce the plays he had in mind. Without money or influence, what might have been a detail for some, proved to be a major task for Antoine. Father Krauss, however, did come to his help in time: he offered to rent his theatre to him for a hundred francs a month. He refused, however, to be involved in Antoine's enterprise. Antoine accepted the offer and used his salary from the Gas Company to pay expenses.

The dress rehearsal, on March 29, 1887, inaugurated the birth of the Théâtre Libre. Three-hundred guests had been invited.   The opening was scheduled for the following evening. Although only three journalists attended (other openings competing with Antoine's) the Théâtre Libre was filled to capacity. More important, perhaps, was the fact that three greats—Émile Zola, Alphonse Daudet, and Stéphane Mallarmé—were present. That such vastly different creative spirits attended was paradigmatic for Antoine.   Paying homage to Naturalists and Realists as he did with his choice of plays, Antoine knew from the very start that he would never imprison himself in an artistic ideology.   Symbolists, Parnassians, and those who belonged to no school, but who showed promise and talent, were also to be invited to share in Antoine's theatrical venture.   Nor was Antoine a chauvinist.   Open-minded in all ways, his interests focused on the quality of a work offered, be it by an unknown or a known writer—French or foreign.   As Henri Becque, the author of the popular play, *The Vultures*, stated: Antoine was "the real leader and master of the whole youthful movement, a man whom we all consider the renovator of contemporary drama."[5]

Chapter 2

Productions at the Théâtre Libre

Antoine produced one hundred and twelve plays as director of the Théâtre Libre (1887-1894). Although he offered audiences a preponderance of naturalistic, realistic, and psychological dramas (by Zola, Goncourt, Alexis, Duranty, Hennique, Méténier, Porto-Riche, Curel, Brieux), lyrical, poetic, and symbolistic plays were also included (Bergerat, Villiers de l'Isle-Adam, Banville, Mendès). Significant as well is the fact that Antoine was the first theatrical director to attempt concertedly to rid the French of their provincial attitude toward foreign dramatists, producing plays by Tolstoy, Ibsen, Strindberg, and Hauptmann. Antoine's endeavors were castigated by most critics, who viewed the works of the above-mentioned "foreign" playwrights as antithetical to French clarity and lucidity.

No amount of negative or destructive responses succeeded in dissuading Antoine from putting his theatrical ideas into practice. Nor did his concepts concerning the performing arts ever cease evolving during the course of his directorship of the Théâtre Libre. Experience was also his master; tours and foreign influences were instrumental in sharpening and broadening his vision.

To this end, Antoine went to Brussels to study the structural elements in performance used by the internationally known company of the Duke of Saxe-Meiningen (1826-1914). With utmost care Antoine examined the intricate drawings made by the Duke prior to and during rehearsals: the placements and displacements of actors, their gestures, the decors, accessories, and costumes. A whole complex dynamics involving stage movements, settings, and costumes triggered intense excitement in the French director. Crucial for the Duke and for Antoine as well was the need for extreme accuracy with regard to the various parts of the stage production. Antoine was impressed by the fact that the costumes, decors, intonations, stances

37, Passage de l'Elysée des Beaux-Arts (Place Pigalle)

MERCREDI 30 MARS 1887

à 8 heures très-précises du soir

Première Représentation

Jacques Damour

Pièce en 1 acte, en prose
Tirée de la nouvelle de M. Emile ZOLA
par M. Léon HENNIQUE

Mademoiselle Pomme

Comédie-Farce en 1 acte, en prose
par DURANTY
et M. PAUL ALEXIS

La Cocarde

Comédie en 1 acte, en prose
par M. JULES VIDAL.

Un Préfet

Drame en 1 acte, en prose
par M. ARTHUR BYL.

NOTA. — Cette invitation étant **rigoureusement personnelle,** prière de vouloir bien retourner, avant la représentation, les places dont on ne disposerait pas.

A. ANTOINE.

Antoine's invitation for the Théâtre Libre's opening night:
Zola's *Jacques Damour*

and other elements in the Duke's productions were in keeping with the period depicted in the play and the social background of the protagonists. Equally impressive was the superb harmony emerging from the highly disciplined troupe. The Duke had abolished the star system, underscoring *ensemble playing* instead.

That Antoine had been so vitalized by the company of the Duke of Saxe-Meiningen was not surprising. Stanislavsky, among other greats, had also been motivated by his meticulous and detailed approach to theatre. Antoine outlined his reactions to the Duke's views on performing arts in a letter to Francisque Sarcey, the critic for *Le Temps*, emphasizing the incredible ease with which this German director handled crowds on stage, while also outlining his future plans for the Théâtre Libre:

> Their crowds are not, like ours, made up of elements put together at random—or people hired during the dress rehearsals, badly dressed and quite untrained to wear bizarre or constricting costumes, especially when these demand precision. Our theatres almost always demand that the extras stand stock still, while those of the Meininger must act and portray their characters. Do not assume therefore that they attract attention and divert the emphasis from the principals. No, the scene is an organic whole, and wherever one looks, he is struck by a detail in situation or character. This lends an incomparable power to certain moments.[1]
>
> In the crowd scenes the protagonist who is the center of the scene can bring about strict silence with a gesture, a cry, a movement. And if the crowd then watches the actor and listens to him, instead of watching the audience, or, as at the Comédie-Française, contemplating the leads with a mute but visible deference, their listening would seem natural and so would their silence. In any case all two hundred must seem really interested in what the dominant actor is saying.
>
> I don't know anything about music, but I have been told that in certain operas Wagner split his chorus into different parts, and that each set of chorus members represented a distinct element of the crowd, even while contributing to a perfect ensemble. Why can't we do that in the spoken theatre? M. Émile Zola wanted to for *Germinal*, but the directors prevented him for budgetary reasons. His plan was to rehearse the crowd extensively and have them supervised by leading actors. As you see, this is the Meiningen approach.[2]

That the Duke's company formed a cohesive whole was due in part to his insistence that *all* performers participate in his theatrical productions, even if called upon to play a walk-on or an extra. Such a situation could never exist in Paris, where stars were the focal point of everyone's attention and directors yielded to their most arbitrary of demands just to please them.

Arresting as well for Antoine was the Duke's acting technique which corroborated his own view of the mise-en-scène. Gestures, facial expressions, gait, demeanor are all to be natural—as if the performers on stage were guests in your own living room. Just as Antoine was later to be praised by some and castigated by others for having actors turn their backs to the audience when the situation demanded it, so, too, was the Duke for the requirements he made of his performers.

Nevertheless, Antoine did have some reservations. He considered certain settings used by the Duke rather "garish and oddly designed" and not as well painted as French decors. As for the costumes, although almost always historically accurate, "they are foolishly rich" and in bad taste. Such conditions were regrettably prevalent in Parisian theatres, and understandably, since actors and actresses had to pay for their own costumes—and these were frequently very expensive—and so they bought gowns they liked. When these fitted the part, it was all to the good; when they did not, they were incongruous. A play taking place in nineteenth-century France might feature a star wearing a Greek or Roman dress, or vica versa. Such anachronisms would not take place at the Théâtre Libre where rigorous discipline was enforced with regard to costumes and decors.

The Duke's lighting effects, "although often striking," were, in Antoine's words, sometimes handled with "epic naïveté."

> ... [W]hen an old man has just died in his armchair, a beautiful ray from the setting sun suddenly shines through the window, without any gradations, to illuminate his beautiful head—this solely to achieve an effect. Again after an extraordinary torrential rain, achieved by electric projections, I was annoyed to see the water stop abruptly, without any transition.[3]

Other distracting effects present in the Duke's company were also noted by Antoine: the rocks, for example, used to depict a Swiss landscape, had been placed on coasters, which might have been effective had it not been for the fact that they squeaked each time the performers walked on them. Antoine judged the acting technique of a great many of the Duke's performers to be quite rudimentary; they had only trained a year or two before joining the Duke's company. Still, there were some who, like Carl Gorner, were excellent.[4]

On the whole, Antoine returned to Paris stimulated by the Duke's incredible innovations and intent upon appropriating some of his ideas when answering a particular need at the Théâtre Libre.   Antoine's problems, however, differed vastly from the Duke's. Money was no problem for the German director. It was crucial for Antoine. His company consisted of working people who could devote only evening hours to rehearsals. Nor could he afford to pay them more than the bare minimum—and frequently not even that.   Borrowing when he could, and asking for advances when the need was overly great, Antoine persevered despite the incredible frustrations and disappointments facing him. Frequently, after having trained his actors, they were invited to perform on a regular basis at other theatres. They accepted, for the security it gave them.   Sometimes he did not know upon whom he could count.

Despite the hardships, Antoine endowed his productions—which were performed only three times (a dress rehearsal, an opening night for invited guests, and a performance for subscribers)—with his own stamp. His actors were trained to act *naturally* and to speak on stage in virtually conversational tones. Despite Antoine's weak voice, criticized as being difficult for audiences to hear, he acted in many of his productions. Praiseworthy, however, was the range of his abilities: the incredible variety of his facial expressions, his meaningful gestural language, and the impressive way he handled his body on stage. The emotional impact of some of his creations, as we shall see, was astounding. Although critics such as Lemaître, Faguet, and Sarcey disagreed in their appraisals of Antoine's productions, they felt he was a superb actor.

> What suppleness he brings into his characters which are so utterly different one another! With what surety of composition he succeeds in giving, in the same evening, to most varied roles, a silhouette so successful that at first one does not recognize him. He never plays Antoine, he always plays his character and, penetrating the soul of his character, he presents him in an unforgettable manner. It is singular, but it seems that there is no stage, and that the raised curtain of the Théâtre Libre discloses people in their houses going about their affairs unconsciously and without knowing that they are watched.[5]

Antoine played as if incited by an inner necessity.

*

Jacques Damour:

Although a much-admired novelist, Zola's plays, *Thérèse Raquin* (1873), *The Rabourdin Inheritors* (1874), and *The Rose Button* (1874), failed in the theatre: overly static, devoid of poetry, paper-thin characterizations. *Jacques Damour* (1880), adapted for the stage by Léon Hennique, differed from the others: it was dramatic in essence, focusing on a man struggling against his "evil" instincts.

Visibly influenced by Balzac's *Colonel Chabert*, Zola's drama tells the story of Jacques, a communard and fugitive, who was thought to have been drowned during his attempted escape from New Caledonia. Some time after his departure, a death certificate was given to his wife. She marries a butcher, after which a daughter is born to them. A few years later, much to the astonishment of all, Jacques returns and wants to assume what he considers to be his rightful place: as husband to his wife. His inner struggle becomes acute when he realizes that were he to yield to his wishes, he would be destroying a loving and harmonious household. After much soul searching, he leaves, sacrificing his happiness for his wife's well-being.

Antoine portrayed Jacques as a stern and grim man: tragic, like many a Greek hero destroyed by destiny. Although pain is explicitly expressed in the part, Antoine underplayed the highly emotional situations on stage, thereby increasing the impact of his character's inner tension. His facial expressions ranged from euphoria, at the sight of his wife whom he has not seen in so many years; to dread, when he discovers she has married; to anger which takes hold when he wrestles with his own conscience. Antoine's controlled gestures and stance point up the protagonist's deeply pathetic situation. So deeply did he feel his character that he confessed to having been oblivious of the audience—even to his own nervousness. Another being inhabited him: Jacques Damour walked the planks at the Théâtre Libre.

Henry de La Pommeraye of *Paris* confessed to having had tears in his eyes when writing about Antoine as performer:

> I do not know of any professional actor who could have better composed the character: mask, clothing, stance, gestures, expression, everything was true and striking.[6]

Antoine's subdued demeanor, his natural stance, and his soft and whisperlike voice, stood him in good stead in his portrayal of Jacques Damour, heightening the tragedy of his character's

Program for *Gringoire* at the Théâtre Libre

situation.[7]   There was nothing "conventional" in Antoine's superb creation of this basically brutal and violent, but also resigned individual, who had struggled so many years against the continuously painful hand of fate.[8]

Antoine had also taken special pains with his mise-en-scène. Everything had to be just right. Without any funds to spare, Antoine asked his mother for permission to borrow her dining room furniture (a table and chairs) to use for sets. She agreed. On the night of the dress rehearsal, after finishing his work at the Gas Company, a friend lent Antoine a hand-cart which enabled him to take the furniture himself down the tortuous streets to Krauss' theatre. Unable to afford real live props and accessories, Antoine had to resort to *trompe-l'oeil* which he would rarely use in future productions. The backdrop for *Jacques Damour* depicted chunks of meat, immediately situating the drama in a butcher shop.[9]

Zola, visibly moved—"enchanted"—by Antoine's production, expressed his full admiration, recounted by Antoine as follows:

> After we finished *Jacques Damour*, Hennique led the master onto the stage, and Zola backed me into a corner under a gas burner. My nerves gave way as his eyes ran over me. A look of astonishment was on his face when at length he abruptly asked me: "Just what are you?" He let me stammer in confusion under his searching gaze before he continued: "It's very good, very good indeed. Hennique, isn't it very good? We'll be back tomorrow."[10]

Alphonse Daudet was "unsparing in his praise," as were Alexis, Céard, and others. Denayrouze of the *République française* commented on the play's "enormous" effect upon the audience as a whole and not merely on the "initiated." He predicted that if the "naturalist theatre produced many plays of this caliber, it could rest easy about its future."[11] *Le Cri du peuple* was also unsparing in its flattering remarks, singling out Antoine for praise: his acting was "breathtaking, unforgettable."[12]

Although critics wrote nothing but laudatory statements about *Jacques Damour*, the three other plays offered on the bill—Duranty's *Miss Apple*, Byl's *The Prefect*, Vidal's *The Vain One*—went unnoticed. Nevertheless, Antoine considered it a good start; and this, despite the fact that he had debts of nearly a hundred francs, was working full time at the Gas Company, rehearsing only at night, and writing letters soliciting subscribers for his Théâtre Libre, which he delivered by hand so as to save on the postage.

*

Zola's *Madeleine*, produced by Antoine in 1889, and based on his novel, *Madeleine Férat* (1868), was spared condemnation by critics out of deference to the well-known author. An early work, written when he was only twenty-five, it recounts the story of a convent-educated girl whose tutor had attempted to seduce her. *Madeleine* is filled with melodramatic and macabre themes: adultery and guilt, which not only shocked the audiences of the Théâtre Libre, but left them uninvolved and detached because of what the critics labeled the amateurish nature of the dialogue and the naïveté and hackneyed nature of its plot.

The Death of the Duke of Enghien:

Léon Hennique's *The Death of the Duke of Enghien* was "a real event" in theatre, Antoine noted. It marked the rebirth of the historical play, acted out in *realistic* and *positivist* style, despite the romantic nature of the situations.[13] This *genre mixte*, as it was referred to, called for authentic set and appointments, and costumes in keeping with the period.

The Duke of Enghien (1772-1804), who had emigrated from France in 1789, was extradited from German territory at the request of Napoleon and transferred to Vincennes, where it had been decreed that he be shot. Although the play itself elicited little enthusiasm on the part of the audience—the character studies were deemed superficial and the suspense factor virtually nonexistent—it was praised by the critic, Emile Faguet, for its "historical naturalism" and its "slice of life reality." The sets were so exact and the mise-en-scène so deftly regulated that it gave some spectators the impression of sequences of "instantaneous" photographs; it reminded others of "documentary theatre." Sarcey, adding his usual discordant note, stated that it "was theatre that was not."[14]

That critics should have commented on the accuracy of the costumes and sets is not surprising. The cut, color, and fabric of the costumes were exact copies of Jean Paul Laurens' painting of the Duke of Enghien. The sets were based on documents of the period. Act III, the Duke's trial, was outstanding in its actuality: the removal of foot and stage lights left the pro-

scenium and orchestra in virtual obscurity, the only illumination on stage coming from lanterns placed on tables in front of
the highest ranking judges.   Every now and then, when the
lights from one lantern would dim, others would be focused on
the Duke's face—particularly during periods of interrogation.
Antoine's lighting effects were seemingly inspired by the
engraving based on Henri Dupray's drawings of the Duke.   So
effective was the interplay of chiaroscuro on stage in underscoring the harrowing events and in heightening the tension
implicit in the scene, that critics and audiences alike reacted with
praise.   Some spectators, however, unaccustomed to such black-
ness in theatre, felt ill at ease at certain junctures, voicing their
feelings verbally during the performance itself.   The Goncourts
were outraged by such tumult, looking upon it as irrespectful of
the historical incident depicted, and cried out, "Silence,
catarrheux!"[15]

*

Antoine not only searched out fine, unknown dramatists,
but was so intent upon disassociating himself from the Naturalists—or any school that sought to limit free thought and artistic
creativity—that he went to all extremes to invite different
schools of playwrights to give him their works to perform.   To
this end he paid a visit to the Parnassian poet and dramatist,
Emile Bergerat (1845-1923), who was also a journalist of no mean
repute at the *Figaro*, writing under the name of Caliban.   So
impressed was Bergerat with Antoine's innovative ideas that he
gave him the manuscript of his three-act verse comedy, *Night of
the Bergamasque*, a work which had had the honor of being rejected by both the Comédie-Française and the Odéon.   A versi-
fied fantasy, *Night of the Bergamasque* is based on one of
Boccaccio's themes: that of an old miser who attempts to dis-
suade a young poet/adventurer from absconding with his
mistress and slave.

Deeply pleased with Antoine's directing and the troupe's
performances during rehearsal periods, Bergerat invited
Coquelin the younger, celebrated actor at the Comédie-Française,
to attend the opening.   Although moved by Antoine's performance, Coquelin saw the part of the old miser differently.   He
should strive for certain "effects," he remarked, such as winking
at the audience to make a point, as if to say, "Just watch how

clever this is." Antoine, however, considered such an artificial, pretentious, unauthentic approach antithetical to *natural* acting, which was at the core of his philosophy.[16]

Antoine directed *The Night of the Bergamasque* with light and humorous banter, with the gusto and inventiveness of the *commedia dell'arte* style. The agility and cheerfulness infused into the mise-en-scène, coupled with Bergerat's poetic verses, delighted and amused the literary-oriented audiences at the Théâtre Libre. A notable was Gôt, who was annoyed by what he considered to be the excessive obscurity injected into certain scenes to heighten tensions. Such devices were unnecessary, he maintained, since Bergerat's stage play was scintillating and his verses brilliant. Indeed, they added nothing to the beauty and ethereality of the text.

Intent upon maintaining some semblance of balance between raw naturalistic drama and vaporous poetic fantasies—and for diplomatic reasons as well—Antoine asked the future founder of the Grand Guignol, the ultra-Naturalist, Oscar Méténier, to produce his one act prose play, *In the Family*.

In the Family:

Méténier was known for a volume of short stories, *The Flesh. In the Family* dramatizes the lower depths of Parisian society in what has been labeled the *tranche de vie apache* style. Comparable in theme to the songs his contemporary, Aristide Bruant, performed in his cafe, *Le Mirliton*, the wretched of the earth—prostitutes, drug addicts, murderers, prisoners, criminals—were singled out for description for compassionate and dramatic reasons. Bruant, who had lived among the derelicts and the poverty stricken, and Méténier, as secretary to a police commissioner, knew well the complex feelings inhabiting these pariahs. The *real* and the *evidential* rang true, therefore, *In the Family*. Thugs, cutthroats, rag-pickers and receivers of stolen objects inhabited the stage of the Théâtre Libre, a fitting background for the sharply delineated characters. Antoine, playing Father Paradis, and Mevisto, Auguste, performed with all the rage, hate, and cruelty demanded of their roles, but also the understanding and love buried beneath their sordid and brutal exteriors.

The decors featured a rustic wooden table upon which a whitish cloth has been placed; some glasses and plates. Four and sometimes five protagonists are seated around this central and

AUGUSTE. — Ah! tenez, le monde me dégoûte!

Antoine's production of Méténier's *In the Family*

focal object. All sorts of stolen objects are visible in the background of this "den of iniquity," lending added authenticity to the scene.

Nor are audiences spared the coarse and vulgar vocabulary implicit in the dialogue of *In the Family:* the *argot* of the drunken and besotted rejects of humanity crying out their despair—their disgust with the world—is used unsparingly. The expression of adversity written over their faces, emphasized by subtle but expert use of make-up, paves the way for the play's climactic description of the execution of a family friend. The monologue revolving around the guillotine happening, new for the theatre, sent shock waves throughout the audience. (Such dramatic depictions had already been performed in song many times by the famous diseuse, Yvette Guilbert, who in raspy but powerful tones sang of the fate of *La Pierreuse* in Jules Jouy's song by the same name.) Terror and dread filled the hearts of many a spectator at the Théâtre Libre as they listened with growing horror to the representation of the icy cold blade coming down on the prisoner's neck.

Poets, actors, writers, sculptors, and painters were in the audience for the opening of *In the Family.* Among them were Jean Richepin, François Coppée, Catulle Mendès, Gôt, Coquelin the younger, Chabrier, Rodin, and Puvis de Chavannes, reacting overtly to what came to be known thereafter as *le théâtre rosse*—daring and violent drama. Critics were impressed by the "the meticulous care and thought" Antoine had brought to the acting and the sets—to the mise-en-scène in general. They did not, however, concur as to the literary value of the play. Sarcey, the critic for *Le Temps,* predicted that Méténier's new-type play would invade French theatre—and he hoped, adding sardonically, that he would not be alive to see this happen.[17]

*

Despite the positive criticisms Antoine received, the director of the Théâtre Libre still had many difficult financial problems with which to deal. Lack of funds, very little money for decors, costumes, technical effects, and performers, made stage problems almost insurmountable. A description of Lemaître, which follows, reveals the burdens—both physical and emotional—placed upon all those associated with Antoine's endeavor.

> The auditorium is very small and rather amateurishly daubed
> with paint, and resembling the concert halls found in the chief
> towns of some districts. One could shake hands with the actors
> across the footlights, and stretch out one's legs over the prompter's
> box. The stage is so small that only the simplest scenery can be set
> up on it, and so near the audience that scenic illusion is impossible.
> If such illusion were born in us, it was because we created it our-
> selves ... [18]

Other hardships added to Antoine's burdens. Since funds
were scarce, rehearsal time was limited and frequently, though
Antoine took meticulous care in his mise-en-scènes, mistakes
were made, mostly on a technical level: lights failed, accessories
were misplaced, stage space was improperly used and often
actors omitted or distorted some of their lines. Nevertheless,
Antoine, the intransigeant idealist, was adamant. He sought to
realize his dream and work with a group of actors who would
not have to rely on outside jobs to live, but could devote themselves exclusively to their art. As for Antoine, he refused an acting position which would have yielded him five-hundred francs
a month, offered him by the director of the Odéon. Ironically, it
had been this very theatre that had rejected Zola's *Jacques
Damour* and whose director had predicted the Théâtre Libre's
demise after its first six months of life.

So that he could concentrate his energies on his work,
Antoine took the drastic step of resigning in July of 1887 from
his job at the Gas Company. Because he had no real home at this
time and could not afford one, he slept in the offices of the
Théâtre Libre at 96 Rue Blanche, which were also used for
rehearsals. His bed? A small cot which folded up when not
used for a stage prop. To add to Antoine's troubles, Krauss
decided to stop renting him his theatre at the Passage de l'Elysée-
des-Beaux Arts. The young director's productions had become
too popular and he feared the publicity would cause too great a
stir with his habitués. After searching all over Paris for a theatre
he could afford, Antoine finally found Hartmann's theatre on
Rue de la Gaîté in Montparnasse, on the Left Bank. There were
both positive and negative sides to the move. Antoine was
given permission to use the theatre and all of its accessories on
Friday evenings for a very reasonable price. The detrimental factors were due to the new location: Montparnasse was considered
outside of the theatre district, which was located in Montmartre.
Disaster, by those in the know, was predicted for the Théâtre
Libre. Its director thought otherwise.

Antoine was a practical man as well as a visionary. Although he continued producing plays by untried and unpublished dramatists, he knew that he needed the backing of well-placed writers, such as Bergerat, whose play he had already produced. Such works would encourage audiences to flock to his theatre. He also knew he could count on the moral support of Stéphane Mallarmé, the head of the Symbolist school, who was himself searching for new stage forms: poems conceived for the theatre alone. There were others who would second Antoine's endeavors: Catulle Mendès (1841-1909), the poet and journalist who also enjoyed a fine reputation, gave him one of his short stories, *Tabarin's Wife*, for adaptation. Theodore de Banville (1823-1891), the celebrated bard who wrote "The Ballad of the Poor People," and the play, *Gringoire*, gave him his *The Kiss*. The Goncourt brothers allowed their novel, *Sister Philomène* to be adapted for the Théâtre Libre. With such plays in hand, Antoine felt secure enough to ask the unknown bohemian/mystic whose works he so admired, Villiers de l'Isle-Adam, for one of his works, *The Escape*.

Sister Philomène:

The Goncourt brothers, Edmond (1822-1896) and Jules (1830-1870), dramatists, novelists, critics, and historians, sought to convey "true to life" portraits and situations in their writings. The events narrated and the protagonists created were based on a scientific system of documentation. The brothers searched out their facts with fervor and exactitude, taking notes constantly, investigating and observing specific areas in cities, suburbs, or wherever their novels took them. *Germinie Lacerteux* (1865) narrated the painful life and loves of a Parisian servant girl; *Madame Gervaisais* (1896) depicted the case of a religious hysteric. Zola was impressed by the "excessive delicacy of their nervous style," alluded to as *écriture-sensation*, which made their analyses that much more penetrating and impressive.

Sister Philomène was difficult to stage because it lacked drama. Critics for the most part saw it as consisting of a series of tableaux which, in Arthur Byl's and Jules Vidal's adaptation of the novel, simply prolonged its inherently static quality. Although based on a true case, that of a nun who fell in love with a doctor, the subtle tensions implicit in the Goncourts' narrative did not come through in the stage play. Moreover, such an unconventional situation was considered by many in the audience at the time to be unpalatable.

Sister Philomène takes place at l'Hôpital Dieu.   Act 1 opens on a large room used by the interns for their consultations, and as a pharmacy and refectory.   The interns, seated around a table, eating and joking as well as indulging in scientific jargon, acted in true to life manner, talking among themselves, their backs turned toward the audience—an absolute violation of theatrical ethics in any other theatre but Antoine's.

Act II, which takes place in a recovery room, where women were sent after being operated upon, was appointed with extreme care, perhaps even more than usual, since Antoine wanted to preserve the stark and ascetic quality implicit in the Goncourts' novel.   Ten hospital beds with lowered curtains which resembled shrouds from the distance, were constructed by Antoine's stage manager and set out in two rows on either side of the proscenium.   In the back had been placed a modest altar with a statue of the Virgin around which had been grouped a few artificial flowers and three candles.

The plot of *Sister Philomène* was simple.   The intern, Barnier, played by Antoine, had met Sister Philomène of the Augustine sect at the Hospital when she was caring for the ill. Both had been moved by tender and pure feelings for each other. The medical student had been and still was in love with a girl from the Latin Quarter, Romaine, who had left him for others. One day Barnier is called to examine a new arrival.   It is Romaine.   She is suffering from breast cancer and must be operated on immediately.   Barnier does just that, and successfully, but Romaine dies from complications.   The intern's grief is profound—as is Sister Philomène's jealousy of his love for another.

Although Antoine had inaugurated his own concept of a real, live theatrical space in other productions, it came through in all of its dynamism and authenticity in *Sister Philomène.* The "transparent fourth wall," behind which people would walk and talk with ease, as if they were in their homes, unaware of the audience, gave spectators the distinct impression of participating in the stage events.   They were not only *voyeurs*; they were there to identify, to react, to judge.

The most talked-about scene in *Sister Philomène* was the prayer sequence, during Romaine's agony and death.   As Sister Philomène begins reciting the prayer, the dying Romaine responds with couplets from a naïve and romantic song, *Little Rosette*, which she had sung in her happy youth.   The fugal quality of such an interchange adds a note of poignancy.   The deeply distressed Barnier accuses Sister Philomène of lacking charity toward the sinner. He walks over to the bed on the left, the only one whose curtains are open, and uncovers the head of the dead Romaine in a sharp and brusk movement, then retracts his statement and asks for forgiveness. Sister Philomène's countenance grows increasingly mysterious and sublime as she says: "I am not a woman, I am only the servant of the World and forgiveness belongs only to God!" Alone on stage at the conclusion, she kneels down, sobbing, in front of the dead Romaine, who *had* known real love.

Drama critic for the *Figaro*, Auguste Vitu, stated that "there was not a word, a gesture, a detail in the play that merited retrenchment." The audience was absorbed continuously by the characters, tableaux, discussions between doctors and the nature of their work. As for Sister Philomène (Deneuilly), "her gestures were rare, her smile ingenuous, her voice discreet as if almost smothered by the inner conflicts she was experiencing. Her white dress accentuated the chastity of her ways. Antoine as Barnier underplayed his role: no cries, no flamboyant antics, no melodramatic effects, speaking most of the time in conversational tones, he was incredibly effective. As for Romaine's death-scene, it was remarkably rendered in controlled and subtle tones.[19]

Alphonse Allais, writing in the *Chat Noir*, was equally impressed. The portrayals were "virtually perfect." The actors lived their parts rather than merely giving the impression of acting them. Antoine's Barnier was "marvelously natural." When he defended the work accomplished by the holy women, crying out his ear-splitting "Name of God!," half reclining on a table rather than standing upright, his usually weak voice reached portentous depths.

Some critics, including Sarcey, were annoyed by the fact that actors turned their backs toward the audience, particularly in Act I, and that he was unable to see their facial expressions. This kind of innovation, he noted, was artificial: Antoine was substituting one convention for another. Had he really wanted to be accurate, he would have gone one step further and had all the actors speak at once, as one does during a heated discussion in real life. No one waits for the other to speak at such times, he maintained. Had Antoine permitted such a shouting match on stage, no one would have understood the dialogue. Then why did he resort to other devices—such as having his actors turn their back to the audience?

The Nation in Danger:

Goncourt's *The Nation in Danger* was a historical *pièce a tableaux*, and not real drama: the tirades were pedantic, the characterizations only silhouettes and not flesh-and-blood personalities. Antoine's mise-en-scène—the mob scenes in particular—was innovative and really saved the play. His lighting techniques—for example, the overhead lamps that illuminated the crowd of five-hundred extras that swarmed through the single door—suffused the atmosphere with incredible tension. Like "a subtle tide," the walk-ons inundated everything with which they came into contact—moving into and about the furnishings in the room. When the lights dimmed, the teeming masses moved about in semi-darkness, evoking feelings of dread. The effect was "extraordinary." The Goncourt's were "thrilled."[20]

The Brothers Zemgano:

More exciting was another adaptation for the stage of a Goncourt novel: *The Brothers Zemgano.* Paul Alexis and Oscar Méténier, who wrote the stage play, had a feel for the boards and for plot lines. They understood how to create drama from the affection two brothers had for each other—an obviously autobiographical theme. The poster designed by Henri Rivière for the occasion generates the proper atmosphere. It features a man walking alone down a snowy street; trees line the way; a light from a street lamp casts its rays upon the lonely individual, accentuating his sadness; a kiosque, with Théâtre Libre written on it, spreads the word to audiences.

The Brothers Zemgano revolves around two circus acrobats. Act I takes place in a courtyard outside of the brothers' home on rue des Acacias. The performers, Gianni and Nello, have finally succeeded in executing a difficult stunt: a fourteen-foot leap to the ground during which they must pass vertically through a wooden barrel. The director of the circus has come to appraise their act; so, too, does the clown Tiffany and the beautiful equestrian lady, Tomkins, in love with Nello, the younger of the two brothers. Delighted with his achievement, Nello teases and jokes with her, never taking her feelings seriously.

Backstage at the circus is the locus for Act II. We hear a crowd impatiently awaiting for the performance to begin. Journalists stand ready with pen in hand to describe the events to follow: the equestrian performing her difficult feats, jumping to the ground and on to her saddle, riding bare-back, in startlingly beautiful positions; the clowns performing their stunts, all in preparation for the *pièce de résistance*. Preparations are made; the spring-board is set up. Silence reigns. Nello walks up to the required height; applause is heard from the audience. The acrobat falls; writhes in pain. How did this happen? Only later do we find out that Tomkins, angered by Nello's flippant treatment of her, had vowed vengeance, substituting for the barrel made of cloth one of wood. The young gymnast's legs were broken.

The brother's home is the locale of Act III. Nello is slowly recovering from his accident. He will be crippled for life. He tries to walk about the room on his crutches and despite his utter despair, he jokes and wears a smile. After Nello has retired for the night, Gianni, who thinks him asleep, leaves the apartment. Having given up his work so as to take care of his brother, he now feels a need to go to the gymnasium—to breathe in the air of that other life. Nello awakens. When he does not see his brother, he pulls himself up and creeping along, goes into the next room. Making his way toward the open window, he hoists himself up to the sill, looks down through an open door at his brother jumping on the trapeze, performing on the bars and the rings with gusto and with the love a real artist feels for his work. "How supple he is . . . How skillful . . . How handsome . . ." Nello remarks, longingly. Then, sobbing, he lets his head fall on the sill. His brother, sensing something is wrong, rushes up, takes Nello in his arms, hugs him tightly. "Child," he says, "kiss me! . . . The Zemgano brothers are dead! . . . Only two fiddlers are left; and they will play from now on, their behinds seated on chairs!"

Antoine who played the role of Gianni, went to Medrano's circus in Paris, to watch, observe, study all types of stunts so as to imbibe himself with the atmosphere needed to create a proper mise-en-scène. Detailed in all ways, Antoine's *real* circus environment on stage elicited praise from reviewers. So, too, did Mevisto's portrayal of Nello; Antoine's incarnation of Gianni, however, left much to be desired in the Goncourts' view. His enunciation was so poor and his voice so soft that most of the dialogue was incomprehensible.

Elisa, the Whore:

Antoine's production of *Elisa, the Whore*, adapted by Jean Ajalbert from the Goncourt novel by the same name, created a furor. "Immoral," cried certain critics and spectators. The grossness of the dialogue was offensive; the shallow characterizations and undramatic plot were dull.   Another thesis play, which speaks out against society for allowing and encouraging prostitution, then casts off its victims like so many unwanted animals. *Elisa, the Whore* was already old-fashioned.   The consensus: the Goncourts were just not playwrights.

The Escape:
      The Escape, a drama based on one of Villiers de l'Isle-Adam's (1838-1889) tales, is both fascinating and terrifying, perhaps because the author of this work was himself a strangely hallucinatory figure.   Although impoverished to the extreme, his clothes threadbare, his demeanor unkempt, Villiers walked the streets of Paris with the dignity of a "provisionally dethroned king."   Almost nightly he could be seen at one of the brasseries in Montmartre, talking to his friends, or reading from his works. His voice was arresting.   It had a hypnotic quality about it—as if it came from another world.   All listened without moving.   Unable to adapt to the real world, he preferred the occult domain, identifying as he did with some mythic hero living in some remote period of time.   Antoine described him as

> magnificently Bohemian with his long locks and strange eyes, under the pretext of instructing his actor, he seizes any opportunity to play the convict who is the hero of his drama and his portrayal is so gripping that, for the pleasure of the thing, I often let him go all the way to the end.[21]

      The Escape takes audiences into "the heartland of the cut-throat"—to an isolated house in the country near Rochefort. Night has fallen.   The curtains part on a living room.   A large curtained window is visible to the left of the stage, as well as a balcony which opens onto a garden, and a door, backstage.   On the table in the middle of the living room are two vases filled with flowers.   A love seat, a rug, a piano and some unlit candles make up the rest of the set.
      Only moon rays light the stage.   A man enters from the balcony; his hair is cut very short, his shirt is dirty, torn, and bloody.   We learn that he is an escaped convict and that he wants to make his entrance into the *real* world by a horrible murder which would put him in possession of a great fortune.   He has already strangled an old servant; he now has to kill the young couple married that very morning, who are going to spend their

Stage set for Goncourt's *Elisa, the Whore*

wedding night in this remote house. Another man, his accomplice, dressed in a sailor's uniform, follows him into the living room. They speak in hushed tones, fearing someone might overhear. The accomplice puts a narcotic in a drinking glass the couple will use for their celebration. Soon, noises are heard from the outside. The newlyweds enter. Their joy is boundless. They drink to long life, then fall asleep on the couch. The convict, who has hidden behind a curtain during the interim, emerges, intent upon fulfilling his deed. So disarmed is he, however, by the uttter innocence of the sleeping couple, that he has second thoughts; he cannot go through with his plan. His anxiety is acute. Audiences see him wrestling with his conscience, torn between his desire to escape from the law and his need to be redeemed. So disoriented is he that the knife he had taken out of his back pocket, to be used for his crime, falls from his hand. The door opens; the police arrive. Someone had informed on him. The criminal gives himself up. There is no struggle; he goes willingly toward his punishment, and says, *"It seems to me that now I AM REALLY ESCAPING!"*

Mevisto's portrayal of the *apache* transcended the usual stereotypic criminal incarnated on so many Parisian stages. His guttural, violent, raspy and acerbic articulations were singled out for praise, as was the restraint he imposed upon his role, which served to increase the terrifying effect of this murderer's appetite for revenge and blood. Critics alluded to him as "a great artist." The reality of his composition, and the fear he instilled in his audience, grew in intensity throughout the dramatic unfolding. Indeed, some critics compared the play to Victor Hugo's monumental *The Last Days of a Condemned Man* and to his *Misérables*, so stark was the portrayal and the viscerality of the episode depicted.

Antoine, as the accomplice, also played well: subtly and in a nuanced manner. As for the young couple, they were dressed in the style of 1830: the young boy in a blue suit with a velvet collar, and curled hair; the young girl in a chiffon dress with puffed sleeves and soft curls in "Ninon" style.

Although *The Escape* smacks of Grand-Guignol gore, its irony, bitterness, cruelty, and poetry both shocked and impressed audiences. Villiers's fervor, the mastership he revealed in creating atmosphere, and his sculpted and sanded dialogue, endowed a work based on a banal incident with archetypal dimension. Praise also went to Antoine for having given Villiers—a recluse and a querulous, misunderstood and singularly unappreciated writer, but a unique creative spirit—a chance to have his work performed at the Théâtre Libre.

The Kiss:

One of Antoine's biggest successes was Théodore de Banville's *The Kiss*, a charming, delicate, poetic pantomimic fairy tale, reminiscent of *A Midsummer Night's Dream*. Like Antoine, Banville had also wanted to alter what he considered to be the circumscribed and banal theatrical scene. Indeed, he labeled Scribe the "Antichrist of literature."[22]

The Kiss takes place in a delightful forest scene—à la Corot—in the outskirts of Paris. The lilting music composed by M. Vidal for the occasion suits Banville's light and sprightly verses. The old Fairy Urgèle knows that a kiss from a young man will render her young again. The handsome youth, Pierrot, who happens into the forest, food-basket in hand and full of life and joy, sees the fairy and soon complies with her wishes. Now that beauty and radiance are again hers, he is captivated by her grace and suggests they marry. She agrees, but suddenly, she hears singularly divine and supernatural music emanating from all about. Her sisters are beckoning to her in tonal modulations to return to them—to the land of Dream and Fancy.

> Instead of marrying,
> Follow me, the heavens are so pure!
> And run about in the dew,
> Fly into the sky!
>
> The dreamy pond reflects
> The surrounding reeds.
> Come now, let us go and drink
> Together with the birds!

Deftly, she returns Pierrot's kiss to him and flies away. Pierrot, heartbroken at first, is ready to die. Soon, however, reason returns. He will live and search for another love.

Antoine, as Pierrot, recited Banville's crystalline verse with point, never maudlin or sentimental; his words seemed to radiate as they poured forth, revealing their myriad facets. As the ingenuous clown, Antoine underplayed his part, thereby accentuating the "naively innocent" side of his character while also playing up the tenderly idealistic aspect. Comic and dramatic, his dreamlike countenance was compared to a painting by Watteau of the clown *Gilles*. Such an analogy is apt, since Banville had always wanted to write very special type plays which would bring to life the idyllic people Watteau had painted on his canvases.

Spectators, much moved by *The Kiss*, responded with an ovation. As for Banville, he expressed his pleasurable reactions to Zola:

> "They act like angels; where the devil did they learn to speak verse?" to which Zola replied: "Here, I believe, are the actors we have needed for a long time."[23]

Tabarin's Wife:

Catulle Mendès' (1841-1909) *Tabarin's Wife* dramatized the well known tragic story of a clown so jealous of his wife that he murders her. Although the story is banal, what is intriguing is the drama's structure: the play within a play technique.

The curtains open onto a stage divided into two parts. On one side, there is a stall-like platform on which Tabarin, a Pagliacci-like character, struts about before his audience, made up of richly dressed lords and ladies, seated on the opposite side of the proscenium. In the center, in back, sit the musicians, performing melodies written by Emmanuel Chabrier for the occasion. The spectators attending the Théâtre Libre, then, have a triple view of the happenings: they not only saw the audience observing Tabarin and the clown himself, but could peer backstage, behind the performers' stall.

As the curtains part, Tabarin's wife is preparing supper. She laments the fact that she has married such a buffoon. Rather than spending his time earning money, he flits about from cabaret to cabaret. Time passes. Tabarin's wife has spied someone she likes: a cardinal's guard. They meet behind a curtain directly in back of Tabarin's stage. Their lovemaking takes place simultaneously with his performance on the outside proscenium. Tabarin tells his audiences that he loves his wife madly; that he would kill anyone who might take her away from him. As he utters these very words, spectators can see the wife in the arms of her lover, behind the slightly-drawn curtain back stage. Tabarin happens to glance back and sees the two in flagrante delicto. Aroused to the point of madness, he asks his audience for a sword, rushes behind the scenes, to the applause of the spectators who admire the reality of his gestures and facial expressions.   Moments later, he returns to his small stage, brandishing the bloody weapon which he then breaks in two in a burst of horror.

Tabarin's Wife, a "brutal" and "poetic" burlesque, was an instantaneous success, soon to be taken over by the Comédie-Française. With Mendès' usual humility, he suggested that the accolades received were due to Antoine's daring direction. He called him "the consolation of old romanticists as well as the hope of the young naturalists." Speaking directly to Antoine, he remarked that it was "from the time of the inauguration of your free boards that one must date the renaissance of real drama, of real comedy and of real farce."[24]

Antoine was also praised for his portrayal of Tabarin. "He brought his science and "his ardor to the terrifying role of Tabarin; he was magnificent in the last scene," wrote Méténier.[25] Other critics referred to his Tabarin as "remarkable"; his supple movements, his powerful rage building up to a climax, revealed technical mastership. As for the faithless wife, protrayed by Marie Fresnes, her emotions ranged from delightful sensuality in her low-cut gypsy dress to feelings of horror, at the conclusion, as her once beautiful throat now becomes a mass of blood.

*

Catulle Mendès' next play, Queen Fiamette, a six-act verse drama with music by Paul Vidal, proved to be a financial and artistic disaster. The cost of fashioning the Renaissance costumes and sets was prohibitive and Antoine found himself in greater debt than ever before. Originally written for Sarah Bernhardt, Queen Fiamette was too flamboyant and old-fashioned for audiences of the Théâtre Libre. Moreover, its intricate structure, its pompous stylization, its protagonists given to extremes, was written in true Hugo and Dumas style—in outworn and outdated tradition.

Lucie Pellegrin's End:
Some critics referred to Alexis' play, Lucie Pellegrin's End, as another Lady of the Camelias, whose Armand Duval would be called Chochotte, and whose unredeemed Marguerite would fare even more tragically.

The action takes place in sequences of flashbacks. The decor features a room filled with strange and haunting mementos. Its owner, once a celebrated cocotte and the rage of Paris, is now grey and ill. In her delirium, she recalls her past, to the accompaniment of the "Waltz of the Roses" played by the orchestra of the Élysée-Montmartre. Those were the happy days when her lovers, male and female, were all at her feet, captivated by her dazzling body and provocative ways. Although fatigue and sickness have taken their toll on Lucie Pellegrin, she refuses to give up and thinks that she may once again be that spellbinder she had been. "I want to begin to live once again. You will see, my life is not over. . . . I can still attract men." Before she dies, her friend enters. Portrayed by Félicien Mallet, the well known cabaret star of the period, Chochotte is dressed like a man; his large hips, however, reveal her sexual identity, making obvious her lesbian relationship with Lucie Pellegrin.

Some critics and spectators were offended by the realistic portrayals of the homosexual. "Scandalous," they said. The dialogue, for the most part in *argot*, was offensive. Vitu, Sarcey, Fouquier, condemned *Lucie Pellegrin's End* outright.

*

A plethora of plays followed. *Serenade,* a cynical, satiric, and coarse *comédie rosse* by Jean Jullien, was designed to provoke anyone adhering to the sacrosanct principles set down by Scribe and Sarcey. It was Jullien who is said to have coined the phrase *slice of life* theatre, thereby transposing Zola's term, *lambeau d'existence,* which was used for the novel. Julien was also the one to have suggested to Antoine that he do away with footlights, arguing that illumination in the *real* world comes from above and not from below.

Antoine was also influenced by the innovative lighting techniques used by the celebrated English actor, Henry Irving. By focusing a kind of spotlight on isolated parts of the set or segments of the stage, Irving succeeded in heightening the intensity of the unfolding drama. Lights, then, were used by him as an element of the stage play and as a kind of protagonist or catalyst, capable of accentuating the emotions of the moment. Antoine began using Irving's lighting technique, focusing his stage lights, one at a time, on certain objects—plants, flowers, etc.—thereby setting them apart from the rest of the accessories and lending both a mysterious and realistic touch to the stage happenings.

Antoine also borrowed from English theatre the idea of a movable platform, thus facilitating the many scene changes required in certain plays. Likewise, he began to set out his decors non-symmetrically and irregularly on stage, reasoning that in so doing he better paralleled the lay-outs in real homes. He also began using hydraulic power and electricity, thereby succeeding in eliminating the distracting noises usually made during scene changes.

Antoine kept up his arduous work schedule, evoking either praise or condemnation, or both, with each new venture. *The Butchers* by Fernand Icres created a sensation—not as dramatic literature, but for its mise-en-scène which some critics considered the epitome of bad taste. Because the action takes place in a butcher shop, Antoine, attempting to be ultra realistic, hung actual pieces of meat on stage. This "bloody" setting, he reasoned, was in keeping with the play's theme: two butchers murder each other over the love of a woman.

Antoine's Rembrandt-like lighting effects—clusters of deep shadows with light infiltrating from the window every now and then—underscored the gleaming steel blades used by the butchers both to cut the meat and commit their murders. Horror dominated this stage play from beginning to end.

Sarcey was incensed. Not only did he consider the sets unartistic, but "odious" and coarse.   "Oh Naturalism!" he exclaimed, "What horrors are written in thy name!" He predicted that if Antoine pursued this course he would be courting disaster: he even renamed the Théâtre Libre "The Montparnasse Cemetery."   Daudet considered Antoine's choice of plays lugubrious—a Feast of the Dead.[26]

Outrage poured onto Antoine with his production of Rodolphe Darzens' mystery play, *Christ's Lover*.   That Christ and Mary Magdalene were portrayed on stage—and the latter, erotically—was considered sacrilegious.   Yet the dramatist, a good Catholic, reasoned otherwise. Hadn't many Renaissance painters depicted Madeleine bending low at Christ's feet? Hadn't Jean Michel, in his fifteenth-century liturgical drama, accented Madeleine's sensual past? Nor were Correggio's Madeleines always sacrosanct.

Such bad publicity did not enhance Antoine's financial situation; nor did his location in Montparnasse draw the sought-for crowds. He decided, therefore, to return to the Right Bank, this time to the more accessible Menus-Plaisirs on the Boulevard de Strasbourg.

A stroke of good luck ensued: Antoine was invited by the very wealthy Mme. Aubernon de Nerville, who lived on the fashionable Rue Astorg, to play the lead opposite the famous star, Réjane, in a private performance of Henri Becque's *La Parisienne*. Not only was it an unhoped-for honor to play opposite one of France's most celebrated actresses, but it also made it possible for him to meet the famous dramatist, Henri Becque, whose works he so admired.

Becque had, since the very birth of the Théâtre Libre, written in praise of Antoine's endeavor. It was Becque who had described Antoine as a "really young, very cultivated" director, underscoring his highly perceptive and sensitive views of things theatrical, and complimenting him for his zeal, his fervor, his open and sincere approach to the performing arts. He does not, Becque remarked, "seek to *stagger*" his audiences, nor create a new style. Still, Becque had not all praise for the new school. Antoine produced too many naturalistic works, too many thesis dramas, he thought, in an attempt to proselytize audiences.

Henri Becque (1837-1899), author of *La Navette* and *The Crows* was a loner in theatre. His plays, rejected by the Comédie-Française among other theatres, did not prevent him from accomplishing on stage what Balzac, Flaubert, Goncourt, and Zola had executed in the novel: to create good theatre within the framework of traditional forms, but divested of the conventions of the well-made play. Becque's skillful dialogue pointed up character, and although mostly negative, unlike the Naturalists he succeeded in evoking compassion and feeling from his audiences.

La Parisienne, in which Antoine performed, is an example of the *slice of life* theatre. A satire on the *ménage à trois*, it has verve and point. The delightful, superficial, but terribly bored, Clotilde, turns her charm onto her lover's rival in order to help her husband secure the position he seeks. Using all the wiles and feminine finesse known to her sex, this paradigm of the *civilized woman* continues to scheme until she reaches her goal.

Critics in general, and Faguet in particular, though rejecting his ultracynical and morose view of life, considered Becque a worthwhile dramatist. Intransigeant in his views, difficult to get along with, Becque had suffered rejection of his work at the hands of so many directors. He was a dreamer, though, and hoped one day to find a director who would produce his plays *in the right way*. He was certain that Antoine was such a director and for this reason, as well as for Antoine's integrity and courage, he held him in great esteem.

Antoine would have wanted nothing better than to direct one of Becque's works. Many a time he asked the dramatist to write a play for the Théâtre Libre. Becque simply could not; he had evidently written himself out. "I have never had any dramatic stock to draw from," he told Antoine. "I don't know what it is to take notes or write scenarios." Antoine never gave up hope that one day Becque's creative talents would again flow forth. To this end he took him to Brittany to spend the summer, leaving him there with paper and writing material. It was to no avail.[27]

Antoine was growing in understanding and broadening in experience. Always interested in studying the directing and acting techniques of others, he learned to assess their results and his own by analogy. He had reached a point in his development when he began questioning the validity of the teaching methods of the Conservatoire—that august school for actors where such matinee idols as Gôt, Delaunay, Maubant, and Worms taught. Students attended a two-hour class twice a week, which meant that they studied around a hundred to a hundred and twenty-five hours a year. What kind of roles did they study? Usually classical ones, which may or may not have suited the temperament of the student performing it. Moreover, to restrict oneself to the classics is to limit the students' perspective concerning art in general and their potentials in particular. During the future actor's three-year stay at the Conservatoire, he or she might win first prize simply by rehearsing a single part while enrolled in school. How can such an actor be expected to create anything but what he has memorized and studied during the three-year period? The entrance requirements were also unfair, Antoine remarked. Although examinations were required, those students with "pull" were accepted; those without it were often rejected. As for the prize-winning students many of them walked the streets of Paris looking for a job. They were not hired and rightly so, Antoine contended, since they were really unequipped to exercise their art with expertise. Even the teachers at the Conservatoire no longer believed in the merits of this system.

In May of 1890 Antoine set forth his own artistic program in brochure form.   His training methods, his choice of plays, based on "keen study and observation," required performers imbued with a sense of reality. Antoine explained:

> These future works, based on a broader and more flexible aesthetic, in which the characters are no longer typed; this new theatre, no longer based—as was the theatre before it—on five or six conventional types, always the same and constantly reappearing under different names and in different plots and settings; this multiplicity, and complexity of characters brought to the stage will, I have no doubt, bring forth a new generation of actors suited to all kinds of roles. *Jeunes premiers*, for example, will no longer be just a single type but will become in turn good, evil, stupid, witty, elegant, vulgar, strong, weak, courageous, and cowardly. In short, they will be living beings—complex beings—complex and variable.
>
> Thus the actor's art will no longer be based, as was that of the acting companies in the past, on physical qualities and vocal gifts: it will thrive on truth, observation, and *direct* study of nature.
>
> We will achieve in the theatre what has occurred in other interpretative arts—in painting, for example, where the landscape-artist no longer works in his studio but in the open air and in the midst of life. The theatre will no longer produce dramatic artists repeating the same roles over and over again, roles which have been created and established for centuries by several generations of famous actors. The actor's intellectual talent will again be directed toward truth and exactness.
>
> Since the theatrical style in the new works tends more toward the use of everyday conversation, the performer will no longer have to *declaim* in the narrow and classical sense of the term, but will have to *talk*, a feat which will be found to be just as difficult.
>
> What at the present time is meant by the term, *the art of elocution*, consists solely in exaggerated enunciation, in developing the student's voice as a *special* organ quite different from the voice he really possesses. For sixty years now, all the actors have spoken only through their *nose*, simply because that kind of elocution is necessary to be heard by the audience in our *too large halls with their poor acoustics*, and also because speaking through the nose prevents the voice from aging and wearing out with the years.
>
> All the characters in the present-day theatre have the same gestures and express themselves technically in the same manner, whether they be old or young, ill or in good health. All the *fine-speaking* artists forego those infinitely numerous nuances which could illuminate a character and give it a more intense life . . .
>
> In most of our theatres, either too huge or badly built, not only do the players not speak, they *yell*; and the unfortunate actors are forced to do this so much that even when they play in the Boulevard theatres they retain these excesses and exaggerations which cause an actor to stand out among ten people chatting.

The same transformation will have to take place in the other spheres of dramatic art. With stage-sets brought back to the actual dimensions of scenes of contemporary life, the actors will play in true-to-life settings, without the constant need to *strike poses* in the customary sense of the term. The audiences will enjoy, in an intimate play, developing simply and naturally, the simple gestures and natural movements of a modern man living our everyday life.

The actual movements on the stage will be modified: the actor will no longer step out of the setting in which he has been playing and pose before the audience. He will fit in with the furniture and the stage-props; and "his performance will be broadened" to include those thousands of nuances and details which have become indispensable in capturing the spirit of a character and building it logically.

Purely mechanical movement, voice effects, empirical and redundant gestures, will disappear with the simplification of theatrical action and its return to reality. The actor will come back to natural gestures and will substitute *composition   for effect achieved solely by means of the voice.* Expressions will be based on familiar and real props: a returned pencil or an overturned cup will be as significant and will have as profound an effect on the minds of the audience as the grandiloquent exaggerations of the romantic theatre.

....

Although it may sound a little paradoxical, one may almost lay down the proposition that: *In an actor, the profession is the enemy of art.*

We mean the professional skill that is abnormally developed, that invades everything; we mean too frequent tricks and cleverness which stifle personality and dominate the supreme quality of the dramatic performer: *emotion,* that kind of special and souble sensitivity which imbues the actor who is a true artist.

Here, moreover, as in all the arts, sincerity, *élan,* a kind of conviction, and the special fever that grips the interpreter are the most precious gifts.

The teaching of drama, as it is applied, snuffs out this special kind of nervousness and levels all temperaments. Individuality becomes rarer and rarer, and we find that our "greatest actors were mediocre students precisely because their artistic temperament resisted traditions and narrow, over-specializing training. How many of the ten noted actors of Paris distinguished themselves in competitions at the *Conservatoire?*

Once someone asked Stendhal if he had ever seen a play perfectly rendered. He replied: "Yes, some time ago in Italy, by mediocre actors in a barn."

Obviously, he was referring to the way in which these obscure and unknown actors had acted as an *ensemble.* And he was certainly right, for is not *ensemble* playing the most complete and the most exquisite joy in the theatre? We must admit that such a treat is almost impossible today; even the *Théâtre-Français*, which nevertheless has in its company the most remarkable actors in Europe, is no longer able to give us such a treat. We have to go back several years and recall the opening performances of *l'Ami Fritz*, for example, to remind ourselves what *true ensemble acting* is like.

The *Comédie-Française* finds itself today in the same situation as the other Paris theatres in which the *star* system has done so much harm to the dramatic art (and to the manager's box-office receipts!). Everywhere, when we spend an evening at the theatre, we are fascinated by one or two first-rate artists around whom everything gravitates and for whom everything is arranged. But in such a state of affairs, what—from the strictly artistic point of view—becomes of the measure, the balance, and the harmony of a dramatic work? Develop this theory before any present-day actor, and he will only be concerned with his performance in the part assigned to him: he will think only of amplifying and developing his own role and its effect, even at the expense of throwing the whole work out of balance.

A very young artist at the *Comédie-Française*, already crowned with success and endowed with a keen intelligence, had to carry in a lamp and a letter in the third act of one of the masterpieces of contemporary theatre. He was very astonished to hear the following said to him: "But my dear sir, even though you have shown so much talent, subtlety, and finesse in the modest part you played this evening, you forgot one of the basic principles in the art of the actor: *keep the character you portray on his own level.* When you carry the lamp and the letter, you are nothing but a slight incident imagined by the author in order to hasten the course of his action. As you hand over the letter to Mlle. Bartet, one of the protagonists in the play, on whom all the attention and interest of the audience are concentrated at that precise moment by the express will of the author, if you find a way of putting on the entire *Les Fourberies de Scapin, Les Précieuses ridicules,* and the five acts of *L'Etourdi,* you will win applause from the indulgent playgoers, but you will introduce an extraneous element into the drama, you will harm the skillful ordering of the work you are interpreting.

This young man certainly did not understand what the other person meant, yet he is one of the outstanding talents in the current theatre.

So the model for an ensemble company would be a group of about thirty actors of moderate talent, all equally gifted. They would be simple people who *always—no matter what happened*—followed this basic law of ensemble acting.[28]

*

Antoine's views were, to be sure, new and provocative. He must also be commended for having produced the works of four outstanding playwrights of the period: Georges de Porto-Riche (1849-1930), Eugène Brieux (1858-1932), François de Curel (1854-1928), and Georges Courteline (1858-1929).

Françoise's Luck:

After having scandalized many a spectator and critic with his *In Love* (*Amoureuse,* 1879), considered a brutal psychological analysis, the discouraged Porto-Riche withdrew from the dramatic scene.   Upon his return some years later, dejection again set in after his new offerings were rejected by the Comédie-Française and the Vaudeville.   When *Françoise's Luck* came into Antoine's hands, he was impressed by the author's audacity and authenticity.   Although the play might invite protests, he thought, it was worth a good fight.   Nevertheless, when it came time to rehearse Porto-Riche's play, author and director did not see eye to eye.   The dramatist did not like Antoine's "new" style acting, the natural and casual way of treating tension-filled incidents.   Understandably, Antoine's zeal and fervor were considerably diminished.   He did not allow enough rehearsal time and as a result, the performers' gestures and vocal tonalities lacked the finesse and nuances they should have had for a drama dealing with a wife whose luck was to have been saved from her husband's infidelities.

Critics decried the sloppiness of the acting.   They also found fault with the decors: they were not only meaningless, but lacked all aesthetic sense.   Approbation, however, was given the play: Porto-Riche's style was reminiscent of those delightful eighteenth and nineteenth-century parlor comedies—à la Marivaux and Musset.   Some critics likened Porto-Riche's cruel irony to Becque's: both had insight into the human heart, both were deft and incisive in their portrayals; the truth they ferreted out, however, must be sparingly decanted to audiences.

Blanchette:

Before Antoine's production of *Blanchette* (1892), he had introduced Brieux to his audiences with *Artists' Households* (1890).   The latter drama could be labeled a *morality* play: married poets must see to the welfare of their families or expect to be punished.   All of Brieux's dramas are *thesis* or *social* plays which fight for a cause, intent upon righting an injustice.   A milieu is given, a character—either virtuous or vicious—chooses his or her direction and is either rewarded or chastised for the ensuing action.   As Brieux stated in his preface to his *Complete Theatre*:

> I always looked upon theatre not as a goal, but as a means. I not only wanted to provoke thought by means of the performing arts, but to modify habits and actions; even more, to change certain administrative matters that I think are desirable. Because of my life, I wanted the quantity of suffering throughout the world to be diminished just a little bit.[29]

Brieux, always concerned with social and moral problems, was a reformer by nature who acquired intimate knowledge of provincial life.   Yet, technically speaking, his characters are mere silhouettes; their problems are superficially treated; their milieux serve only to prove a point.   Despite these failings, Antoine's production of *Blanchette* earned acolades for both dramatist and director. Not long afterwards, it became part of the repertory of the Comédie-Française and played throughout the world—with unfaltering acclaim.

A comedy of manners, *Blanchette* tells the story of a young peasant girl who was given a fine education, which resulted in an appointment to a government school. While waiting to begin her new post, Blanchette returns home to her father (Antoine), the owner of a wine shop/cafe. Imbued with new ideas which she considers superior to her parents' old-fashioned, retrograde, and boorish ways, she takes it upon herself to modernize the family's shop/cafe. She also informs her parents that she has decided not to live in the country, but in Paris instead.   Her goal in life is to acquire wealth and to travel. When her rich friend from boarding school calls on her, Blanchette is visibly ashamed of her parents peasant ways. So irate is Blanchette's father with his daughter's attitude and the *costly* transformations she has made in his shop that he sends her away from home. Blanchette leaves for Paris. Soon disheartened, she realizes that the dreams of wealth and love she has had nurtured were unrealistic. The shock of recognition encourages her to attempt suicide. She is rescued just in time. She becomes the mistress of her friend's brother who eventually tires of her. When Blanchette learns that her father's property is being sold for debt, she offers him the funds to pay it. Never would he touch her "tainted" money! Despairing, Blanchette returns to Paris to live the life of a prostitute. As the curtain falls, she cries out, "Suckers beware!"

Because Brieux knew that his painful ending might prove offensive to some spectators, Brieux offered Antoine three different conclusions to *Blanchette*.   The first, recounted above, was *rosse*.   The second was overly dramatic: Blanchette returns home purified after her ordeal, begs her father to accept her money, which he does, after which the family sits down to their meal and recites the *Bénédicité*.   The third features a virtuous Blanchette who returns to a thriving shop/cafe and marries a country-boy of her own class. Antoine chose none of these endings. He concluded his production with Act II—with Blanchette's departure—on a strong and powerful note.

As to be expected, Antoine's sets were realistic: the inside of a small country shop/cafe with two windows in back adorned with checkered curtains; a slightly raised counter on which bottles of liquor and empty glasses had been placed. In the foreground stood a small round table, and some stools; another table, covered with an oil cloth, right of center. A shelf on one wall was filled with liquor bottles. Blanchette's framed diploma hung on another, among other ornaments typical of the environment and the class.

Although *Blanchette* was a work of propaganda and Brieux was a social reformer, compassionate audiences responded overtly to his profound sympathy for the poor, the unwanted, and the outcast. *Blanchette* was neither maudlin nor bombastic; it had neither rhetoric nor preaching, thereby accentuating the interest of a play dealing with such eternal themes as the generation gap and the problem of the over-qualified who seem not to be able to fit into society's hierarchy.   Despite Brieux's limited imagination and rather pedestrian style, he had the faculty of breathing life into his characters.   So, too, did Antoine, particularly when portraying Blanchette's father—a tormented man who knows he cannot see eye to eye with his daughter nor cope with altering circumstances.

*

Antoine was not a theorist, as we know; he did, however, express his ideas on the performing arts every now and then, either in brochure form, or in statements to friends, or in letters. To the well-known actor, Le Bargy, he wrote on the art of the actor:

I should like to convince you . . . that actors should have no
theories about the works which they perform. Their business is
merely to play them, to interpret, to the best of their ability, characters which they may fail to understand. They are in reality man-
ikins, marionettes, more or less perfected in proportion to their talents, whom the author dresses and moves about at will. Certainly,
after long years, they acquire at times a sort of material experience;
they can tell an author why a character should come in or go out on
the right rather than on the left, but in no case can they, or should
they, without departing from their true function, try to modify a
character or a dénouement.

The intellectual gap between the poet and his interpreter is so
impossible that never can the latter satisfy the former. The actor
always deforms the vision of the author who accepts a characterization that is nearly right, and who most often resigns himself to
the impossible. . . . The absolute ideal of the actor should be to
make himself a keyboard, an instrument, marvelously tuned, on
which the author may play at will. It is sufficient for him to have
a purely physical and technical training, to make his body, face,
and voice more supple, and an intellectual training that will permit him to understand simply what the author would have him
express. If it is asked of him to be sad or gay, he ought, to be a good
comedian in the exact sense of the word, to express in masterly fash-
ion, sadness or gaiety, without appreciating why these sentiments
are demanded of him. That is the author's business; he knows what
he is doing, and he is the only one who is responsible to the spectator. You will agree with me that the actor's art, thus reduced to
its limits, still remains a conspicuously honorable and difficult
one.[30]

The Other Side of a Saint:

The story of how Antoine chose to produce two of Curel's
plays is amusing. Curel, who had received so many rejections at
the hands of directors, decided to sign the names of three of his
friends to the drama he sent to Antoine: *Love Weaves, The
Walk-on* and *The Other Side of a Saint.* Incredible as it may
seem, of the five-hundred plays he received, Antoine picked the
three by Curel, though each was signed by a different name.

The Other Side of a Saint is a psychological drama which
probes the savage and repressed psyche of Julie Renaudin. We
learn at the outset of the play that she had loved her cousin,
Henri, who had left for Paris. Not only did he forget her in the
big city, but when he did return, it was with Jeanne, his wife.
Overcome with jealousy, Julie pushes the now-pregnant Jeanne
down a ravine. Christine is born prematurely. Julie's guilt is so
great that she enters a convent. She remains there for eighteen
years, hoping all the while to purify her soul. The play begins

after Henri's death. Julie returns home only to learn that she who had wanted Henri to think of her as a "martyr to love" had been told by Jeanne the truth about her crime. Angered anew, Julie again seeks revenge. This time she encourages Christine to take the veil and not marry the young man to whom she is engaged. When, however, she is told that before Henri died, he had asked Christine to be kind to Julie whom he had wronged, her rage dissipates and she returns to the convent only after convincing Christine to marry the man she loves. Before leaving, in a moment of unconscious brutality, Julie crushes to death the little bird she holds in her hand—before its owner can return it to its cage. This act, considered symbolic at the time, was designed to reveal Julie's still-powerful unconscious murderous instincts; it also symbolizes the hateful life she leads, incarcerated in a convent.

> Poor little bird, they are going to put you back into a cage . . . a prisoner for life! . . . Hopping from your perch to your eating tray and back again, from your eating tray to your perch . . . and singing so sadly.

The in-depth study of the anger and violence inhabiting a passionate and primitive nature such as Julie's was a difficult role to cast. A complex individual, who is neither strictly flesh and blood, nor a theoretical essence, Julie stands above the mundane individual, resembling more closely a Racinian figure—a fire-brand—a mythological creature. Although Curel probed Julie's psyche and the instincts revealed were authentic, audiences at the Théâtre Libre felt uninvolved. Curel explains:

> By a singular contradiction, my mind, naturally inclined to seek the reason of things, expresses itself easily only in dramatic form. What shall you say of a soul in which the meditative curiosity of a Montaigne is united to the fanciful outpourings of a Musset? . . . Characters present themselves to my imagination passionate and vibrating, but I am tormented with a desire to go back to the causes which make them act, whence it results that in my plays the thought goes hand in hand with the action. A combination fraught with difficulty if I want to conquer my public upon which is imposed the double task of getting interested in my plot, of assimilating my idea. . . . Yes, thought is the worst enemy of a dramatic author, and each time that he brings it into a play without meeting disaster, he accomplishes a miracle.[31]

The Other Side of a Saint required only one set: a living room in a wealthy household. The highly polished floors, heavy curtains, colored rugs placed evenly in front of each arm chair, the liquor cabinet, the backgammon set, the photograph album, set off the uninteresting but expensive-looking furniture. That there were neither books nor newspapers in the room was commentary enough on the inhabitants of a hate-filled home.

Although fascinating in its insights and poetic in its dialogue audiences reacted adversely to *The Other Side of a Saint*. Overly analytical and slow-moving, and though free of bombast and rhetoric, viewers felt detached from both the events and the protagonists. They felt outside of things because *The Other Side of a Saint* did not follow the "usual formula"; rather, it introduced viewers to *new* and *vital* elements which were for the most part unpalatable. Despite the adverse criticisms, Antoine considered the play's value to be *internal*: its drama was lived within the human being and not outwardly, heightening, thereby, the austerity and asceticism of the participants.

Despite the generally poor reactions, there were some critics, such as Lemaître, who singled out *The Other Side of a Saint* for praise. "The most original and interesting play," he wrote, "which the Théâtre Libre has given" in the past two years. He pursues:

> The play has tedious moments, awkward spots, useless repetitions—the same things are echoed many times in it, and not at all where they should be for the clarity, interest, and movement of the drama. The play is a bit too close to a very good novel in dialogue form. Even so, it is beautiful and has an exquisite quality.[32]

René Doumic concurred:

> M. Curel's play is composed of a series of conversations in which the characters tell about themselves and analyze themselves. The conversations are repetitious and as a result, the whole lacks vivacity, but, still, except for these reservations, *The Other Side of a Saint* recommends itself by rare qualities—a highly elevated conception, a delightful curiosity about the secrets of the internal life, the boldness to carry a study of a psychological case through to its end, an analytic vigor pushed to its limit, and finally, the gift of breathing life into imaginary characters.[33]

Henry Bauer of the *Echo de Paris*, could not praise *The Other Side of a Saint* highly enough: "Finally, we have gone back to the

real way of art and literature, above purely plastic realism, repug-
nant exceptions, facile brutalities, tetralogical incidents." Curel's
mastership was immediately discernible, he continued, speaking
as he does directly to and *about the soul* in "strong, clear, nervous," language.[34]

Understandably, Curel was deeply grateful to Antoine for
producing *The Other Side of a Saint* and conveyed his feelings to
him and to his troupe in an introduction to his *Complete
Works:*

> He, Antoine, exercised a prodigious influence over his company of
> actors; he was an apostle teaching new doctrines, and a master in
> indicating the way to apply them. His most insignificant judg-
> ments were listened to religiously. When he announced the coming
> of a man of genius, all the faces about him were illuminated with a
> look of triumph. Thanks to a little act played at the Théâtre-
> Libre, an author had the sensation for a year of being a great man.
> As for me, the glorious hours that I have lived in the humble room
> in the Rue Blanche remain the most beautiful of my literary life.
> The people whom I met there really deserve the name of artists, a
> name usurped by so many second-raters. . . . They loved their art
> with a disinterested passion and played with a heart that gave us
> interpreters which the highest official theatres were incapable of
> equalling.[35]

The Fossils:

The Fossils, produced a year later, received high praise
from most critics—although begrudgingly from Sarcey. Its poetry was likened to the alexandrines of Corneille; its depth and
understanding reached universal proportions. Some viewers,
nevertheless, found its theme of *incest* unpalatable, distasteful,
immoral.

"The Fossils" are those aristocrats who consider their heritage, their past—their fossilized ways—to be sacrosanct. Robert
de Chantemelle, the last in line of a decadent family, is dying of
tuberculosis. He leaves an illegitimate son, who is destined to
maintain the family traditions and rule over their vast estate
and holdings. A question remains: did Robert or his father, the
Duke, beget the child? Both men had had the same mistress.

The decors: an old manor house in the Ardennes. The
immense reception hall is filled with panoplies and hunting tro-
phies, ancient armaments, genealogical trees, and plans of the
estate, lending a feudal and severe note to the atmosphere.
Seemingly banal, the sets, nevertheless, were unusual. The

Stage sets for Ibsen's *The Wild Duck*

three acts, although played in the same reception hall, were viewed from different angles each time the curtain went up, as if the sets were turning on themselves. Never once did the audience view the same section of the room twice.

Antoine, as the Duke of Chantemelle, received poor criticisms. Rather than speaking his words clearly, he mumbled them, thereby denaturing his character. Yet, in the crucial scene, when the father informed Robert that the girl he loves and the mother of the child was also his mistress, he did so with restraint and dignity, befitting his aristocratic heritage. The dignity of his avowal lent heroic grandeur to his portrayal and by extension to the entire drama.

Mention must be made of Curel's extraordinary dialogue in *The Fossils*. Like an ancient Greek tragedy, it is bone-hard and biting. Words are not minced, nor are thoughts or feelings diminished in intensity merely to placate the puritans. In Act III, for example, Robert's harrowing dilemma is made that much more poignant by Curel's expert use of the metaphor and the personification. Indeed, while seemingly wrestling with eternal themes, such as the legitimacy of Robert's son and the authenticity of his mistress's feelings for him, Curel penetrates mythic climes.

> In me the aristocrat worships those lofty trees which are as old as ourselves, whose branches protect a whole people of shrubs. Are we not brothers of the oaks and gigantic beeches? It is impossible for me to walk among them without sharing their arrogance. I soar above the dwarf sapplings, I take for myself all the light, and scatter disdainfully beechnuts and acorns to the famished dwellers of the moors. Here, in the presence of the sea, a different man is awakened in me. The waves, one just like the other, come in battalions dashing upon the shore, all equally glittering in the sunshine, all equally smooth in calm weather, all equally rough in the storm. Then I say to myself that here is a picture of humanity totally different from that of the woods. The uniformity of those waves, each bearing its share of the weight of ships, and on which the gulls alight where they will, disturbs a little my forest instincts. I ask myself whether man could not advance in unison like the waves, which, without clashing, rush together to the shore. But immediately a fear assails me.[36]

Despite the play's brilliance, both Lemaître and Sarcey deprecated Antoine's sloppy acting. The poverty of his delivery succeeded in obfuscating the beauty of Curel's poetry, its harsh rhythms and powerful images. Curel disagreed, commending

Antoine for not having declaimed his lines and for having spoken in soft rather than in loud and brash tones. After all, Curel questioned: does one speak loudly when at home and chatting?[37]

Critics also disapproved of Antoine's mise-en-scène: it lacked focus and, therefore, did not succeed in pointing up the drama's lugubrious and decadent atmosphere. Nevertheless, Antoine created some startling effects, particularly in the last scene when Robert's dead body lies in full view of the audience, while his sister reads the will before the entire family. That she stands next to the bed of the deceased increases the tragic grandeur of the situation. Berthe Heldy, who made her debut in this play, although reading rather awkwardly, was unforgettable. "She has an admirable voice and a vibrant sensitivity," Antoine noted, which she projected outside the acting area, directly onto the audience. So intent was Antoine in creating a tableau effect in this scene that he was not at first aware of the difficulties involved. Because the actor portraying Robert had to remain absolutely immobile throughout the long act, he had a sculptor cast a mask of his face. This was easier said than done. "It was quite agonizing for our comrade to have his whole face covered with liquid plaster and to have to wait while it dried, breathing through straws in his nostrils and mouth, but he bore the thing with the resignation of a martyr."[38] The tableau was exceptional!

Although Antoine finally did admit to "having massacred the play" in part, *The Fossils* was a tremendous success. Reminiscent of classic tragedy, where a powerful will leads to the heroic immolation of morality, it transformed dream into nightmare.

*

Antoine not only chose his plays, directed and acted in them, but also frequently called upon painters to create program covers, posters, decors, and backdrops for his productions at the Théâtre Libre.

Toulouse-Lautrec placed his stamp on one of Antoine's productions, *The Missionary*. With his typical satiric verve, he depicted a woman with orange hair, yellowish skin and red lips, seated in a box decorated in flamboyant reds, looking down with her lorgnette to the crowd below. For Emile Fabre's comedy,

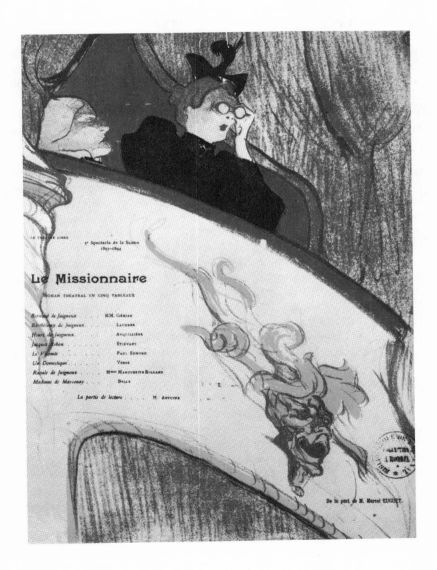

Toulouse-Lautrec's poster for Fabre's *Le Missionary*

Money, Lautrec designed a program daubed in red, black, ochre and ivory tones, focusing on a couple drawn in sharp and incisive lines.

Henry-Gaspard Ibels (1867-1936), a lithographer and caricaturist whose scenes of the Butte Montmartre with their little theatres and dives were printed in the *Courrier de Paris,* also worked for Antoine. His feature drawing for the program of Georges Courteline's *Boubouroche* and Maurice Vaucaire's *Valet de Coeur* depicted a barge, bridge, and background landscape in flat tones. The image of two men huddled in the foreground was memorable for the pathos injected into their stance. He also designed a program for Curel's *The Fossils,* featuring two old women and a nanny on the beach with a child, with boats in the distance lending both a staid and an expansive view to the scene. For the program of *Snow White, Moneyed Marriage,* and *Ahasuerus,* he drew five men with top hats seated in a restaurant reading their newspapers. The greens, yellows and browns lend richness to the fluid lines of the drawing itself.

Jean-Louis Forain (1852-1931) also added an artistic note to some of Antoine's offerings. Best known for his drawings in *La Revue illustrée,* the *Courrier français,* the *Figaro,* and *l'Echo de Paris,* his ironic scenes are filled with verve as well as bitterness. His ever present caustic intent, his sober lines, and acute observations fill his works with an element of severity and sadness, paralleling the frequently painful atmosphere inherent in so many of Antoine's productions. In his program illustration for *Une journée parlementaire,* a man stands outside a prison smoking as he peers into a barred window. For *Elisa's Daughter,* he featured a woman and soldier seated at a table in a cafe, on which has been placed a bottle of wine and a glass.

Adolphe-Léon Willette (1857-1926), the illustrator of so many Pierrots and Colombines and frequently alluded to as the Montmartois Watteau, also designed program covers for Antoine. His works, revealing the witty, fantastic, and poignant side of *commedia dell'arte* figures, also blended into Antoine's theatrical offerings.

Auguste Rodin's (1849-1917) program cover for Curel's *The Lion's Repast* featured a rough drawing of a draped figure in virtually constant motion—enigmatic and mysterious in its intent.

Edouard Vuillard (1868-1935), the Intimist painter who concentrated on simple, everyday subjects, created a program cover for the Théâtre Libre: a strong peasant-like figure bending low to the ground, as if intent upon uprooting something invisible from its depth. In the background a spiral-like tree trunk with some leaves drawn here and there fills in the background. The pastel tones, light blues, ivory and flat yellows, add a warm and moving note to the scene.

Paul Signac (1863-1935), a Neo-Impressionist, whose aim was to increase the interplay of lights on his canvases, thus lending the images a sense of eternalness, designed a stark program cover for the Théâtre Libre. Amid circles and squares, and in *pointilliste* style, it features the back of a man's head; the deep reds, greens, purples, and roses add to the enigmatic quality of the image.

*

To produce French plays only, no matter how fine they might have been, did not always answer Antoine's continuous craving to internationalize his theatrical endeavors. One of his greatest contributions to theatre was his introduction to France of some of the outstanding foreign writers of his day and ours: Henrik Ibsen, August Strindberg, Gerhardt Hauptmann, Edgar Allan Poe, and Leo Tolstoy.

André Antoine, Director of the Théâtre Libre

Chapter 3

Productions of Foreign Authors

To produce the works of Tolstoy, Ibsen, Strindberg, Hauptmann, Poe, and other foreign playwrights in ultra-nationalistic France was either to court disaster or inspire heroism. To be sure, the works of Shakespeare had been performed many times in Paris, but in watered-down translations, in lamentable mise-en-scènes, declamatory and artificial speech, and bombastic acting styles. Foreign plays were considered unworthy and unappealing in the land of the great Racine, Corneille, and Molière.

Despite the well-meaning, and not so well-meaning, advice of friends, Antoine had a mind of his own and persevered, producing such works as Leo Tolstoy's *The Power of Darkness*; Baudelaire's adaptation of Edgar Allan Poe's *The Tell-Tale Heart*; Henrik Ibsen's *Ghosts* and *The Wild Duck*; August Strindberg's *Miss Julie*; Gerhardt Hauptmann's *The Weavers*.

Tolstoy: The Power of Darkness

Dumas predicted failure as soon as Antoine announced his decision to produce Tolstoy's *The Power of Darkness* (1886). "It was too melancholy" for French audiences; "not one of the characters is sympathetic." Although "a cruel truthfulness and a real beauty," is implicit in Tolstoy's drama, Sardou remarked, "it was the kind of work that should be read and not staged;" it was "unpresentable." Augier stated categorically: "It is less a play than a novel in dialogue form; its length alone makes it impossible for a French stage."[1]

Antoine admitted that *The Power of Darkness* was different from French works. Its coruscating energy and cruelty were colossal and tremendously impressive. That Tolstoy's play had been banned from the stage in Russia might also have whetted Antoine's appetite: he reacted powerfully to such a challenge. There were difficulties involved in staging *The Power of Darkness*. In certain scenes, twenty-two characters would be on stage at the same time; their movements had to be handled both dramatically and with clarity of purpose; an ambiance of Russian peasantry had to be created on stage—otherwise the play would surely fail. The first problem was resolved by his talent as director; the second, by a strange quirk of fate. Russian political refugees had recently arrived in France and were willing to give him their native costumes for the occasion. The colorful fabrics on stage lent just the perfect note to the dramatic event.

The Power of Darkness is an example of *direct theatre*. It attempts to communicate with all types of audiences, both untutored and tutored. Tolstoy, who wanted brutal moujiks to be moved and purified by stage happenings in general, and by his play in particular, considered theatre a moralizing agent—an edifying experience. In "What is Art?" (1897), a study on aesthetics, he stated that, since theatre is a human activity, it must have some value and, therefore, serve people. Art "is a means of union among men, joining them together in the same feelings, and indispensable for the life and progress towards the well-being of individuals and of humanity."[2]

Tolstoy's play was based on a grim incident which had taken place near his estate in 1880. A peasant told the guests assembled at his step-daughter's marriage that he had killed the child he had by her and then tried to kill the six-year old daughter he had had with his wife. Tolstoy, whose goal was to underscore the dark and hidden areas of the human soul and psyche, succeeded in his adaptation of the incident to suit his needs.

In Act I we learn that the thirty-seven year old peasant, Nikita, has seduced the young Marina. After abandoning her, he became the lover of Anissia, the wife of Peter Ignatitch, his master. When Nikita's mother, Metrena, learns of the illicit relationship and realizes that Anissia cannot get along without Nikita, she tries to make the most of the situation. She suggests that Anissia poison her husband Peter and marry Nikita.

The crime takes place in Act II. Anissia is calm and collected as she blends some poison with her insomniac husband's sleeping medicine, and then watches him writhe in pain. With complacency, she steals Peter's money before he dies and gives it to Nikita to put in a safe place. They marry and pay for the wedding feast with the stolen money. Soon Nikita becomes Akoulina's lover, Peter's young daughter from a first marriage. Anissia cannot bear such a situation and decides to find the now-pregnant Akoulina a husband. They hide her condition from her peasant fiancé and a large dowery makes the relationship acceptable.

In succeeding acts, Anissia and Metrena, her mother-in-law, convince Nikita, the guilty and adulterous father, to kill his newborn infant. He will do so in a barn and simultaneously with the wedding ceremony. Fearful lest he be discovered, he quickly digs a whole in the cellar of the building. Meanwhile Anissia brings him the baby. When she notices his hesitation, she resorts to threats. It is then that he decides to go through with the murder: he throws the crying infant on the ground, places a wooden beam over him, sits on it and crushes him to death. The scene was so realistic that audiences could actually hear the bones of the dead baby cracking. Nikita, terrified by his deed, rushes out, leaving his wife and mother to bury the infant. He interrupts the wedding ceremony, confesses his crime, begs Akoulina and others he had deceived for their forgiveness and accepts his punishment of forced labor as *expiation*.

Antoine, whose goal was not to give audiences lessons in morality, but rather to perform fine plays, cut sections of Tolstoy's work which he thought French audiences might find tedious: the lengthy confessions and avowals which slowed down the pace. Like Greek tragedy, *The Power of Darkness* bore within its plot and characterizations mythic and mystic qualities. For great theatre to be born, Antoine believed, truth alone—and not idealism—must live on stage. And Diderot's great law must be adhered to, he remarked: "Truth!   Nature!   the Ancients! Sophocles! Philoctetus!"[3]

Melodramatic as well as mystical elements abound in *The Power of Darkness*. Unlike French thrillers, where crimes are multiple and extreme, and endings climactic and most usually positive, the sequences and tenor in Tolstoy's work are grave. The graphic nature of the happenings—the drunken scenes, the poisoning, and the infanticide—were devastating in power and horror, portentous in intent. As for its spiritual message—the protagonist's redemption or ascension toward light after his horrific crime—lends a supernatural aura to the entire work.

Although Sarcey had reservations about the play, he not only admired Antoine's production of *The Power of Darkness*, but was also moved by the verisimilitude of the atmosphere created on stage and by the acting. He suggested, however, that unlike Aeschylus and Sophocles, whose poetic flights were masterful, Tolstoy's language was repetitious, even whiny and pathetic at times. The Russian writer does not succeed in evoking the *terror* and *pity* which are Aristotle's parameters for tragedy. Because Tolstoy's creatures are inferior, living as they do on an instinctual and animal level, they cannot evoke the sympathy of cultured spectators.

> All these people are beasts with human faces; they eat bread instead of chewing on grass; these beings are not of my species: I cannot feel for them, neither pity nor hate, nor indignation. I look at them anxiously as they go about their dirty and monstrous labors; they will never touch my soul.[4]

Zola approved of Antoine's production. It inspired him to write some of the grueling scenes in his novel, *The Earth*. Adolphe Brisson was astounded by Tolstoy's understanding of the psychological factors and motivations involved. He was also impressed by the fact that *The Power of Darkness* transcended the usual theatrical cliches. It disoriented viewers, creating a kind of malaise among the spectators—a positive comment on Brisson's part since he felt it forced the people watching the play to think about their own bestial ways and perhaps do something to remedy them.

The consensus as to the acting? Never had a play been better served. Mevisto as Nikita was the paradigm of the moujik: savage and ferocious, boorish and churlish. When drunk, he was scurrilous and obscene, his foulness reaching unheard-of proportions. Mevisto's incredible portrait was the outcome of his own natural gifts and intelligence. He had allowed his imagination free rein; it had not been repressed or spoiled, Antoine remarked, by traditional theatrical training. On the contrary, the performers at the Théâtre Libre were taught a new view of acting based on reality and naturalness—and *experience*.

Antoine as Akim, the devout, addle-pated, besotted, old fool of a father, was commended for his fine performance. Enclosed as he is in his narrow religiosity, he stutters along throughout the play, broaching only two subjects: God or cesspools. It is he who stands for consciousness and morality and encourages Nikita to confess at the end.

Henry Bauer, of the *Echo de Paris*, wrote of the coolness of Nikita's wife and mother as they poisoned Peter. Placid and adroit in every way, these two archetypal women performed their deed with dexterity, without feeling. They, like the Medea of past centuries, transcended earthly moral women, victims of their own fears and superstitions. No scene evoked more horror among critics, however, than the infanticide: not since Shakespeare had theatre attained such truth—as "life in all of its intensity burst onto the stage."[5]

The sets were rustic, with the usual fireplace at the far end of the stage, benches on the side, tables, and chairs. What did upset some critics, however, was Méténier's translation. Rather than trying to render the flavor of Russian peasantry, he used the slang of the faubourgs of Paris. A corruption of the refined language used in city life, it in no way conveyed the primitive language of the moujik and, therefore, on this level, lost the real flavor of Tolstoy's Russian play.

Ibsen: Ghosts

Ibsen's *Ghosts* (1882), censored in Norway, Germany, and England, had caused a veritable battle at the Freie Bühne in Berlin and at the Independent Theatre in London—both modeled on Antoine's Théâtre Libre.

Ghosts, which dealt with such taboo subjects as hereditary venereal disease, incest, and euthanasia, and the rigid conventions which weigh so heavily on a decadent society, was Ibsen's declaration of war against "the blackest group of theologians." Unlike the trendy dramas in France at the time, Ibsen's dialogue, characterizations, and plot, which rests on sequences of revelations and the protagonist's inability to face the truth, are pruned down to their essentials.

Antoine understood the all-encompassing nature of Ibsen's message and his work method, which the Norwegian dramatist described as follows:

> Before I write down one word, I have to have the character in mind through and through. I must penetrate into the last wrinkle of his soul. I always proceed from the individual; the stage setting, the dramatic ensemble, all that comes naturally and does not cause me any worry, as soon as I am certain of the individual in every aspect of his humanity. But I have to have his exterior in mind also, down to the last button, how he stands and walks, how he conducts himself, what his voice sounds like. Then I do not let him go until his fate is fulfilled.[6]

Ghosts tells the story of Mrs. Alving, who, ten years after her husband's death, is about to open an orphanage dedicated to his memory. The intellectually emancipated Mrs. Alving has suppressed and repressed all the facts concerning her husband's profligacy. Her son, Oswald, who has just returned from abroad, is as dissipated as his father had been and is also marked with syphilis. His liaison with the maid is revealed to be incestuous since she is his father's illegitimate child. The sudden burning down of the orphanage at the conclusion of the drama symbolizes the fire eating away at Oswald's brain: general paresis. The play's ending is moot: will Mrs. Alving administer a lethal dose of morphine, as she had promised to do, to her son who has gone insane?

Antoine was deeply impressed by *Ghosts*: "It is like nothing in our theatre; a study of heredity; the third act has the somber grandeur of Greek tragedy."[7]   Ibsen's play injects "a new accent and force" into French theatre, Antoine further suggested. The profound void and "wilderness" inhabiting Mrs. Alving and all those entering her "gaslit parlor" parallel to a certain extent Antoine's own aesthetics: his understanding of "the slice of life" concept. "The play's effect," Antoine wrote, "depends to a great extent upon the impression of reality of certain scenes that the spectators hear and see on stage."[8]

Antoine who acted the part of Oswald was so deeply excited by the role, that after the performance, he remarked:

> I myself underwent an experience totally new to me—an almost complete loss of my own personality. After the second act I remember nothing, neither the audience nor the effect of the production, and, shaking and weakened, I was some time getting hold of myself again after the final curtain had fallen.[9]

Zola had encouraged Antoine to produce *Ghosts*, a play he considered truly "magnificent."   Catulle Mendès, on the other hand, discouraged him from doing so because the French could not possibly understand Ibsen's "problem play." Céard agreed. "Yes, it is quite beautiful, but it is not clear enough for our Latin minds." It is not surprising then, that some critics found *Ghosts* "foggy," "cold," "aloof," and "enigmatic." Although Faguet remarked on its clumsy construction, he nevertheless stated that *Ghosts* was one of the great dramas of the century. Paul Desjardins called Ibsen "the greatest living dramatist." Lemaître said that, even though *Ghosts* needs explaining for audiences to understand its meaning, it was a "beautiful and strong tragedy" which reaches deeply into the depths of the soul.[10]

Ibsen: The Wild Duck

Antoine was so encouraged by the positive reactions to *Ghosts*, despite the dire predictions, that he decided to produce *The Wild Duck* (1884). Ferdinand Bac made the poster for the play. A representational drawing—an attic with a skylight, some rough hewn chairs, a table and mirror, a father sobbing as he bends over his daughter who lies dying on a couch, the doctor and three friends looking on in painful disbelief—it conveys most potently the pain implicit in the drama.

The Wild Duck seemed "to reveal another side of the master's genius," Antoine wrote; "to the pathetic grandeur of *Ghosts* is added a picturesque life, of uncommon quaintness."[11] It substantiated in fact what Ibsen looked upon as a profound imbalance in society: "The prolific growth of our intellectual life, in literature, arts, etc.—and in contrast to this: all of mankind gone astray."[12]

The Wild Duck is not only a tragedy; it is also a satire aimed at those pseudo-idealists whose poetic fantasies are based on illusion and not the real world. The kind, weak and self-deluded Jhalmar Ekdal believes himself to be on the "verge of a great invention." Gregers Werle, his old school friend, seeks to break down his phantasmagorias in which he believes him to be entrapped. During the course of events, Werle discloses a devastating truth to him: he is not the father of Hedvig, his beloved daughter. So traumatized is Ekdal by this news that he rejects the young girl. Werle, who tries to rectify a bad situation, tells Hedvig that her adored father will return to her if she sacrifices what she loves best—her wild duck. Instead, she commits suicide.

What is the wild duck? critics asked. Does it represent one or all of the characters? Modern society? Civilized people? Is there an answer? James Joyce wrote that "one can only brood upon it as upon a personal woe."[13] It is to Antoine's credit that he underscored the strange and haunting qualities of Ibsen's drama: its symbolism, with all of its mysteries, and the prismatic and shadowy regions buried deeply within everyone's unconscious.

Thus audiences and critics alike responded coldly at first to this arcane drama, far more difficult to assess than *Ghosts*. "Hostile" and "bantering" remarks were audible throughout the first part of the play on opening night. By the fifth act, however, the audience seems to have been won over by the play's powerful overtones which served to underscore its supernatural and poetic qualities.

Despite some rave reviews, however, when the light of consciousness returned and critics began articulating their reactions, some of their remarks were vitriolic. Sarcey condemned outright what he considered to be Ibsen's obscure and symbolistic writing style, which was far from his liking. It was devoid of French clarity. Antoine responded in kind: "Just as I was the first to open my doors wide to naturalistic drama, so shall I open them wide also to symbolist drama, provided it is drama."[14] Nor did the Goncourts respond positively, commenting as they did on the Arctic Pole atmosphere inherent in *The Wild Duck*; moreover, they added, its dialogue was bookish. Although Lemaître found that Ibsen's play required great concentration to understand the deeper dimensions involved in the piece, he nevertheless hailed it as fine drama.[15]

Strindberg: Miss Julie

Antoine remained undaunted, despite severe financial reverses and defections from his company. Some of his cast left the Théâtre Libre, lured by the Comédie-Française, the Odéon, the Variétés, and the Gymnase—established theatres which offered them economic security. What was more devastating, however, were Sarcey's continuously harsh criticisms and those in the *Echo de Paris* by Henry Bauer, formerly one of Antoine's staunchest allies.

To produce Strindberg's *Miss Julie* (1889) was in itself an act of courage. Banned in Denmark, *Miss Julie*, marked as the first Scandinavian Naturalistic play, opened in 1892 at the Freie Bühne theatre in Berlin. The drama revolves around a sexual encounter between Miss Julie, a neurasthenic young girl from a noble family, and Jean, the footman, a vulgar arriviste. Their liaison, which is brief but powerful, takes place during Midsummer's Night's Eve. Because it occurs at a time in history when "the classes are not yet ripe for fusion," when economic, political and psychological situations are swiftly changing, one understands why Miss Julie's sexual relationship with Jean cannot possibly last. Strident, bitter, and acerbic bickerings take place. Only when Julie's father returns does Jean revert to his servile state. Then, Miss Julie's dignity resumes its former pseudo-normalcy. In time, however, she discloses her schizoid personality. That she commits suicide comes as no surprise.

Such deeply introverted and troubled beings as Miss Julie, though longing to communicate with others and with themselves, are unable to do so and are, therefore, food for trauma. Victims of difficult temperaments and sick psyches, of hereditary and repressive educational disciplines, they convey their feelings and sensations in mysterious ways: through imagistic, nonpalpable statements and symbolic gestures. In Strindberg's simple and brutal world, audiences face characters with obscure tendencies and heretofore repressed instincts, who suddenly burst forth, only to withdraw, moments later, humiliated, brutalized, guilt-ridden.

Different—and fascinating to Antoine—were Strindberg's concepts of theatre. It would seem, he wrote *Miss Julie* with the Théâtre Libre in mind. No longer would his characters remain catechists, asking ridiculous questions on stage so as to elicit the answers they want to hear. Nor would he link hands with French classical drama by replicating their structurally symmetrical and parallel scenes. On the contrary, Strindberg sought irregularity, imbalance, and the unforeseen. A play should not be divided into acts, which call for intermissions; such interruptions destroy illusion. *Miss Julie*, which runs for one hour and a half of condensed, concentrated time, encourages audiences to reflect upon their world and themselves as projected onto the stage happenings—that is, under the continuous influence of the "authormesmerist." There should be no respite, no pauses except those for which the actions calls. Tension should increase progressively and cumulatively until the breaking point.[16]

Like Antoine, Strindberg was also looking for new theatrical forms, intent as he was to integrate modern ideas and situations into existent molds. He succeeded in this, most particularly in his characterizations, as he himself wrote:

> My souls (characters) are conglomerates of a past stage of civilization and our present one, scraps from books and newspapers, pieces of humanity, torn-off tatters of holiday clothes that have disintegrated and become rags—exactly as the soul is patched together.[17]

Miss Julie, an archetypal creature, is described by the dramatist as a "half-woman" and a "man-hater"—a kind of creature that has existed from time immemorial. Because of the density of the emotions conveyed and the complexity of the role, Strindberg did away with all intermissions. To stop the action would serve only to disrupt the increasingly troubled atmosphere he sought to maintain. Instead of a pause, he provided audiences and actors with "momentary interludes (or rest stops)," during which time they could catch their breath, thus finding release from the extreme tension of the drama without diminishing its impact. These time zones or "momentary interludes" were made up of three art forms: monologue, pantomime, and ballet. Nor were these genres new, having been used in ancient tragedies, "the monologue having been derived from the monody and the ballet from the chorus," Strindberg remarked.[18] In Strindberg's hands, however, they were at once authentic and symbolic in cast. The sexual encounter, for example, which took place during the festive Midsummer's Night's Eve, included dancing, music, and general merriment on stage as it did in real life. It also took on the dimensions of a religious ritual—a *hieros gamos*—mortal and immortal fitting together into a cohesive whole.

Strindberg was influenced as well by the seventeenth-century Italian acting troupe's rendition of *commedia dell'arte*. Known for their spontaneity and creativity, these comedian/mimes performed on stage knowing only the play's outline and very basic dialogue, developing and amplifying upon the play during the performance. In like manner, Strindberg suggested that the long monologues in *Miss Julie* should not be written out, but only indicated. A gifted actor may improvise such a scene better than the author can, because the actor has become part and parcel of the situation and is imbued with its mood. In short, the author has no way of determining in advance how much small talk may be used and how long it should last without awakening the spectators from the spell of the play.[19]

Strindberg, as previously indicated, liked asymmetical structures. In this regard he was influenced by the Impressionist painters who used light to accentuate illusion and to trigger the imagination. Like Antoine, he insisted that furniture and accessories be real and not *trompe-l'oeil*. As such, the stage in *Miss Julie*, was transformed into a kitchen "with the fourth wall removed."[20] The three actors, in natural stances, show full and half-profiles during the course of the performance and when seated opposite each other at table turn their backs to the audience. Nor was canvas used as a backdrop, with the usual doors and shelves painted on it. When Julie's father wants to show his anger, for example, he slams the door, virtually shaking the entire house. If the door had merely been painted on cloth, it would have only rippled, thereby destroying the effect. Sets for Strindberg and Antoine were not only part of the action, but of the environment as well.

Another of Strindberg's monumental innovations, adopted by Antoine, was the construction of a rear wall which ran at a slight angle diagonally across the stage from right to left, thereby giving the impression of increased reality.

> I have placed the rear wall and the table obliquely across the stage for the purpose of showing the actors full face and in half-profile while they face each other across the table.[21]

Like Antoine, Strindberg called for the abolishing of footlights. The French director had done so since his production of *The Death of the Duke of Enghien*. Lights from below were too brash, Strindberg commented; they obliterated the performer's subtle facial expressions—the cast of the eyes, the shape of the nose—so important in revealing character.

Significant as well—and Antoine and Strindberg were again in complete accord—was the belief that actors should not stand motionless in the centre of the proscenium, wearing their highly studied and effected poses in dramatic scenes, singing out their lines as they do—as waiting for applause. Asymmetry is again the rule. Performers must stand off center: be malleable, lifelike, and move around and not pose. Make-up should serve to heighten temperament and disposition, particularly in psychological dramas. "The soul must be reflected by facial expression rather than by gesture, shouting and meaningless sound."[22]

Strindberg wanted to go even further than Antoine: to alter the shape and form of the orchestra and to remove the boxes. He called for a small stage and a small house so that a new dramatic art form catering to the cultured could be brought into being. He also advocated the raising of the orchestra so that the spectators' eyes would be "focused on a level higher than the actors' knees."[23]

Antoine considered Strindberg's preface to *Miss Julie* of such import that he had it translated and distributed to his audiences prior to his production.

That *Miss Julie* played to mixed reviews is understandable since it was innovative in so many ways. Some considered Antoine's production a masterpiece, praising with unreserved admiration the ease and realism of the acting, the dramatic interplay of the lighting effects, the assymetrical mise-en-scène, the dancing, singing and pantomime Others, like Goncourt, reacted with furor and shock: "I am convinced that this Slavic fog should be left to Russian and Norwegian minds, and not forced upon our lucid intellects." Such "sickly" writing can only harm theatre in general. If models must be had, the French should turn not to the Scandinavians, but to Beaumarchais, the author of *The Barber of Seville* and *The Marriage of Figaro*.[24] Needless to say, Antoine pursued his own course, as always looking forward—and if he did look backward, it was to the greats!

Hauptmann: The Weavers

Antoine's production of *The Weavers* (1892) by Gerhart Hauptmann (1862-1946) was to create another milestone in French theatre. Extremely demanding for Antoine because of the many characters that had to be on stage at the same time, *The Weavers* was also satisfying in that it revealed once again his expertise in handling groups on stage—a technique he had learned *grosso modo* from the Duke of Saxe-Meiningen, but which he had personalized for his own use.

Considered one of the first German socialist dramas, *The Weavers* depicts in compelling terms the suffering of Silesian weavers after their unsuccessful revolt in 1844 against their exploiters. Epic in dimension, because of its historical setting and because it substitutes the individual hero for the collective—the masses—it is also revolutionary theatrically speaking: this is the first time that the impact of group power was dramatized on stage. The rebelling weavers marching out in full force, are seen as strikers, to be sure, but the energy expended by them in attempting to win their cause adds another dimension to the play: as the irrepressible instinctuality of the workers builds up, these flesh and blood beings on stage take on the quality of elemental powers, their rage reaching incandescent proportions. Nothing can stop this growing wave of human anger/fire as it reaches out to the audience. Spectator-actor identification was incredible. The poster created for *The Weavers* by Ibels was in itself moving: standing in sharp relief in the background, like so many silhouettes, are the houses of the wealthy company owners; in the foreground, in darkened tones, the dank and decaying hovels of the poor; in front of these, groups of men—hunger and dissatisfaction haunting their gaze.

The series of tableaux which make up Hauptmann's drama feature workers, women, children seated on benches, each weaving his or her material; or those who come to ask for their salaries. Some complain because their pay is so poor; others argue, burst into violent political discussions. All types of characters come into view: old and frail men, their bodies bent from years of toil; women, also marked by suffering, poor food and disease; children, thin and pale. At the home of one of the workers, a dog has been killed and served to the family for food. The old man eats and drinks, then vomits it all up. Throughout the drama audiences hear *The Song of the Shroud*, which Hauptmann borrowed from Heine:

> With our daughters and our sons
> It's our shroud that we are weaving!

A cabaret scene follows. The place of forgetfulness and dream, alcoholism and perversion—sometimes poison and death. These forgotten beings would do better if they gave their pay to their wives than to squander on drink. Here, too, political discussions break out as does *The Song of the Shroud*. Suddenly, the police break in and rough up the workers. The song had been forbidden. Despite the interdict, it is sung in chorus-like modulations.

Scenes at the homes of the wealthy company owners point up the terrible dichotomy between rich and poor. Riots begin as some workers, wearing their threadbare clothes and armed with sticks, hatchets, some reeling from drink, enter the elegant residence and begin carrying off the silver and other precious mementos.

The climax of the play takes place in Old Hilse's workroom. A confrontation between soldiers, called in to quell the rioters; and the workers, who fight back with such intensity that they claim victory at the end. The battle between opposing forces takes place off-stage. Various episodes are described by people looking upon the events from the window. Heads bob up and down during the scene, adding to the scene's triturating effect as well as lending it an anonymous quality. The interaction between the outside world, which is invisible to the audience, and the inner domain, which can be seen from the orchestra, accentuates the explosiveness of the situation.

Old Hilse stands for the status quo: the workers who accept their earthly lot and bless God for his magnanimity. In good Naturalist tradition, decors are described in detail by the dramatist, and Antoine adhered to Hauptmann's meticulous notations.

> On the left a small window, in front of which stands the loom. On the right a bed, with a table pushed close to it. Stove, with stone-bench, in the right-hand corner. Family worship is going on. . . . A winding-wheel and bobbins on the floor between table and loom. Old spinning, weaving, and winding implements are disposed of on the smoky rafters; hanks of yarn are hanging down. There is much useless lumber in the low narrow room. The door, which is in the back wall, and leads into the big outer passage, or entry-room of the house, stands open. Through another open door on the opposite side of the passage, a second, in most respects similar weaver's room is seen. The large passage, or entry-room of the house, is paved with stone, has damaged plaster, and a tumble-down wooden stair-case leading to the attics; a washing-tub on a stool is partly visible; dirty linen of the most miserable description and poor household utensils lie about untidily. The light falls from the left into all three apartments.[25]

The volatility of the scene stems from the sharp division in the Hilse household, which has become a warring camp. Old Hilse, a religious man, believes that people are fated to live out their earthly suffering and must accept a continuation of the things as they are. Gottlieb, his son, is torn between his family's religious views, which spell passivity and resignation, and feelings of rebellion expressed by his wife, Luise. She stands for the new way, and although anguished because she is aware of the bloody schism occurring in the home, she refuses to prolong a past which has brought her humiliation and pain. She rejects the bigotry and pusillanimity of her entourage.

Unlike Tolstoy's *The Power of Darkness*, where the woman represents the forces of evil and destruction, in Hauptmann's work she is the hero. It is she who conveys the new virile way of life; it is she who stands for Liberty and not Fatality, Revolt and not Resignation. A *visionary*, she cried out her lines on stage with vigor and valor:

> You an' your piety an' religion—did they serve to keep the life in my poor children? In rags an' dirt they lay, all the four—it didn't as much as keep them dry. Yes! I set up to be a mother, that's what I do—an' if you'd like to know it, that's why I would send all the manufacturers to hell—because I'm a mother!—Not one of the four could I keep in life! It was cryin' more than breathin' with me from the time each poor little thing came into the world till death took pity on it. The devil a bit you cared! You sat there prayin' and sing-

in', and let me run about till my feet bled, tryin' to get one little
drop o' skim milk. How many hundred nights have I lain an'
racked my head to think what I could do to cheat the churchyard
of my little one? What harm has a baby like that done that it
must come to such a miserable end—eh? An' over there at Dittrich's they're bathed in wine an' washed in milk. No! you may
may talk as you like, but if they begin here, ten horses won't hold
me back. An' what's more—if there's a rush on Dittrich's, you'll
see me in the forefront of it—an' pity the man as tries to prevent
me—I've stood it long enough, so now you know it.[26]

Old Hilse is outraged. Antoine, who played this part, used
his voice to point up the pain he feels: his voice grows trem-
ulous, it wavers at times, grows husky and strong as he expresses
his religious views. He does not fear mankind, he bursts out,
only God's Judgment. What counts for him is Eternal life and
not earthly existence which is ephemeral. As for Gottlieb, he
reveals his strength when he hears the weavers battling the
army and, despite his father's interdict, grabs his axe and rushes
out to join the fighting workers—and his wife. "He gave himself to the devil," Old Hilse mumbles in desperation. Or is it
God who dictates? he questions as he looks heavenward. Turning back to his loom next to the window, he resumes his work.
Suddenly, a volley of shellfire explodes; he is hit and dies. At
the very same moment, spectators hear cries of joy. The soldiers
have been forced out of the village.

Antoine understood Hauptmann's mystical vision: two
ways of life, two worlds struggling against each other—the old
on the way out and the new being born in blood and agony.
Religion, based on the ill-founded notion of earthly existence as
a vale of suffering as mortals await future happiness after death,
has been superseded by a different outlook, based upon understanding and compassion for humanity. The individual hero,
representative of the collective—like Egmont or Judas Maccha-
beus—participated in the Power Struggle. It is he who will try to
bend the uncontrollable forces which are at stake to suit his
needs rather than accepting destruction as the outcome. It is he
who will build for the future and spread the message of love
throughout the land, not passively, but actively. Hauptmann
introduced a new note in theatre with *The Weavers*—that of
mob psychology. Antoine made the most of it in his mise-en-
scène by his use of crescendos and diminuendoes in the sound
effects accompanying both the mob scenes and the descriptions
of the volatile conflagrations which the audience could not see.

Antoine, as Old Hilse, and Gémier, as a weaver, received accolades. *The Song of the Shroud,* which served as the play's *leitmotif,* issued nearly continuously from the wings, and was singled out for praise. The mounting terror generated when the mob overran the manufacturer's home was so powerful and so evocative "that the entire orchestra rose to its feet." As for the last scene—" amid the shooting and shouts of the crowd," and Old Hilse's death—it earned acclamations.[27]

"No playwright in France is capable of creating a fresco of this scope and power," Antoine remarked. "It is a masterpiece of the developing theatre." Although its message is one of hope through revolt, the audiences at the Théâtre Libre looked upon *The Weavers* primarily as a "cry of despair and misery." Because they identified so strongly with the workers, agitators, and idealists, they cheered from the moment the curtains parted to the end of the play. Jean Jaurès, the founder of the French socialist party, was so impressed that he sent word to Antoine stating that "such a production accomplished more than any political campaigns or discussions."[28]

*

Despite the laudatory articles and testimonials in favor of Antoine's contribution to theatre, he was growing tired. The energy and courage needed to pursue his arduous work was being dissipated by his constant concern over money and his search for good plays and trained performers. His decision was to hand over the directorship of his theatre to Larochelle, the son of the director of the Théâtre Cluny in 1895. Then, he left on tour with some members of his troupe for Belgium, Germany, and Italy. Upon his return to Paris, he acted both at Larochelle's Théâtre Libre, at the Renaissance, and was made co-director of the Odéon, with Ginisty, but resigned because of a disagreement with him. After touring France and South America, Antoine returned to the Menus-Plaisirs Theatre, where he continued to produce plays; and on September 30, 1897, changed its name to the Théâtre Antoine. He remained its director for the next nine years, producing some of the finest plays of the Théâtre Libre repertoire: Courteline, Brieux, Ibsen, Tolstoy, Hauptmann, Strindberg. In 1906, Antoine was made director of the state-subsidized Odéon, where he remained until 1914. Afterward, he freelanced as director, and as drama critic for numerous periodicals and newspapers, remaining continuously involved in things theatrical until his death in 1943.

*

Antoine was a pioneer in theatre. Although committed in many ways to Zola's brand of Naturalism, and considering him "the greatest, the most clear-sighted of the whole group of revolutionists," Antoine was not a slave to any group, school, or credo. Nor did he opt to placate the Romantics and produce their works exclusively; nor the Symbolists—nor any other group. The play was what counted!

Antoine had trained a whole generation of actors according to his own natural and true to life methods. He was, in Becque's words, "the real leader and master of the whole youthful movement, a man whom we all consider the renovator of contemporary drama."[29]

PART II

Aurélien Lugné-Poë

The Théâtre de L'Oeuvre

1893-1899

Chapter 4

Aurélien Lugné-Poë (1869-1940)

Aurélien Lugné, known to the theatre as Lugné-Poë, the last name having been added ostensibly out of admiration for the American writer, was as indefatigable, as zealous, and as innovative as Antoine, in whose company he performed. Like Antoine, Lugné-Poë was drawn to the avant-garde; unlike him, he was taken with Symbolist and Impressionist mise-en-scènes. His vision of the theatre went beyond the visible world, directly into the occult, sometimes nightmarish, transcendental domains. His goal, he wrote, was to "to bring to theatre in whatever manner, the work of art; or at least, to stir ideas."[1]   As founder and director of the Théâtre de l'Oeuvre, his productions included works of Maeterlinck, Rachilde, Bataille, Shakespeare, Jarry, Ibsen, Gogol, and Sanskrit dramatists.

*

The Parisian born Lugné-Poë was excited by theatre at an early age. Although his father earned only a modest income as banker, supplementing it by giving private English lessons (one of his students was Pissarro), his parents always found enough money to take him to the marionette theatre. He was fascinated and traumatized by the antics of Guignol and Gnafron, wooden puppets pulling, hitting, striking each other and voices which seemed to come out of nowhere.[2] So much did the young lad enjoy the idea of theatre that he participated in the plays performed in Sunday school classes.   Later, at the Lycée Fontanes (renamed Lycée Condorcet) where he was enrolled, he developed an appetite for reading in general, and the theatre in particular. Familiar with the works of the Naturalists and Symbolists, he preferred the suggestive, warm and imaginative climes of the latter group to the cold, objective, and bleak view of life offered by the former. The hidden and amorphous sensate world, which manifested itself through suggestion rather than concrete reality, had allure for him. He became a devotee of the new magazines which sprang up here and there: *La Nouvelle Revue Gauche* (1882), *Lutèce* (1884), *La Basoche* (1884), as vehicles for the publication of poems by former students of the Lycée Condorcet: Pierre Quillard, Stuart Merrill, René Ghil, Ephraim Mikhael, André Fontainas and others.

Symbolism was far from being a new movement. Baudelaire was its precursor, his theory of *correspondances* (infinite analogies) having made deep inroads among novelists, poets, and dramatists after him. The word viewed as sign was endowed with an independent existence: it conveyed impressions through suggestion, rather than by direct objective statements. Poets such as Rimbaud, Verlaine, and Mallarmé experienced the symbol in their own unique and individual way: subjectively as well as objectively. Rimbaud introduced a new verse form, *le vers libre* in *The Illuminations*; Verlaine considered the musical factor in verse the most significant element; Mallarmé probed esoteric and ineffable domains in *Igitur*. Symbolists in general considered the world of the imagination as *reality*. Their ideas and works burgeoned, influencing the world of poetry (Laforgue, Moréas, Régnier, Kahn), the theatre (Maeterlinck and Villiers de l'Isle Adam), and music (Debussy).

Important, too, was the influence of German culture on the French Symbolist movement. Despite the Franco-Prussian War (1870), which had ended with the enemy's occupation of Paris, the German hold in the field of philosophy (Hegel, Kant, Hartman, and Schopenhauer) and music (Beethoven, Bach, Wagner) was of great magnitude. Though *Tannhaüser* had been disastrously received by Parisians when first performed (1861), Baudelaire's essay on this opera and Wagner's music in general—notably its synesthetic aspects—were instrumental in creating a *Wagner cult* among the young. The founding of *La Revue wagnérienne* (1886) gave it impetus.

Emile Faguet, critic and Lugné-Poë's much-admired teacher at the Lycée Condorcet, was also effective in arousing his *passion* and that of his schoolmates for symbolism and for the performing arts in general. Heated discussions between Lugné-Poë and his friends, revolving around everything that was innovative in the domain of the arts, was the rule of the day. Several persons, including Georges Bourdon and Lugné-Poë, founded the "Cercle des Escholiers" (1886), a theatrical group which continued to function long after the students had left the Lycée. Enthusiasm ran high at each of their meetings, rehearsals, and performances of such works as Ponsard's *Charlotte Corday*. Intent upon having celebrities associated with their group, Lugné-Poë asked Gustave Worms (1836-1910), the celebrated actor of the Conservatoire, to become a honarary member, and he accepted.

It was also at the Lycée Condorcet that Lugné met the future painter, Maurice Denis, who was to become so closely associated with him in his future theatrical enterprises. By 1890, Denis had become one of the chief theorists of the Nabis (from the Hebrew word, prophets). Sérusier, Vuillard, Bonnard, Maillol, and Vallotton were also included in this group. Influenced by Gauguin, the Nabis, enemies of Impressionism, developed a style characterized by flat areas of bold color and heavily outlined surface patterns.

Although literature and painting beguiled Lugné-Poë, the theatre was his *obsession*. When, in 1887, he failed his baccalaureate, he decided to prepare his entrance examination for the Conservatoire. As Antoine had done before him, he, too, joined the *claque* at the Comédie-Française, which offered him the opportunity of studying the methods of the great actors of the day: Mounet-Sully, Worms, Delaunay, and the Coquelins. Lugné-Poë also took private lessons from Léraval, a former student at the Conservatoire. To increase his experience and his finances, he took as many acting jobs as possible with small touring companies in the Paris region. Faguet, who had seen him act, commended him for his "comic verve," his fine voice, and for the clarity of his diction.

Lugné-Poë also auditioned for Antoine and was accepted into the Théâtre Libre as actor and stage manager (1888-1890). He had been impressed by Antoine's production of *Jacques Damour*, and deeply moved by Tolstoy's *The Power of Darkness*. Although his hours were long and arduous, and Antoine was a hard task-master, Lugné-Poë was learning about theatre from the ground up, absorbing the "unconventional" methods implicit in Antoine's *slice of life* technique. Antoine also knew how to fire the young man's love for theatre and inspire in him the spirit of work and dedication that goes into this art. Although he played only minor roles, at least at the outset—in *Cavalleria Rusticana* by Verga, *Christ's Lover* by Darzens, *Cousine Bette* by Balzac, *The Tell-Tale Heart* by Poe, etc.—he gained in experience, even earning praise for his portrayals. There were times, however, when Antoine's criticisms were sharp and cutting, particularly for what he termed Lugné-Poë's "mumbling." At the outset, their relationship was good, Lugné-Poë even accompanying Antoine on some of his short tours, to London, for example, where he played in *The Death of the Duke of Enghien;* to Brussels, with *Christ's Lover.* It was after the Belgian venture—or adventure—that he and Antoine had an altercation and Lugné-Poë's predictable break with Antoine occurred. They were two creative, authoritarian, and independent people in one company, neither willing to accept subordinate roles. What was unusual, however, was that their enmity toward each other lasted throughout the years.

Lugné-Poë fended for himself, performing in theatres and café-concerts—wherever he could find employment as actor or stage manager. Between 1887 and 1893, he acted in nearly fifty plays. To say that his training was eclectic is an understatement. Nevertheless, experience alone seemed not to satisfy Lugné-Poë. He wanted conventional classical training. He was accepted into the Conservatoire in 1888. There he studied gestural, declamatory, and physical arts, and all the other important disciplines connected with performance.[3] Worms was Lugné-Poë's idol at the time, despite the fact that he considered his gestures frequently awkward and his stance affected. The novice was deeply impressed by the meaningful nature of this seasoned actor's facial gestures, which paralleled so closely the emotions he sought to convey. Worms alone *really* knew how to recite Racine.

Despite his enthusiasm, Lugné-Poë's life was not easy: he experienced many hardships, including foodless days. He felt unable to ask his parents for funds since his father had himself suffered financial reversals; furthermore, he had never approved of his son's choice of careers. In fact, Lugné-Poë had had words with his father concerning his future and had moved out of his home in a huff.

Lugné-Poë pursued his multiple activities, intrigued most particularly at this juncture with the idea of joining forces with Paul Fort, the eighteen-year old poet and founder of the "Théâtre Mixte" (1890).

Although he much admired Antoine's work at the Théâtre Libre, Paul Fort was drawn instead to Symbolism, but not to the exclusion of other literary techniques, providing they triggered both his imagination and sensibilities. The "Théâtre Mixte," soon to be called the "Théâtre d'Art," sought to conciliate divergent views by producing works of great aesthetic worth. Like Antoine, Fort would program unpublished as well as long-forgotten works. Unlike his predecessor, Fort was a dreamer. He lacked organizational qualities and financial ability. Nor did he have the knack of choosing works that would intrigue and excite audiences—at least not in the beginning, as attested to by his opening program, consisting of a long prologue in verse by Marc Legrand, "Concerning the Théâtre Mixte"; "Pierrot and the Moon," a lyrical one-act comedy; *The Florentine*, also by the same author; and *At the Fountain*, adapted for the stage by J. B. Rousseau—banal, old-fashioned, uninteresting. The critics were less than impressed; the acting, moreover, was mediocre. Fort, like Antoine and Lugné-Poë, was not one to be discouraged. He continued soliciting subscriptions for his theatre and claimed Maupassant, Banville, and other well known writers as honorary members of his group.

Lugné-Poë's theatrical career came to a sudden halt in November, 1890, when he was called into service. Five months later he returned to Paris on sick leave, but only temporarily. It was at this time that he moved into a studio which Maurice Denis, Edouard Vuillard, Pierre Bonnard, and other painters shared at 28 rue Pigalle. Although poor, their kindness was felt by Lugné-Poë, whom they kept on though he was so frequently unable to pay his share of the rent. Discussions were many and heated among these young people, particularly when Sérusier and Gauguin visited. The Nabis were always seeking to concretize their views: inviting mystery *per se* to inhabit line and contour, light and darkness—every aspect of their pictorial forms.

The Nabis frequented Paul Fort's Théâtre d'Art, enjoying and frequently participating as decorators and painters in his innovative, though sometimes financially disastrous productions. A case in point was Fort's decision to produce Shelley's so-called "unplayable" five-act tragedy, *The Cenci* (January, 1891). Closely paralleling Stendhal's so-called translation of the sixteenth-century account of an historical event which told of murder, incest, parricide, sado-masochistic orgies, and perversions, unlike the French writer's swift moving, clear, and simple style, Shelley's work was heavy and portentous. Indeed, it was really more than Fort should have attempted at the time. His actors and his own directing and production techniques were sorely inadequate.   Laughter, rather than shock and consternation over the sordid events depicted, was heard during the performance and always at the wrong moments.   Was it simply that Shelley's dramatic poem was just not theatre?

Fort was still experimenting, still probing various forms of expression.   For some productions, curtains would part on a silent stage featuring a tableau which audiences would view for three or four minutes, after which the play would begin.   At other times, Fort would have certain musical motifs played for specified time periods, after which he would have the theatre sprayed with perfume, his goal being to fuse the senses so that the stage play could be experienced viscerally as well as intellectually.   According to symbolist credo, what had been heretofore divided, prior to the creative act, had to be united in the work of art.   Hadn't Baudelaire revealed the key to his literary and mystical notions in his poem, "Correspondances"?   Hadn't he suggested that "Perfumes, colors and sounds answer each other?"

Fort attempted in like manner to find a common denominator linking the disparate views of the poets and artists of the period—Symbolists, Nabis, Idealists, Decadents.   Indeed, it was the Nabis who invited Lugné-Poë to attend a performance at the Théâtre d'Art (1891).   Impressive, yes; but also faulted, technically and dramatically.

Rachilde's *Madame Death*, a "cerebral" drama whose novelty resided not in the work itself, but rather in the intriguing sets for Act II, was arresting.   The sets featured a fantasy garden in the shape of a human skull.   To enhance the intended nightmarish and ghoulish atmosphere, actors suppressed all gestures and banished any vocal or verbal emotional outbursts.   An ingenious idea!   But because the actors were not sufficiently skillful, the effect was lost and the play, dull and routine to begin with, became increasingly so.[4]

The recitation of Mallarmé's "Le Guignon" and Pierre Quillard's one-hundred-and-fifty-line verse drama about a girl who was fiercely proud of her virginity, *The Girl with Two Cut Hands*, followed.   The actors, standing behind a transparent curtain which unfortunately veiled Sérusier's decor—a golden gauze framed by red draperies and flaked with multicolored angels—recited their lines in slow, lugubrious, and portentous tones.   The narrator, dressed in a long blue tunic, stood in the front of the proscenium, as he explained in crystalline prose the meaning of the characters' various feelings and gestures as well as the significance of the unfolding events. In so doing, he fused the disparate theatrical factors into a melodious and rhythmic cohesive whole. Both Mallarmé's poem and Quillard's verse-play earned Fort a modicum of success. Critics praised the new type diction used in the production. The lyrical and sometimes strident harmonies, with their rhythmic alternations, lent fresh vigor and vital flavor to the works. Certain critics, as to be expected, had reservations and suggested that actresses as well as actors should have been used to balance out the preponderance of heavier timbres that prevailed. The last play, *Prostitute,* by Chirac, designed to ridicule the Naturalists, invited chaos. Anti-Symbolist reactions were violent. Some spectators screamed "Long live Zola"; while others stridulated, "Long Live Mallarmé."

Lugné-Poë, thrilled by what he had witnessed at the Théâtre d'Art, wrote years later: "Everything started right here!"[5] Before joining forces with Fort, Lugné-Poë continued his life as a wandering actor and minstrel, performing, among other places, at the Théâtre d'Application run by Charles Bodinier. A vir-tually unique enterprise, Bodinier's custom was to invite students from the Conservatoire to perform, and diseuses, like Yvette Guilbert, to enact their song-dramas. Lectures were also given by such well known writers and critics as Brunetière, Lemaître, Barrès, and Donnay. Since Bodinier was intent upon maintaining sound finances, he rented his theatre to writers such as Edouard Dujardin, the Symbolist poet and devotee of Mallarmé. It was at the Théâtre d'Application that he produced his trilogy, *Antonia's Legend.* The play, conveying in lyrical terms his belief in humankind's eternally tragic fate, suggested that man's earthly lot is to suffer and woman's is to betray. Although Lugné-Poë was given only a small part in this produc-tion, his portrayal was so impressive that he was awarded the lead in the second and third parts of Dujardin's trilogy. Lugné-Poë knew exactly how to underscore the lyrical qualities of his lines, while blending these with subdued and virtually mute tones. In so doing, he succeeded in making manifest a whole inner dimension—which is exactly what Dujardin sought.[6]

Mallarmé's views concerning the performing arts, which he expressed in an article in *La Revue Indépendante,* attempted the fusion of the stage play with music and rhythmic verse. The poet, Gustave Kahn, seconding his master's voice, suggested that each actor should be given a tonal personality, while also main-taining his own individual musical sonorities.[7]   Such experi-mentation indulged in by Mallarmé and his disciples, such as Kahn, also fascinated the Belgian dramatist, Maurice Maeter-linck. Fort, in turn, was intrigued by Maeterlinck's avant-garde plays, and introduced one of his symbolic one-acters, *The Intruder*, at a benefit to raise money for the ill and poverty-stricken Verlaine, as well as for Gauguin, who was leaving for Tahiti.

Maeterlinck: The Intruder

Maeterlinck's *The Intruder*, with Lugné-Poë playing the lead, was one of the works to be performed on May 21, 1891; the others were Charles Morice's very mediocre *Chérubin*, which centered on the theme of avarice; and a curtain-raiser, Verlaine's "The Ones and the Others," recited by Marguerite Moréno, which was greeted with applause.

The Intruder, original in every way, is constructed almost exclusively on the exteriorization of inner states.   The actors, nearly immobile throughout the performance, pared their ges-tures down to the barest nuances of movement, underscoring by their very restraint the mounting terror of the situation.

The Intruder, a play about death, features a family consist-ing of a blind Grandfather, an Uncle, a Father, and three girls, who await the Mother's recovery after childbirth. A relative is expected. The Father and Uncle are convinced the Mother is out of danger. Only the blind Grandfather senses the hopelessness of the situation. The visitor finally arrives—in the form of Death.

The dialogue is sparse. Words, enunciated with objec-tivity and yet with infinite tonal and rhythmic variations, some-times sounded metallic, giving a choppy effect; at other moments they took on the solemnity of a religious chant. Nor did Fort and Lugné-Poë, so deeply involved in the visual arts, neglect this aspect of *The Intruder*. The troubled characters, grouped together on stage, hid behind their own mask-like anxieties that corroded their lives. The glazed eyes of one, the enigmatic smile of the second, the deeply furrowed brow of the third, were reminiscent of the canvases of certain Flemish primitives: Dirk Bouts and Roger Van der Weyden.

Lugné-Poë, as the Grandfather, succeeded in concretizing sensations, stifling feelings, and imposing the stamp of eternity on Maeterlinck's work. Indeed, the entire cast divested their characters of personal elements, giving the impression that myth-like and mediumistic beings inhabited the stage. They flayed each other in the subtlest of ways, seemingly compelled to do so by some invisible network of fatal forces.[8]

For Maeterlinck—and this was emphasized in the Théâtre d'Art's production of his play—theatre reflected an inner search based on an intuitive experience. A mood had to be created so as to make man's soul manifest through a silent stage language and through rituals devoid of nearly all motion. Each restrained gesture became a sign or symbol suggesting some profound and mysterious reality. Maeterlinck believed that a nearly static condition had to reign on stage, thereby permitting the intrusion of occult forces into the dramatic happenings. Thus was created an atmosphere weighted with tension, as each of the protagonists slowly became acquainted with his *karma*.

Technically speaking, though *The Intruder* adhered to the French classical unities of time, place, and action, it was a modern piece, simple and poignant. There are no extraneous peripateia and nothing superfluous. Everything on stage emerges directly from the body of the text. Action and playing time are the same: one and a half hours. The set does not change. It consists of a room with three doors and a window, the window opening onto a garden. The door to the left leads to the dying woman's room; the one to the right to the infant's room; the third, back center stage, leads to the outside world. The doors may be looked upon as three aspects of existence: death, life, and chance. Hovering over this ultrastationary and lugubrious atmosphere of doom are, as Maeterlinck wrote in his preface to his *Théâtre* (1929), "enormous invisible and fatal powers."

Appealing to Symbolists was the fact that Maeterlinck's protagonists were not to be looked upon as flesh-and-blood beings, but rather as archetypes—primordial images arising from the profoundest layers of man's unconscious. The fact that the blind Grandfather is the only one to sense his daughter's imminent death may be regarded today as a theatrical cliché. However, if examined in the light of the latest psychological knowledge, it becomes a *nouveauté*. The Grandfather's outlook upon the world is termed *synchronistic* or *acausal*. Because he has been exiled from the visible world, cut off symbolically from the realm of Ideas (or the rational principle in man), he finds solace in a world of senses and feelings. He, therefore, experiences life on a different level than do the others in the family—intuitively, premonitorily in a realm where the limited linear time and space factors of rational beings have been transcended.

The Intruder was a success and Lugné-Poë's acting was acclaimed for its restraint and its subtleties. The Symbolists admired Maeterlinck's play for its power of suggestion, its depth and artistry. Henri Bauer, Antoine's one-time friend, but now his avowed enemy, wrote: "Nowhere has the impression of the reality of nonmaterial sensations been rendered with such intensity."[9] Quillard considered it "the revelation of the day." Jean Jullien confessed to having been "subjugated by the authority of dominion and novelty of this art."[10] Maeterlinck was now looked upon as the painter par excellence of the inner experience. Some of the old-guard critics, ready to reject any innovative work, castigated The Intruder and everything about the production—its "incredible follies" along with its "ridiculous inconsistencies." Sarcey was bored from beginning to end.[11] Fort's reputation, along with Maeterlinck's and the artists associated with their group, was spreading. Three months later, two of Denis' illustrations for The Intruder were exhibited at the chateau of Saint-Germain-en-Laye, along with some new works by Bonnard, Ibels, Sérusier and others.

*

Meanwhile, Lugné-Poë, still a student at the Conservatoire, received only second prize at his competitive examination, the first going to the future matinée idol, De Max. Sorely disappointed, Lugné-Poë uttered his dismay openly in an article in Art et Critique—reminiscent of Antoine's feelings expressed years earlier on this state subsidized theatre—accusing the judges of favoritism. Another, perhaps more mundane reason, enraged Lugné-Poë and was at the root of his disappointment: had he succeeded in winning first prize, he would have been exempted from further army duty. Although another two years of military service awaited him, he succeeded in so arranging his affairs as to be able to remain in Paris most of the time, contributing critical articles to such magazines as Art et Critique, La Plume, and Le Chat Noir, and performing in some memorable performances at the Théâtre d'Art: Maeterlinck's The Blind, Jules Laforgue's The Fairy-like Council (Le Concile féerique), Rémy de Gourmont's Theodat, and works by P. N. Roinard, Stuart Merrill, Adolphe Rette, and Camille Mauclair.

Maeterlinck: The Blind

The Blind has no real plot. A play of metaphysical dimension, it dramatizes the *dying complex*, conveying in so doing a profound sense of despair and futility, while also revealing a need to hope based on the need to wait for some illusory salvation to earthly anguish. Paradoxically, a desire to put a stop to new beginnings, thereby ending the life cycle of human beings—birth, life, and death—is also evident. The strength of Maeterlinck's play lies in its economy of language, its emotional restraint, and virtual condition of stasis. Whatever action is inherent in the drama has already taken place before the curtain rises. Suspense consists in waiting.

Twelve blind people from the home for the blind have been led into the forest by their leader-priest. He had wanted them to become acquainted with the mountains and the sea surrounding the island on which they live to broaden, so to speak, their knowledge of the world. He tells the people to wait for him while he investigates their whereabouts. And there they remain: six blind men seated on stone slabs opposite six blind women, three of whom pray throughout the performance; one, a young "crazy girl," holds a baby on her lap. The audience, however, sees (back center stage) the old priest, dressed in a thick black coat and hat, leaning against a large cavernous tree trunk. He is dead. The drama consists in the growing anxiety of the twelve as they await the priest's return; their terror and feelings of abandonment when they discover their leader's death; and their plea at the end for "pity" as they face eventual death from cold and hunger.

For Maeterlinck, the sightless protagonists represent those who have been exiled from the Godhead, the Garden of Eden, souls thrust into the material world, fallen into so-called evil—that is, have become human beings. They grope about in the forest, limited in their capacities, vainly attempting to find their way back to the safety and security of their institution—that is, conventional attitudes and frames of reference.[12]

The blind are, psychologically speaking, living out a *shadow* existence, not able to experience life in terms of themselves as individuals, but rather as followers of their priest-guide. The priest, a self-sacrificing figure, has certain Christlike attributes. He was always attempting, through his instruction and protection, to help the blind during their years in the home. As they followed his dictates and lived within the security of the institution ("within the shelter of the walls"), they felt comfortable because there was "nothing to fear when the door is shut."

A way of life is germinated within the home for the blind. The validity of the resulting ideations, however, could be tested only by a confrontation with the outside world—the "open door." Growth, a dynamic process, needs conflict and activity. Binary opposition is obligatory if existence is to be experienced fully. Should introversion dominate for too long a period—as symbolized by the life spent in the institution—a condition of stasis, which is antithetical to life, occurs. The blind, therefore, had to leave their institution and make their way to the outside world; they had to experience the terror of isolation, to live in a sphere where opposition existed in order to understand the significance of their own lives.

Critics, such as Lemaître, Fouquier, and Wolff, were deeply moved by the increasing anguish emerging as the play was being performed. Fort's mise-en-scène emphasized Mallarmé's views on the work of art which must be experienced on several dimensions, depending upon the depth of the spectators' feelings and understanding. Lugné-Poë's vocal tones, as one of the blind, were singled out for praise: his cry of terror in particular: "There is a dead man in our midst!"—which shook the audience so deeply that they applauded at that very moment. So, too, were the vocal pitches of the other actors, sequenced in a nuanced interplay of harmonious and cacophonous interludes. Such tonalities were praised for the outer-wordly quality they conveyed. François de Nion, writing for *La Revue Indépendante*, compared Maeterlinck's ability in conveying horror and terror to that of Aeschylus and Shakespeare. Sarcey's reaction, as to be expected, was negative: he couldn't see or hear a thing, he said, as he groaned and sighed throughout the production.[13] Julien Leclerq, of the *Mercure de France*, considered *The Blind* too static a piece. Although Maeterlinck rarely interfered in his plays' productions, he vetoed Lugné-Poë's suggestion to have a dog on stage even though the play called for such a presence. The dramatist's suggestion, unfortunately, was not obeyed and the performance suffered because of it: the dog remained close to the priest, ignoring the blind people he was supposed to first approach.[14]

*

On this same evening of December 11, 1891, Lugné-Poë performed the lead part in Remy de Gourmont's one-act prose play, *Theodat*, revolving around the theme of temptation. Such a role gave him added opportunity to reveal his potential: the very demanding role required great virtuosity on his part since he had to express a wide range of emotions—from great containment to sheer abandon. Maurice Denis, who designed the set and the costumes, also emphasized the dichotomy existing within the protagonist's psyche. François de Nion considered *Theodat* "sobre . . . wise, contained . . . overly wise even, a youthful fault which he will outgrow," he predicted. Most critics, including Sarcey and Fouquier, considered Gourmont's drama valueless.

Laforgue's poem, *The Fairy-like Council*, also performed on the same program, received the brunt of many a reviewer's wrath. Sarcey expressed his anger as follows:

> It's night; a man is standing at an open door to the right; a young man and a young woman are leaning on the window sill to the left. A man is lying down in the middle of the stage. The three begin to dialogue. Are they speaking in verse? I think so, because the noise made by the incessant hammering of bizarre rhythms is just like a half-dozen house bells being shaken at the same time. But these verses sometimes have fourteen syllables and at other instances, four. Impossible, however, to understand a word. I cannot even guess what is going on between the three groups. The curtain comes down and whistles are heard.[15]

Jules Lemaître did not understand the meaning of Laforgue's poetry. Julien Leclerq, however, considered it "exquisite"; Willy, "sensational."[16]

The pièce de resistance—or so it has been suggested—was P.-N. Poinard's adaptation on that same evening of Solomon's *Song of Songs*. A paradigm of poetic theatre at its best, it invited spectators to experience the sensual pleasures involved in a world of images, rhythms, tonalities, conveyed paradoxically in both a realistic and mystical manner. In an attempt to arouse the olfactory senses of the audience by spraying the theatre with perfume, with only two atomizers at Fort's disposal, only the orchestra pit benefitted from the delicate aroma intended to reach out into the entire theatre. Instead of encouraging audiences to blend sight, smell, and sound, thereby expanding their enjoy-

ment, many proved to be allergic to the cheap quality of the perfume used and sneezed and coughed instead.   Perhaps synes-
thesia should be experienced only in the mind and soul—in the
limitless world of the imagination—and not in the restricted
material world!

*

Problems were arising at the Théâtre d'Art.   Lugné-Poë
was aware that, although Fort had imagination, he was no business man.   He never developed the knack of soliciting funds or
of managing them.   His choice of plays, Marlowe's *Faust*, for
example, was a good one.   This powerful and rich work would
surely please.   What he did not take into consideration was the
inanity of the French translation.   As a result, the performance
was dismal.   Nor did Van Lerberghe's *A Sense of Death*, or the
recitation of Rimbaud's "The Drunken Boat," for which Paul
Ranson had created the decors, fare much better.

Fort realized—unhappily—that his theatrical enterprise
was coming to an end.   His last production, on March 28, 1892,
was composed of anodine works: *Satan's Sabbath* by Jules Bois,
The First Song of the Iliad, adapted by Mery and Melnotte, and
two scenes from *Vercingétorix* by Edouard Schuré.   The audience
left soon after the last piece had begun.   A "somber and ridiculous" spectacle was the consensus: old fashioned, banal, esoteric,
and dull.   Lugné-Poë's participation in Fort's Théâtre d'Art as
actor, however, was singled out for praise.   He was cited for his
power, objectivity, depth, and ability to penetrate a world beyond
the material and visible domain.[17]

Although Paul Fort had multiple projects in mind—and
good ones—he was, nevertheless, the subject of calumnies from
many critics.   Some of their negative judgments were certainly
valid: the anarchical spirit that reigned at the Théâtre d'Art, the
troupe's lack of cohesion and discipline, and its rudimentary
training techniques.   Fort either did not know how to instruct
his actors or stage technicians properly or he did not have the
necessary time to do so.   As a result their work was rarely satis-
factory, dreaded mistakes occurring during nearly every performance.   To Fort's credit, however, was the scope of his imaginative and intuitive powers—his need to step out of the bounds of
the real world and experience the transpersonal realm.   The fact
that he was the first to have produced Maeterlinck's plays—a

dramatist recognized by some today as the father of the twentieth-century Theatre of the Absurd—is praise enough.

The Théâtre d'Art closed its doors in March 1892. Lugné-Poë was again on his own. Nevertheless, he had learned from Fort's mistakes and when, a year later, he opened his Théâtre de l'Oeuvre, he knew how to train and discipline his actors and technicians; and although his choice of plays was not always felicitous, some, like Fort's, were ground-breaking. Lugné-Poë maintained his friendship with Fort and with all the marvelous pictorial artists who had helped the director of the Théâtre d'Art to create his extraordinary decors and program designs: Vuillard, Bonnard, Sérusier, Denis and others. Like Antoine, Lugné-Poë's taste was eclectic and he branched out whenever he could to reach into the heart of the matter, forever broadening and enrichening his singularly intuitive ways.

Chapter 5

Productions at the Théâtre de L'Oeuvre

In the late spring 1893, Lugné-Poë and some friends, including Veuillard, were discussing their future plans. Vuillard,
so the story goes, happened to open a book at random; his eye
fell on the word *oeuvre*, and he suggested that the theatre Lugné-
Poë wanted to bring into existence be called the *Théâtre de
l'Oeuvre*.[1] And so it was.

Before beginning his new venture, Lugné-Poë thought
back upon past mistakes as well as onto previous successes. The
Cercle des Escholiers, for example, which he had helped found
during his lycée days, had grown in stature and reputation.
Although he had broken with them in 1887, he again renewed
ties with this artistic group shortly thereafter. Indeed, they had
invited him to direct and perform in some of their productions:
a pantomime, *Colombine's Suggestions*, by François de Nion; an
ironic piece, *Flagrant Délit*, by Paul Ginisty; and *The Family*, a
poetical drama by Adolphe Thalasso. Lugné-Poë received particularly commendable criticisms for Thalasso's play. The critic
Croze commented on his excellent diction, his meaningful
gestures and his sensitive concern for effects, all of which were
instrumental in his exceptional portrayal.[2]

Lugné-Poë was well aware of the amateurish nature of the
Cercle des Escholiers' productions. He not only realized that this
group of performers would never achieve any professional rank,
but he also understood the fact that he would have to look elsewhere for inspiration and for regular work. Nor had he any
illusions. After finally winning first prize at the Conservatoire
and thus freeing himself from further military obligations, he
knew jobs were hard to come by and, therefore, accepted as many
acting roles as he could: large, small, in and outside of Paris, in
regular and fly-by-night theatres. He appeared in a disparate
brew of plays, including Alphonse Daudet's *Sapho* with Réjane
and Lucien Guitry; Maurice Donnay's *Lysistrata*; in Molière's

Toulouse-Lautrec's poster for the Théâtre de l'Oeuvre

The Hypochondriac.   But these were just stop-gaps until he could find just the right play which would allow him to branch out on his own. And he did.

For years, Lugné-Poë had been haunted by Ibsen's symbolic drama, *The Lady from the Sea*.   Finally, when he broached the possibility of directing this work to the board of the Cercle des Escholiers, they agreed to his plan although well aware of the abstruse nature of this drama.   After all, they reasoned, Ibsen was in vogue in Paris; they would not, therefore, be taking the same risks as had Antoine who, against the advice of critics, dramatists, and friends, produced *Ghosts* and *The Wild Duck*.   Lugné-Poë's *The Lady from the Sea* was performed on December 16, 1892 and with success. (See discussion of *The Lady from the Sea* in Chapter 6.)

Maeterlinck: Pelléas and Mélisande

When Lugné-Poë suggested to the Cercle des Escholiers that he direct a production of Maeterlinck's *Pelléas and Mélisande*, their reading committee vetoed his proposal. It was overly ambiguous, they said. Since Lugné-Poë was not one to be easily discouraged, he turned to Paul Fort, who was in the process of making plans to revive his Théâtre d'Art.   Fort greeted Lugné-Poë's project with favor and thought of producing *Pelléas and Mélisande* in his theatre, but unable to acquire the necessary funding, he subsequently abandoned all thought of reactivating his theatre and of producing Maeterlinck's play.

Meanwhile, Maeterlinck, with whom Lugné-Poë had grown very friendly, encouraged him to produce *Pelléas and Mélisande*.   He advised him, however, to take his time and devote a lot of attention to costuming, decors, and the mise-en-scène.   All details pertaining to this difficult work were of extreme import, Maeterlinck told him, and haste or bad judgment could ruin the entire production.   With the help of Camille Mauclair, a writer himself, Lugné-Poë's project came to fruition.

Lugné-Poë, who had only wanted to assume a minor role in *Pelléas and Mélisande*, was convinced by the dramatist, who considered him a "great artist," to play the lead (Golaud). Maeterlinck also cautioned him on the ultra-simple manner in which his play must be enacted: the characters must be viewed as childlike, innocent, naïve beings. Nor should harsh or overtly realistic gestures, tones or expressions be used.[3]

Maeterlinck also maintained that a Medieval atmosphere must prevail, situated sometime between the eleventh and fifteenth century.   A single tonal nuance should predominate as well as harmonize with other subordinate colors.   The ensemble of hues must suggest and convey *feeling*—in an imprecise way. Nothing brash or overt should interfere with the subdued, secretive atmosphere.   Nor should there be any explicitly delineated objects on stage—only essences and symbols.   The function of decor is virtually ornamental, Maeterlinck argued; it is there to foster illusion through analogy and implication.   Drapes that hang in folds to the floor may serve to heighten feelings or diminish them, depending upon how the light strikes them and the various pleats.[4]   The paintings of the Flemish artist, Memling, should be the inspiration for the costumes.   Lavender, instead of green, would be most suitable for Mélisande's long dress, with ribbons of the same color braided into her long blond hair. Pelléas would be best served in green.

Pelléas and Mélisande, performed on May 17, 1893 at the Bouffes-Parisiens, made theatrical history.   The curtains parted, Octave Mirbeau wrote, on a set of flat and "graduated muted tones of dark blue, mauve, orange, moss green, moon green, water green, blending with the dimmed violets and blue greens of the costumes"—working up to Mélisande's lavender costume, clearer and lighter than the other hues.[5] Diffused and dim rays of light shone now and then like moon beams, creating a floating, indistinct, dream-like ambiance; otherwise, the stage was bathed in darkness.   No footlights stood between audience and actor to impede a close rapport.   All extraneous accessories and sets were banished.   There were no *trompe-l'oeil* decors, even in the forest or garden scenes.   The gauze veil placed across the acting platform emphasized the play's spiritual qualities, its dreaminess, and mystery.   Evocative and suggestive rather than explicative, the entire stage vision was reminiscent of the canvases of Puvis de Chavannes.

As the characters ambulated about the stage, more like phantasmagories than flesh-and-blood beings, uttering their monosyllabic feelings and sensations, illusion and poetry prevailed.   Maeterlinck's intent was respected: the characters portrayed souls in shock as they confront those many and disquieting unknowns implicit in life.[6]

The vagueness, ambiguity, and outer-worldly impression of the mise-en-scène paved the way to a whole new orientation in the theatre. Strange and murky happenings, which took place in a forest, in a palace, in subterranean passageways, became visual expressions of pictorial patterns existing in the unconscious. Archetypal images, embodied in a series of rhythmic and poetic progressions, were given form and depth, thereby emphasizing the fairy-tale atmosphere of *Pelléas and Mélisande*.

The central theme of Maeterlinck's play revolves around the birth and burgeoning of love and the destruction of the protagonists by passion. The plot is simple. Golaud, the grandson of Arkel, lord of a manor, is out hunting. He sees in the forest a young girl, Mélisande, who comes from a distant land. En route she has lost her crown, which Golaud offers to search for, but which she no longer wants. Golaud and Mélisande marry and go to his somber castle by the sea. Here Mélisande meets Golaud's young brother, Pelléas, who was supposed to leave on a journey to visit a dying friend. His mother, Geneviève, has requested he remain at the castle because of his father's serious illness. Arkel accepts Mélisande into the family, even though he had hoped for a politically more advantageous union to bring riches to the famine stricken community. Yniold, Golaud's little son by his first marriage, is always at Mélisande's side. Pelléas and Mélisande fall in love. One afternoon, Mélisande loses her wedding ring while playing with it at the edge of a fountain. Golaud observes the entente between Pélleas and Mélisande and grows jealous. He has Yniold spy on the lovers, surprises them in each other's arms, kills Pelléas, and wounds Mélisande. She dies, shortly after giving birth to a pitifully tiny baby girl.

The tragic love motif in *Pelléas and Mélisande* has been compared to the devastating passion experienced by Paolo and Francesca da Rimini, to Othello's blind love for Desdemona, and to Poe's child-lovers in "Annabel Lee." The fairy tale structure, with its unaccountable dangers, and its obstacles, inexplicable appearances and disappearances, seems the perfect vehicle for conveying Maeterlinck's metaphysical concepts.

The first clue to the evil fate to befall the protagonists occurs in the opening scene of *Pelléas and Mélisande*. The servants are washing the doorstep leading into the castle. Despite the fact that they bring a lot of water and scrub hard, they seem discouraged and claim they "will never be able to wash all of this clean." The impurities on the threshold of Golaud's castle remain embedded in the stone.

The forest sequence that follows—with its already

described shadows and evanescent illuminations—is of extreme importance. Golaud has lost his way. Such a lack of orientation indicates an inner need to transcend the confines of his existence and transform the worn pattern of his life. He comes upon a girl standing next to a fountain. She is petrified. "Don't touch me!" she says, or "I'll throw myself into the water!" She is lost. More important, perhaps, is the fact that she has mislaid her crown and does not want the stranger to retrieve it. Mélisande's appearance in the forest is not explicable along rational lines. The fact that she is lost reveals a confusion, and her unwillingness to look for her crown spells a desire to dissociate herself from her past. When Golaud asks detailed questions about Mélisande's family, her nation, and so on, her answers are vague and ambiguous, as if she herself were not sure of them.

It is not by chance that Golaud finds Mélisande next to a fountain. Since medieval times, and even before, the fountain has always represented the infinite possibilities that await a person when starting out in life or on a creative venture. Mélisande is child-like, nonworldly; she has appeared almost magically on the scene as in any fairy tale domain. She is pure, naïve, and graceful, and wears the intangible, remote, and passive features of the women depicted by the English artist, Burne-Jones.

Mélisande may be looked upon as an anima figure (a soul image). She is therefore revelatory of Golaud's feelings and unconscious state. Her presence indicates, to a certain degree, the void in his life: its lack of beauty, radiance, tenderness, and idealism. Because Golaud projects his unconscious ideal on Mélisande, he is unable to differentiate between his vision of her and the real person. His relationship with her, therefore, can never evolve and will always remain on a superficial level. Mélisande comments at the outset of their meeting on his graying hair, an indication of the course of their relationship: father-daughter (creator-creation), never husband and wife (mutual understanding).

That both get lost in the forest is revelatory of their lack of vision. Because the forest is usually dark and large, it has been associated with the unconscious. Thickly wooded and fertile, it has also been linked to the Great Mother, the female principle in nature that causes growth. In many fairy tales, monstrous froms appear in forests and a forbidding atmosphere is created. In *Pelléas and Mélisande*, the opposite is true. Golaud has a vision and sees the exquisitely beautiful girl in the purity, luster, and freshness of youth.   But being the personification of his ideal female figure, she will never take on any reality.   She is not of this world and is in no way related to it.[7]

Maeterlinck was so nervous on opening night that he did not attend the performance, walking about the Palais Royal area instead.   Mallarmé, Hervieu, Céard, Mr. and Mrs. Whistler, Maurice Barrès and his wife, Octave Mirbeau, Claude Debussy, who were present, admired the production and commented on the subdued color schemes, the slow-paced gestures and walking sequences, the economy of language, the evanescent atmosphere and the metaphysical dimension of the piece.   The old guard was, as to be expected, unanimous in its disapproval.   Interest lagged, wrote Jules Lemaître.   Francisque Sarcey remarked in no uncertain terms:

> Ah! yes, that's the mistake in the play; everyone is mysterious, everything takes on an air of mystery. One emerges from such a tenebrous area an absolute dolt, as though one were wearing a lead skull cap on one's head.[8]

Octave Mirbeau considered Maeterlinck's play the work of a great poet who is endowed with a "strange sensitivity concerning the supernatural" and a "lofty faculty of being able to move about so lucidly in abstract spheres."[9]   Other critics commented the colors were like a symphonic accompaniment of the work itself.   The hieratic postures of the actors, their threnody-like incantations were, for some, including J. Jullien, "annoyingly monotonous."[10]   Mallarmé, whose opinion Lugné-Poë respected, said that *Pelléas and Mélisande* was the paradigm of the theatre of the future.   Debussy wrote the opera.

*

The Théâtre de l'Oeuvre was launched.   Though its headquarters at 21 rue Rochechouart consisted of a very small room built beneath an archway designed for a carriage entrance, enthusiasm ran high.   With forty borrowed francs to his name, Lugné-Poë, together with his friends, Vuillard and Mauclair, a bank employee, Gros, and Adolphe van Bever—all poor—set out to stun the theatrical community.[11]

They had good reason to adopt a positive view.   Not only did they believe in their artistic credo—a poetic, symbolistic, imaginative theatre; they were also convinced that such an approach would enable them to penetrate many levels of *being*: the real and the occult, the causal and the synchronistic. Lugné-Poë's vision was transpersonal. He looked toward the world of reality, to be sure, but also beyond it, intent upon immersing the stage happenings with outer-worldly happenings. His goal was to create *a work of art* while also triggering new ideas and fresh currents: to struggle against the inertia which pervaded contemporary theatre; to rebel against commercial enterprises—a difficult task.[12]

A blending of the arts in Renaissance fashion was Lugné-Poë's intent. To this end, he would invite puppeteers, pantomimists, clowns, musicians, and dancers to perform on his stage. Circulars were printed, describing the Théâtre de l'Oeuvre's credo and plans, and soliciting subscriptions as well. To defray costs, they were hand-delivered by Lugné-Poë and Mauclair—as Antoine had done in 1887, when he founded his Théâtre Libre.

Help came rapidly from critics writing in journals (*L'Hermitage*, *La Plume*, and *Le Mercure de France*) and subscribers, such as Georges Ohnet, Victorien Sardou, Émile Zola, Puvis de Chavannes, Jean-Paul Laurens, and M. and Mme Curie. Lugné-Poë's friends—Vuillard, Denis, Sérusier, and Bonnard—invited the artist colony to contribute their artistic acumen to the enterprise.

Lugné-Poë produced many French works—among them Rachilde's *The Crystal Cobweb*. As depressing and pathogenic a work as Edgar Allan Poe's *The Demon of the Absurd*, Rachilde's drama relates the story of a melancholic young lad who tells his mother that he has a morbid fear of mirrors. He had seen a mirror shatter in front of him as a child and had never recovered from the terror of seeing the spider-like fissures it had made. These kept appearing and reappearing in his mind's eye—as if indelibly engraved—menacing and monstrous in their configurations. One night, awakened by moon rays reflecting and deflecting on the mirror in his room, the dreaded image reappeared in all of its ghastliness. The crystal-spider, reaching bizarre and grotesque proportions, overwhelmed him. Mesmerized by the hallucination, he rushes unknowing toward the mirror. The violence of the impact crushes his head.

Rachilde's play made little impression upon audiences. Banal and pedestrian in its vision and theatrical technique, it paralleled the Gothic novel structure, a form which had had its heyday in the early nineteenth-century, but was devoid of that fire necessary to bring a really creative work into existence.

Gabriel Trarieux's *An April Night at Chios* fared not better and was just as morbid as Rachilde's drama. It focused on certain ancient customs practiced at Chios by magistrates who, when they decided they were tired of living or that their lives were too painful to bear, killed themselves at a time deemed appropriate to them. Despite Denis's set, with its chiaroscuro, its cacti, its golden sea bordered with white houses, and a relatively subtle and nuanced dialogue, replete with repetitions and evocative metaphors, so dear to the Symbolists, the play was dismal. No empathetic reaction on the part of the audience was evident.

Beaubourg: The Image

Nor did *The Image*, by Maurice Beaubourg, author of *Tales for Assassins* (1890) and *Passionate Short Stories* (1892), and a partisan of Idealist theatre, elicit praise. An eclectic group which included Symbolists, Decadents, and other creative spirits, the Idealists emphasized an aesthetics of poetry rather than of drama, combining the more innovative and creative aspects of realism with the esoteric and occult features of metaphysics and mysticism. The difficulties resided in putting these disparate ideas into practice. What works for poetry, the short story, and the novel, may not always be possible in theatre. Theatrical dialogue, for these Idealists, would be evocative and not descriptive, yet geared, strangely enough, to the realistic conventions required of theatre. Influenced by Mallarmé's views concerning the performances, as expressed in his work *Divagations* and in articles appearing in the *Revue Wagnérienne*, the Idealists also believed that, just as leitmotifs exist in musical compositions, they also should be implicit in spoken language. "Verbal orchestration" interwoven into the stage happenings would lead to the birth of a universal art form—total theatre. Mallarmé wrote:

> The highest work of art must put itself in the place of real life; it must dissolve this Reality in an illusion, by means of which Reality itself appears to us to be no longer anything but an illusion.[13]

To mesmerize, to tempt, to lure audiences into a secret, ideal, mystical, and symbolistic world, is to adapt atemporal to temporal factors, which is what Lugné-Poë attempted to do in his production of *The Image*.

A play which some of Lugné-Poë's friends discouraged him from producing because of its unsuitability to the stage, *The Image* focuses on the world of artists and poets. Newlyweds, Marcel and Jeanne, happy at first, are soon headed for moral incompatability. Marcel, living in his illusionary realm, grows increasingly fond of the image of his wife conjured by his fantasies than the flesh and blood being. Tension and anguish increase during the drama, as the dichotomy between dream and reality becomes more pronounced. He also begins to look down upon his friends and colleagues who live in the workaday world and who are unable to transcend pedestrian views and give free rein to their imagination. He sees them as arid, dried up, dead spirits; while he, who experiences multiple worlds on wings of song, is the only one to know the meaning of *life*. He alone has access to transpersonal spheres.

To adapt such intellectual concepts to the stage was accomplished through an interesting use of dialogue, gesture, and facial expressions, all serving to create a *state of mind* or a pathological condition, which mounts in intensity as the play progresses. At the outset, for example, as the twenty-year-old couple sit in their study, the husband, Marcel, at his table, and his wife, Jeanne, relaxing in an easy chair, they talk literature, philosophy, and ever so often rise to exchange kisses. This idyllic world soon grows cold. Jeanne, gentle and loving, cannot account for the change which has occurred in her writer husband. Soon, however, she stumbled on to the problem. "Whom do you love," she questions, "me or my image?" Audiences see him struggling against his fantasy world—the dream image which obsesses him. In a most poignant scene, filled with the rarest of emotions which moved so many of the spectators, she cries out disconsolate, but in simple, just, and restrained tones: "Ah! You don't love me any more; it's the image whom you really love." By the third act, Marcel sees his wife as an implacable enemy, robbing him of his mental image, which has not taken on concrete dimensions. When Marcel can no longer contain it, the dramatist makes the image manifest in a striking scene, with the help of subdued lighting effects. The image becomes strangely evanescent as it climbs some stairs, enters the room, walks, near a curtain, and then takes its place between the once loving couple. Other scenes were equally portentous. One in particular stunned audiences: Marcel strangles his *real* wife, then passionately caressing the amorphous and lifeless form which, for him, had taken on human dimension.

Berthe Bady, incarnating the wife, was acclaimed for her more than sensitive portrayal. As for Lugné-Poë, in the role of the husband, he was, in Albert Samain's words, a "true comédien, personal and understanding, the artist one knows him to be."[14] Lugné-Poë did not merely *act* his richly textured character, but drew upon a panoply of emotions buried within his own inner depths to portray this idiosyncratic being.

Compliments were also aimed at Maurice Beaubourg's poetic, rhythmic, and suggestive style, which not only captured the imagination of theatregoers, but mesmerized and haunted them with its subdued and lilting refrains and strange visualizations.

Some in the audience, however, voiced their annoyance; they claimed they were unable to distinguish fact from fiction and, as a result, wondered about their own sanity.

Critics seemed to be growing tired of this virtually continuous stream of morose, melancholic, and somber pieces enacted at the Théâtre de l'Oeuvre. They asked for respite: something comic, droll—perhaps less profound, but pleasanter. Still, such critics as Pierre Veber were impressed, and lauded Idealist drama and the imaginative qualities that went into the creation of phantasms on stage. Hadn't Maeterlinck, he and others pointed out, succeeded brilliantly in this domain with *The Intruder, The Blind,* and *Pelléas and Mélisande?*

*

Lugné-Poë's production of Henri Bataille's *Sleeping Beauty,* a play about a Prince who rescued a girl from incarceration, was itself unrescuable. The critic's reactions to Burne-Jones' captivating but oppressive program illustration, featuring a fragile and evanescent drawing of a Sleeping Beauty, were negative. Even the sets for the first and last acts, inspired by the English artist's painting, *Love in the Midst of Ruins,* failed to please. The decor for the second act was considered unsuitable and even grotesque. It featured dim rays filtering into a sumptuous drawing room, making visible a couch heaped with furs and rare silks on which a princess, in the most modern of dresses, lounged. Although the costume for the Evil Fairy, designed by Burne-Jones and Georges-Antoine Rochegrosse, seemed appropriate on paper, when transformed into a dress, it looked absolutely weird. The sleeves, which were supposed to resemble wings, looked more like wet umbrellas, particularly when the actress raised her arms.

Sleeping Beauty was judged anti-scenic and the production was deemed badly directed and poorly acted. Uninteresting as well were the lengthy tirades, the philosophical and spiritualistic discussions—more like soporifics, the critics said, than theatre. The voices of the actors, although powerful enough to be heard over the din of the orchestra, were uninspiring.[15]

Régnier: The Guardian

To try to redeem his poor showing, Lugné-Poë offered Henri de Régnier's dialogued poem, *The Guardian*. A Symbolist in Mallarmé's entourage and known for his *Ancient and Modern Poems*, Régnier's verses were virtually unintelligible; audiences neither heard nor understood the modulations of the sonorities, rhythms, or multiple nuances of meanings inherent in the images. The evanescent beauty and charm, the fleeting sensations of Régnier's lines were lost to all those unfamiliar with the poet's work. Because the poem included dialogue only at the outset, the spectators remained on the outside of Régnier's symbolic verse, never able to penetrate those nebulous inner climes.

The green gauze curtain and the greenish lunar hues for *The Guardian* created the wanted eerie and mysterious mood. They also triggered vague and evanescent qualities in the spectators' unconscious, paving the way through suggestion for the dream world to come into being. Jules Lemaître described Vuillard's painted backdrop as follows:

> The backdrop consisted of a dreamy landscape, with blue trees, a violet palace, a Puvis de Chavannes-like fresco painted by the uncertain hand of a color-blind new-born—like stammering painting.[16]

The mise-en-scène was innovative. The stage area had been divided into two separate parts: the reciters were hidden in the orchestra pit while the actors, remaining silent, stood on stage behind a green gauze veil. As the latter replicated the feelings enunciated below in slow pantomimic language, such vocal and visual dichotomies increased the already intense sense of remoteness and mystery inherent in the play. By severing tone from the optical image in his mise-en-scène, Lugné-Poë accentuated a malaise already present in Régnier's poetry. Because the voices and pantomime were not synchronized, the technical aspect of the productionwas faulty. The words frequently preceded or trailed behind the gestures, inviting waves of laughter to ripple forth at the wrong times, disconcerting both performers and those in the audience who were familiar with Régnier's poems.

Although *The Guardian* was considered one of Lugné-Poë's "follies," the techniques used in his mise-en-scène would be copied by many twentieth-century writers, including Apollinaire, Cocteau, Strindberg, O'Neill, Anouilh, and others.

*

For Lugné-Poë, theatre was a spring-board to higher spheres.

> The spring-board is made of solid pieces of wood, which take on a certain suppleness beneath the actors' feet. It becomes elastic as we turn about, as we move; it provokes, arouses a power, an élan; and this elasticity which I felt when I took my first steps on stage accounts for the sensations it triggered in me as a beginner.[17]

An actor must be light on his feet, Lugné-Poë maintained, elastic, ready to bound, jump, and gyrate. A pantomimist, a puppet, a clown, he must be a man for all seasons, an incarnator, a magician—a demiurge. The Symbolists required that the actor be endowed with other qualities. He must be humble and capable of vanishing behind an image, of banishing his own personality and allowing his feeling and sensation world to prevail.

> Isn't the actor's acceptance of identification with another, an example of a kind of mad abdication, of incredible humility—this disdain for all of one's powers, all of one's palpitations, one's words?[18]

In a letter to Jean Jullien, he conveys the prodigious scope of his ideas concerning performance.

> I perceive dramatic art on such a prodigiously high level that nothing around me can help me realize it. Let's see! this abyss between you and me—which makes you judge me to be a *deplorable comédien* (perhaps you're right)—is the result of a constant search to attain

> the audacious goal of the artist creator . . . If I could spend some evenings with you, I would explain what I see to you; you would feel it and would *also explain it to me*. . . .[19]

Lugné-Poë put some of his views to use in his production of yet another Maeterlinck drama: *Interior.*

Maeterlinck: Interior

Interior is a meditation on death. The play's action takes place in a house, visible through three ground-floor windows, and in a garden in front of the mansion. The family inside the house consists of a father, a mother holding a baby in her lap, and two young girls dressed in white. These characters do not speak; they merely rise, walk, gesticulate in "grave, slow, sparse" ways, as though they had been "spiritualized by distance." In the garden are an Old Man, his two daughters, and a Stranger. They are talking, trying to determine the best way of breaking the terrible news—death by drowning of a daughter—to the seemingly peaceful family within.

The emphasis Lugné-Poë placed on the mimetic art was unsettling. The dialogue in the garden, consisting almost exclusively of a series of comments and conversations concerning the family in the house, creates a close rapport between them and the emotions expressed through bodily movements of the people within. The dissociation of speech and action, novel for the period, though it had been tried in *The Guardian*, breaks to a certain extent the conventional empathy usually existing between actor and audience. Although distance separates the two groups, the thoughts articulated by the old Man and the Stranger are for some inexplicable reason sensed by those in the house and mirrored in their pantomime, in a kind of *active silence*. When, for example, the Old Man and the Stranger speak of the corpse that was found in the lake, the two sisters in the house turn their heads toward the window as though aware of some mysterious feelings, some excruciating presentiment.

A sense of secrecy and uneasiness pervades the atmosphere. The young girl's death is mysterious. Had she wanted to die? The Stranger says that the peasants had seen her wandering by the river. They thought she was looking for a certain flower. The Old Man insinuates the possibility of suicide: "She was perhaps one of those who wishes to say nothing . . . who has more than one reason for not living . . . For years one may live next to someone who is no longer in this world."

Anguish rises in the contrapuntal rhythmic effect set up
by the village folk who follow the undulations of the path and,
bearing the dead girl's body, slowly make their way toward the
garden. The Old Man must speak out now. He remarks: "One
does not know in advance the march of pain." He must inform
the family. As the crowd approaches, the Old Man enters the
house. Then, before he utters a word, the Mother walks forward.
She has already understood the tragedy that has befallen her and
hides her face in her hands. The Old Man nods slowly to the
crowd, indicating he has completed his mission. The family
rushes into the garden; the infant sleeps on.

Interior is an extraordinary and excoriating work. The
inevitability of death is made so powerful by both the stage
happenings and the pace of the drama as to become unbearable.
The contrast between the peaceful family scene, visible through
the window, and the sorrowful news that must invade this
atmosphere accelerates in intensity as the drama unfolds, reaching its apogee at the end. As in classical drama, all unessential
material has been eradicated; the play's theme (the obligation of
informing the family) is uppermost.[20]

Not only had Lugné-Poë brought Maeterlinck—the real
Father of twentieth-century Absurdist theatre—to the fore, but
he had also continued the tradition begun by Antoine. By producing foreign plays—Scandinavian theatre in particular—he
broadened and deepened the views of the French theatregoer.

Chapter 6

Productions of Scandinavian Authors

When Lugné-Poë announced his intention of producing works by foreign authors—among them, Ibsen, Bjørnson, and Strindberg—some critics took umbrage, as they had when Antoine introduced Scandinavian dramatists to Parisian audiences. To produce anything but French authors was, they argued, to slight one's countrymen. Lugné-Poë thought otherwise. To seek out authors from different lands would be to enlarge the horizons of the French—to internationalize their thinking.

Lugné-Poë felt attuned to Ibsen, the playwright. He had familiarized himself with the works of this Norwegian dramatist when Antoine had produced *Ghosts* and *The Wild Duck* at the Théâtre Libre. The poetic and elusive nature of *The Lady from the Sea* was so alluring to him that he suggested to the Cercle des Escholiers, prior to his founding of the Théâtre de l'Oeuvre, that he direct Ibsen's drama, and his idea was accepted. (See chapter 5.)

Ibsen: The Lady from the Sea

Audience reacted favorably to Lugné-Poë's production of *The Lady from the Sea* (December 16, 1892), which stressed the haunting and symbolistic nature of the drama. The protagonist, Ellida Wangel, trapped in a mundane marriage to a country doctor and the victim of a deterministic environment, believes that some hidden understanding existed between her, the Sea, and a Stranger—a mysterious seaman to whom she had once been affianced. She longs to experience the real love and fulfillment she associates with this phantasy figure. When the mysterious seaman (existing within her unconscious) takes on real shape and reclaims his bride, she is torn by indecision as to which *path* she should choose. With fortitude and great sadness, she finally

Denis's program for Ibsen's *The Lady from the Sea*

decides to remain with her husband and his two daughters from a previous marriage. No longer will she dwell on the "unattainable . . . limitless . . . infinite." Rather, she will spend her time attending to mundane matters. The adolescent has given way to the mature woman.

Two cosmic principles were at odds with each other in Ibsen's work: the metaphysical as opposed to the scientific side of life. In Ibsen's preliminary notes to *The Lady From the Sea*, he writes: "Everywhere limitation. From this comes melancholy like a subdued song of mourning over the whole of human existence and all the activities of men."[1] Rationalism versus Idealism is evoked through imagery. Ellida's wistful need to break out of her strictured and confining environment is depicted via vistas of fjords and alpine peaks. These figurations, representing the fluidity of relationships rather than their concreteness, pave the way for psychological regression to a past where the world of fantasies dominates.

Lugné-Poë, as Doctor Wangel, acted with punctilious accuracy, gestures, words, and facial expression revealing the utterly scientific bent of this objective and rational being. He cannot understand his wife's needs, her yearnings, her fascination with the sea. Nor can he relate to her emotionally. Indeed, he treats her like a mental case or as a child who needs a pacifier. To emphasize the rationality of the character, Lugné-Poë spoke in grave and serious tones, walking slowly about the stage, stopping every now and then to reflect and meditate upon one or more points. Jules Lemaître did not like Lugné-Poë's portrayal and compared his Dr. Wangel to a "somnambulistic clergyman." Henri de Régnier, on the other hand, admired Lugné-Poë's efforts and wrote of the strange double world existing on stage: each character seemed to be itself and its own ghost at the same time. Compliments, however, were forthcoming for Georgette Camée, as Ellida—a strange creature dressed in layers of white fantomatic veils and a duplicate of the lithograph Maurice Denis had created for the occasion. Her hieratic gestures, lyrical intonations, and feeling for the beauty of language, made for some deeply moving moments.

Ibsen's friend, Herman Bang, was distressed by the production and wrote the dramatist telling him that he would have "wept blood or stared into his hat" had he witnessed the performance. It was a betrayal, he stated categorically, and accused Lugné-Poë of having copied the worst German theatrical techniques and applying them to Ibsen. Sarcey agreed: "In German theatre it has become a tradition . . . when they play Ibsen, to strive to make the audience forget that the characters treading the boards are real flesh and blood people. They move but little, use almost no hand gestures and, when they do, they are broad, almost sacerdotal. Their speech as a whole can be characterized as a slow recitation, which seemingly emanates from supernatural and symbolic lips."[2]

Lugné-Poë defended his production, remarking that this so-called monotonous and religious intonation he and his cast used when performing Ibsen solved certain textual problems. Lugubrious and melodious vocalizations and modulations lent an ambiguity, an unuttered and esoteric climate to the scenes, so important, he felt, in accentuating the mysterious nature of the happenings. The uncertainties aroused by such intonations, however, triggered a sense of wonder and marvel in some spectators, but annoyance in others, who needed to have everything cut-and-dried. Although praised by the Symbolist magazines, *Mercure de France* and *l'Ermitage*, for its disquieting and perplexing obscurities, Lugné-Poë's production, interestingly enough, became a conversation piece in cafes and restaurants. The consensus: the interpretation of *The Lady From the Sea* given at the Théâtre de l'Oeuvre was a paradigm of how *not* to interpret Ibsen. The dramatist himself told Lugné-Poë that he should avoid any German influence in his future mise-en-scènes of his works. Despite their divergent opinions, a great theatrical relationship ensued between the French director and the Norwegian playwright and, as a result, Lugné-Poë was to produce more Ibsen plays than any other French director.[3]

Ibsen: Rosmersholm

Rosmersholm, translated by Count Prozor, was chosen for the opening of the Ibsen series at the Théâtre de l'Oeuvre on October 6, 1893. Lugné-Poë, who did not have the funds to rent a permanent theatre, found temporary quarters for *Rosmersholm* at the Théâtre des Bouffes du Nord near the Gare du Nord (on the Boulevard de la Chapelle). The lack of heat or other amenities in the old theatre obliged the actors, during rehearsals, to wear heavy clothing and galoshes—a good but arduous preparation for the production of this Nordic writer's work.

Vuillard was in charge of the group of artists—Sérusier,

Bonnard, and Ranson—who contributed their artistic talents in
the creation of decors.   All worked from seven in the morning
until eight at night in the cold and dirt—always in a spirit of
dedication. Vuillard made the lithograph for the program.

Ibsen's friend, Herman Bang, who had had such harsh
words for Lugné-Poë's production of *The Lady From the Sea*,
was called upon this time to help direct *Rosmersholm*.   It is he
who steered the actors along the right path: "Be true! . . . profound! give of yourself . . . think . . . and . . . extract everything
you have."[4]

A lecture given by Leopold Lacour, a drama critic,
preceded the production of *Rosmersholm*.   Designed to famil-
iarize audiences with the works of the Norwegian dramatist,
Lacour's stunningly sensitive and polished manner fascinated
the thousand people in the audience.

Rosmersholm is wilfully enigmatic.   As in *Ghosts*, the
past takes precedence over the present, and is the raison d'être
for the motivations of the characters and the emotional climate
of the work. John Rosmer, a pastor and widower, has been living in his ancestral home, Rosmersholm, with his housekeeper,
Rebecca West. She had entered the family's employ a year prior
to Mrs. Rosmer's suicide by drowning in the millrace. Since that
time, John and Rebecca are living out their passionate, thwarted
and guilt-ridden relationship.   The drama consists of series of
conversation/revelations revolving around the mysteries associated with their actions and their unconscious intents.   During
the course of the action, we discover that Rebecca is both mani-
pulative and ruthless; that it was "blinding, uncontrollable
passion" that drove Mrs. Rosmer to suicide. But there is more to
it than that: it is insinuated that Rebecca, who cared for her
adoptive father (probably her real one) after her mother's
demise, had lived an incestuous relationship with him. Because
Rebecca "exposes one motive in order to conceal another," this
theatrical type represents something new, alive, and very real in
theatre. Unlike many of Ibsen's characters, she has a sense of
freedom and feels no guilt. Nor is she ashamed of giving vent
to her lust. Not so for Rosmer, who has never had the courage
to experience real sensuality with his wife, so incarcerated was
he within his cloistered Christian ethos. In time, she inculcates
Rosmer with her ideas of emancipation and with her belief in
the nobility of his soul.   His brother-in-law, Rector Kroll, who
represents reaction and repression, blames Rebecca for the trag-

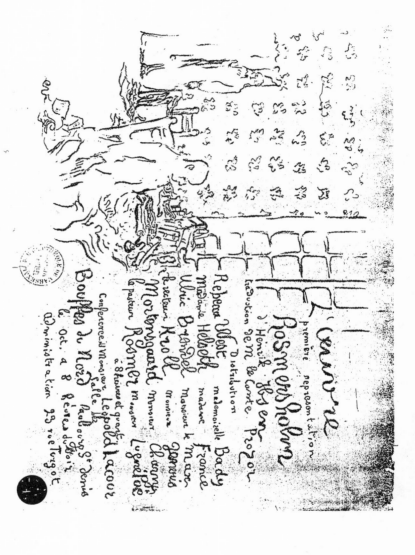

Vuillard's program for Ibsen's *Rosmersholm*

edy besetting the household. He attempts to crush her spirit and
to chastise Rosmer for harboring such dangerous ideations. Rosmer, unheeding, asks Rebecca to marry him.   She declines.
Drained and without courage, her will has grown lethargic since
her rival's demise.   No confrontation; no scheming; no planning. "The time is past when I was afraid of nothing. I have lost
the power to take action, John." Rosmer is crushed by his moral
dilemma. He no longer knows what to believe. Was she sincere
in her feelings toward him?   Only one way would quell his
doubts and prove the depth of her passion for him: to sacrifice
their lives—each for the other. When Rebecca agrees to this act
of courage and self-abnegation, Rosmer gazes at her with infinite
tenderness as his eyes fill with tears. They join in marriage in a
symbolic ceremony. Walking together in close embrace, the two,
overcome with the thrill of great passion, rush toward their abys-
mal demise.   In death alone can they find release, fulfillment,
and escape from the past.

The curtains part on an old, somber manor belonging to
Rosmer's family for ten generations.   The lighting is dim and
shadowy; mystery hovers; silence reigns; laughter is unknown.
A young woman, Rebecca, is seated near the window, bloodied
by the last rays of a setting sun. She is awaiting Rosmer's return.
The furnishings, in Empire style, are arranged symmetrically,
the willed order that prevails masking the mood of
psychological chaos. A flower-stand to the right side of the stage
counter-balances the wild flowers and birch branches to the left.
Moreover, the many flowers and birch branches placed by
Rebecca around the room are antithetical in spirit to the extreme
elegance and grave simplicity of the surroundings. During the
course of the drama the large white shawl Rebecca is crocheting
will come to symbolize a shroud for the death of the two lovers.

The house, a metaphor for "rigid and high-minded moral
traditions," is not only given an eerie cast by the shadowy luminosities infiltrating the room, but also by the sound effects. The
roaring waters of the millrace is heard throughout the drama in
graded nuances.   Likewise, the portraits of Rosmer's ances-
tors—soldiers and priests—add to the already powerful sense of
doom and decay of traditional values. "It's the dead who cling to
Rosmersholm, almost as though they couldn't free themselves
from the ones left behind."

Lugné-Poë, as Rosmer, wore his austerity.   A redingote,
which buttoned all the way to his chin, emphasized his rigidity

and puritanism. His portrayal was considered masterful and grandiose. His suffering and his apostolic fervor were rendered by facial expressions, but also by a flat, sing-song quality in his voice, resounding like so many incantations throughout the theatre.[5]

Berthe Bady's Rebecca was restrained, sensual, and powerful. Flaunting her feelings of independence and proud of the fact that she has succeeded in discarding those superstitions which plague the feeble, she stands out at the beginning as strong and aggressive. The interplay between her vibrant personality and Kroll's measured ways (he takes such pleasure in humiliating her and breaking down her pride) emphasizes the more enigmatic aspect of her personality. Her serenity is superficial; it breaks down slowly, as do her humanitarian views, riddled as they are with the suspected depravity indulged in years back—with her father! What is she really like?

Despite the many accolades given to Lugné-Poë's direction, Adolphe Brisson contended that the play, acting, and sets were antithetical to the French personality.

> Ibsen's dramas exude a black melancholy; they are drowned in fog and mystery. Not a ray of light, except perhaps a ray from the midnight sun—whose pale clarity can in no way warm the Norwegian fjords. And this explains the reason why Ibsen's dramas will never captivate the French bourgeois who cherish gaiety and good wine.[6]

Alfred Valette, on the other hand, praised Lugné-Poë for his courage in choosing such a profound and multi-leveled drama. For him, every element of the stage production—gestures, facial expressions, pace, vocalizations, and costumes —were regarded as *signs* of the superior world of *ideas*.[7]

Clearly *Rosmersholm* played to a divided audience: poets and painters set against the bulk of journalists who neither made the effort to understand the unusual nor to seek a broadening of their views. Theatre for these people was considered *entertainment* and nothing more—like the Folies Bergères. The critic Marcel Bailliot struck just the right note when he wrote: "Ah! naïve influential cretins of critics, you think you have gotten rid of Ibsen. He is now stronger than ever."[8]

Ibsen attended the opening of Lugné-Poë's *Rosmersholm* in Christiana, Norway, in October of 1894. The French director recorded the "Master's" reactions:

> During the whole performance Ibsen remained motionless. He seemed to wish to restrain the audience from demonstrating in any way. Only at the end of every act did he applaud, without manifesting pleasure. After the final act he rose, bowed to us actors, then to the audience who were applauding him. That was all.[9]

The following morning Lugné-Poë was invited to visit Ibsen.

> He received us, as before, with that exceptional amability which I have often remarked in him, like a doctor receiving a patient. . . . Dare I say without lack of respect that morning Ibsen was *"dans le décor"*? . . . Very *soigné*, his hair and beard shaggy yet combed in a curiously fastidious style, his glasses on his nose, just as I had seen him in the Grand Hotel. From time to time Bang came to my assistance. I felt so tall that the furniture, the knick-knacks, the paintings on the wall, even my host himself, all made me feel gauche and clumsy. I waited for Ibsen to indicate that I might sit. He, somewhat small compared with me, seemed visibly ill at ease. His eyes bored deeply into mine as though exploring me.[10]

Ibsen added:

> French actors are more suited than many others to act my plays. People have not fully appreciated that a passionate writer needs to be acted with passion, and not otherwise.[11]

Ibsen: An Enemy of the People

Unlike *Rosmersholm* or *The Lady From the Sea, An Enemy of the People* (1882) was didactic and topical. The protagonist, Dr. Stockmann, is outspoken in his condemnation and defiance of the members of his community for attempting to cover up the pollution affecting local bathing areas. Should he publish his remarks, the community whose livelihood depends on these baths would suffer devastating commercial consequences. At first, the townspeople look upon him as a public benefactor; but when they discover that his forthrightness might lead to a diminution of their incomes, they turn against him and call him "an enemy of the people." Dr. Stockmann's dilemma causes him great sorrow. His patients leave him, his daughter is fired from her job, and a mob shows their anger by breaking his window. Rather than leave, which was his option, he will suffer his isolation and remain to re-educate the townspeople, for, as he says, "The strongest man in the world is he who stands most alone."

Lugné-Poë captured Stockman's multivalent nature as well as his gregarious, impulsive, and tempestuous moods. His gestures assumed alacrity and the tone of his voice rose when he was unable to control his passion. A smoother and more mannered approach was revealed when he took it upon himself to attack the hypocritical officials. At times, he even assumed a bombastic stance, to the extent that there were moments when comedy rather than drama took over.

That the opening of *An Enemy of the People* nearly turned into a riot was not due to the political temper of Parisians nor to Lugné-Poë's mise-en-scène. Anarchist demonstrations had broken out all over the city on first night. The fact that Lugné-Poë had called upon Laurent Tailhade, a noted anarchist, to lecture on *An Enemy of the People* before the beginning of the performance accounted for the chaos that invaded the theatre. Tailhade, taking advantage of his position, used the occasion not so much to analyze the drama but to attack in violent terms "all the 'leading men' in French literature and politics," labeling "the recent Franco-Prussian *fêtes* as an act of collective insanity." After such statements, bedlam broke loose in the theatre and lasted for fifteen minutes.[12]

Invectives, vocal epithets, and general murmurings were heard throughout the performance, supporters and detracters expressing their reactions overtly to certain lines in the play. Despite the interruptions and outbursts, particularly during the fourth act, when extras on stage screamed imprecations at Dr. Stockmann, which paralleled those coming from the audience, Lugné-Poë continued, unflustered. When, however, it came time for him to speak the following lines with conviction, "The majority is never right. Never, I tell you!" the spectators hollered yesses and nos; finally, one spewed out: "Long live anarchy!"[13]

Lukewarm appraisals greeted Lugné-Poë's production of *An Enemy of the People*. His friends, however, marveled at Lugné-Poë's ability to portray such complex and ambiguous types—Rosmer and Stockmann—with relative ease. Avant-garde magazines, such as *La Revue Blanche*, were also helpful to Lugné-Poë. The artists Vuillard, Roussel, Denis, Ranson, Bonnard, Vallotton, Toulouse-Lautrec, and Sérusier who produced an illustration monthly, each created backdrops, programs, or posters for the Théâtre de l'Oeuvre. They were naturals for Lugné-Poë's projects: they loved to paint on large surfaces and

Vuillard's program for Ibsen's *An Enemy of the People*

impose their bold colors and heavily outlined patterns on these empty spaces. Such extensive surfaces transcended the "detestable" conventional limitations which they felt imprisoned the artist's free-flowing imagination. For Sérusier, the virtual spokesman for the Nabis whose ideas had much in common with the Symbolists and Lugné-Poë, decors was a paradigm for a whole hidden dimension:

> A correspondence between the material world and that of thought reverberates throughout the immutable world. . . . The work of art invites one to perceive a universe of unnamable things through the harmony of matter and the soul of the artist.[14]

Ibsen: The Master Builder

Not only did Lugné-Poë want to satisfy his own aesthetic inclinations, but he also reasoned that since Ibsen already had a following in France, it might be wise, financially speaking, to produce his latest drama, *The Master Builder*. He did just that on April 3, 1894.

The Master Builder dramatizes the plight of a man who seeks desperately to fill the void within himself. His life, his heart, his home are barren, cold, damp, hollow inner spatial areas that lie fallow. Solness, the protagonist, is a middle-aged man who has achieved fame in his profession as architect and builder. His chief employees are dependent upon him and he wants to maintain this situation, fearing the young might usurp his power. We learn that Solness' wife is ill and melancholy. A fire destroyed her ancestral home about twelve years prior to the outset of the play and though she, Solness and their twins were spared, she caught an infection shortly after the incident, which was fatally passed on to her infants in her milk. Was it Solness' neglect of the old house that caused the fire? He had noticed a split in the chimney flue in the attic, wanted to fix it, but something always held him back. A young girl, Hilda Wangel, enters the scene. She is a kind of *femme inspiratrice*, attractive and very independent, even aggressive. She claims to have met Solness ten years earlier, when she was only a child. He was building a tower on an old church at the time. She reminds him that he promised to build a "kingdom" for her then, and now she has come to claim her due. Although Solness suffers from a fear of heights, in time he acquiesces to her demands and climbs to the top of the tower he has just completed. Hilda, who watches him from the ground, cries out, "Higher and higher!"

Vuillard's program for Ibsen's *The Master Builder*

Solness, unflinching, reaches the topmost planks and waves his hat. "Hurrah for the Master Builder Solness!" she cries out. The inevitable happens, and he falls to his death.

So little money was spent on decors that the right atmosphere seemingly was not achieved. The few old and worn chairs, the small square coffee table, the narrow drawing table, the small stove, the rather vague-looking sofa in the back, and the ramshackle walls, did not, one critic remarked, give the impression of a thriving architectural firm. Indeed, the furnishings were so out of place that when Hilda questions Solness concerning the crack in the chimney, peals of laughter resounded throughout the theatre.[15]

Critics and spectators alike found *The Master Builder* ambiguous, difficult to understand, murky and inaccessible. When the words, "I don't understand this" were uttered by one of the protagonists several times during the course of the play, several spectators parrotted the remark: "Neither do we."

Despite Herman Bang's efforts to liven the pace of the play and to stress its realistic side, Lugné-Poë, as Solness, and the other members in the cast as well, still intoned their lines, as if reciting mass, thus injecting into Ibsen's work a kind of mystique which the dramatist did not want. Nevertheless, the critic, Gunnar Heiberg, stated that although Lugné-Poë's Solness was "tastefully and intelligently" acted, in no way did it suggest a living person.[16] George Bernard Shaw, who saw the Théâtre de l'Oeuvre's *The Master Builder* a year later in London, wrote:

> Comparing the performance with what we have achieved in England, it must be admitted that neither Mr. Waring nor Mr. Waller were in a position to play Solness as M. Lugné-Poë played him. They would never have got another engagement in genteel comedy if they had worn those vulgar trousers, painted that red eruption on their faces, and given life to that portrait which, in every stroke, from its domineering energy, talent and covetousness, to its half-witted egoism and crazy philandering sentiment, is amazingly true to life. Mr. Waring and Mr. Waller failed because they were under the spell of Ibsen's fame as a dramatic magician, and grasped at his poetic treatment of the man instead of at the man himself. M. Lugné-Poë succeeded because he recognized Solness as a person he had met a dozen times in ordinary life, and just reddened his nose and played him without preoccupation.[17]

Maeterlinck, perhaps better than others, explained the Théâtre de l'Oeuvre's veiled and mysterious interpretation of

Ibsen's theatre in general and *The Master Builder* in particular, which "was one of the first modern dramas which shows us the gravity and the secret tragedy of an ordinary and static life."[18] Like the great works of the past, Ibsen's dramas also border on eternity. Maeterlinck continues:

> What did Ibsen add to ordinary life in *Solness* that it should appear to us so strange, so profound, and so disquieting beneath its puerile exterior?[19]

The power of Ibsen's creative genius lies in the fact that Solness and Hilda are not only flesh and blood, but archetypal in dimension

> within the soul's atmosphere, and they have discovered this essential aspect of life in themselves, which makes them dread ordinary existence. . . . In all lengthy friendships, there comes a mysterious moment when we perceive, so to speak, our friend's exact situation with regard to the unfathomable that surrounds him and destiny's attitude toward him. And when by chance, we meet one of those whom we know to be of this kind, while chatting about the falling snow or women passing by, some little thing within all of us greets itself, examines and interrogates itself without our being aware of what is happening; interested in conjunctions, it speaks about events that we cannot possibly understand. . . . I believe that Hilda and Solness are of this kind and see themselves in this fashion.[20]

Signals or signs abound in each of Ibsen's plays, be it *Rosmersholm*, *The Wild Duck*, *The Lady From the Sea*, or *The Master Builder*. So, too, do death, suicide, disappearances, and the return of people long vanished. Each represents an aspect of the soul, a pattern of behavior, an invisible essence hovering about, ready to manifest itself, to affirm its needs and its longings for fulfillment. To play Ibsen realistically, Maeterlinck remarked, would be a travesty. Mystery exists beneath or behind each word and figure; phantoms seem to hover, gesturing, plaintively at first, impressionistically perhaps, like so many emanations or hallucinations. Another critic, Fouquier of *Le Figaro*, disagreed. He rejected Lugné-Poë's threnodies and his psalmodizing. Ibsen's characters should be interpreted as real, living, acting, feeling beings. What disturbed yet another group was the lack of cohesion they felt in Lugné-Poë's troupe. Gémier, for example, a superb actor, was borrowed when necessary from the Odéon. He played his Ibsenian roles without any preconceived notions—simply and openly. No nuanced gestures or vocal subtle specter-like qualities were implicit in his acting, unlike Lugné-Poë's portrayals. Was such disparity of tone due to a lack of authority or singleness of purpose on Lugné-Poë's part? Did he fail to impose his vision of Ibsen onto the others? Or did he want a pluri-dimensional quality to reign in his productions?

*

By 1894 Scandinavian dramatists were in style. *La Plume*, *La Nouvelle Revue*, *Le Revue dramatique*, *La Revue bleue*, *Le Mercure de France*, published studies and discussions of the works of Ibsen, Bjørnson, and Strindberg. Volumes such as Ernest Tissot's *Norwegian Drama* and René Doumic's *From Scribe to Ibsen* appeared. Critics, such as Henry Bauer of *L'Echo de Paris* and Henry Bordeaux in *La Revue Blanche*, wrote blatantly in favor of the work done at the Théâtre de l'Oeuvre.

For these reasons, in addition to his own inclinations, Lugné-Poë decided to produce yet another of the "Master's" works: *Little Eyolf*, on May 8, 1895.

Ibsen: Little Eyolf

Little Eyolf is perhaps the most complex and hermetic of all of Ibsen's plays. Despite the simplicity of the plot, the march of events seems baffling. Allmers, writer and teacher, has married the wealthy Rita, owner of "gold and green forests"; he is also drawn to her because of her "consuming beauty." Their sexual life had been active until the accident: little Eyolf, their infant son, fell from the table on which he had been asleep while they were making love. Crippled for life, he remained a paradigm of their sin—and poisoned their relationship. Allmers was left impotent, unable to assume his share of the responsibility for the misfortune. It was also while making love that Allmers told his wife that the name Eyolf was his secret name for Asta, his half-sister whom he loved, revealing his psychological incestuous relationship with her. To escape his corrosive feelings he submerges himself in his work. He is writing a book, *The Responsibility of Man*. He also forces Eyolf to study for so many hours each day that his eyes grow tired. Nor can Rita cope with the reality of her situation: she takes out her rage in bouts of jealousy directed towards Asta, Allmer's book, and even her own son.

The play opens with Allmers' return from a six-week walking tour in the mountains. He feels transformed and decides he will no longer write about human responsibility, but will devote his time instead to bringing up Eyolf. He tries to explain his feelings to Rita, who cannot seem to fathom her husband's mysterious transformation.

> I was alone up there, in the heart of the high mountains. Suddenly I came to a large, desolate lake. And I had to cross that lake. But I couldn't, for there was no one there, and no boat. . . .
>
> I went all alone, with no one to guide me, into a side valley. I thought that way I might be able to push forward over the heights and between the peaks, and so come down on the other side of the lake . . .
>
> Yes, I lost all sense of direction, for there was no kind of road nor path there. I walked all day—and all night, too, I began to think I would never find my way back. . . .
>
> I struggled along the deep crevasses, exulting in the peace and serenity of being in the presence of death . . .
>
> I had no fear. I felt that Death and I walked side by side like two good fellow travellers. It all seemed so natural. So logical. After all, in my family we do not live to be old. . . . That night settled the problem. I turned back and came home. To Eyolf. . . .
>
> We are earth-bound, Rita, you and I.

When, some months later, Eyolf is accidentally drowned in the fjord while playing with other boys, Allmers and Rita are again corroded with feelings of guilt. Had they been responsible parents they would have watched over their crippled son. The play then focuses on the protagonists' reconstruction of past events, their reactions and reminiscences, and their self-conscious explorations of themselves and their relationships. When it is discovered that Asta is not Allmers' half sister, but the fruit of her mother's illicit union with another man, she is invited to remain with the family—to be their Eyolf. She refuses, however, and will marry a man she does not love simply to leave the painful environs. The last act, dealing with Allmers' and Rita's inability to live with what they consider to be their crime, is static and talky, and extremely difficult to realize scenically. The audience must follow the characters' psychological involutions and the conclusion that they must face their tragedy together and no longer seek escape. They decide to work for others in Little Eyolf's name—as social servants caring for and rearing the poor village children. That such a mythic death/rebirth conclusion imposes itself upon a structured and outwardly realistic plot, lends an elliptical and atemporal quality to the drama, which is summed up at the end: "A birth. Or a resurrection. A transition. To another way of living."

Lugné-Poë's mise-en-scène was arresting. As for his portrayal of Allmers, though some found his intonations monotonous and his gestures irritating, others were relieved to hear that he no longer chanted or psalmodized his lines. Nor did he hesitate or repeat his words in litany-like fashion. He spoke clearly, vibrantly, naturally, and tenderly, enunciating his text with metallic emphasis or poetically nuanced tones when his part called for such. His stance was casual and more effective in creating suspense than if he had ritualized his poses, as was his habit at times.[21]

Asta, played by Suzanne Deprès, Lugné-Poë's future wife, was delicate and charming. Her voice was pure in harmony, rising at times, at other moments lowered in pitch; its rhythms were varied and meaningful. Her tones "resounding softly, so fraternally appeasing," were both endearing and enticing. Her diction was fleeting and anxious, as if she were fearful about pausing on a word or focusing on a "painful impression."[22]

Rita, played "excellently" by Marthe Mellot, spoke in a studied and stylized manner throughout the play. The mysteriously intriguing impressions emanating from her portrayal are described as follows:

> Her eyes stared, as if she were half-conscious, far, far, into the distance. Her hand rose as if to gather to herself the sonorities she heard in that terrible song of the crutch intermingled with the sound of church bells. Her body seemed to be stretching, her hands pressed against her chest, breathless, during those most painful moments when she feels the transformation operating within her. Then, she has made her decision, she rises, rigid and stiff . . . as in the paintings of Italian primitives. Her arms are glued the length of her body, her hands stir to scan each reply. Her head moves about slowly . . . her words fall heavily . . . There is within her . . . that inexorable rigidity of decision which has been taken. And when Allmers (Lugné-Poë) points the way up to charity, he raises his arm in the manner of a pointed arch as in Gothic cathedrals, indicating the summits, the stars, the great silence.[23]

That critics responded with a clear vision of stage happenings to *Little Eyolf*, a far more difficult play to understand than his other pieces, is a tribute to Lugné-Poë's own growth as actor and director: "one no longer considered the comedians at the Oeuvre as the apostles of error, but as the justified revealers of Scandinavian literature."[24]   The English critic, William Archer, remarked pertinently: "I rank the play beside, if not above, the very greatest of Ibsen's works, and am only doubtful whether its soul-searching be not too terrible for human endurance in the theatre."[25]

Lugné-Poë's production was no longer labeled Symbolistic.   Both he and Ibsen prided themselves on their independence of all literary and aesthetic movements and considered set credos as "monstrosities." In fact, Ibsen went so far as to say that the Symbolists were "disfiguring his plays." He further stated: "Everything that happens in life follows certain laws which are made manifest when faithfully presented. In this regard, then, I feel I am a Symbolist. Not otherwise."[26] Nor did he consider his plays doctrinaire or dissertational. "They describe life as I see it . . . I am not a professor, I am a painter, a portrait painter."[27]

Ibsen: Brand

Prior to Lugné-Poë's production of *Brand* (June 22, 1895), Lugné-Poë and Suzanne Deprès visited the "Master" once again, hoping to absorb greater insight into the play. Described as "brilliant madness," *Brand* was taken so seriously in Sweden as to become a devotional book. Strindberg wrote that in *Brand*, Ibsen spoke with "the voice of a Savonarola." He suggested that it was not a celebration of idealism, but "an autobiographical anti-idealist extravaganza." Shaw did not see Brand as a hero. "Brand the priest is an idealist of heroic earnestness, strength, and courage," and as he pursues his ideal, "he plunges from depth to depth of murderous cruelty," finally dying "a saint, having caused more intense suffering by his saintliness than the most talented sinners could possibly have done with twice his opportunities." For Shaw, Brand should be a "Warning."[28]

Brand tells the story of a passionate and uncompromising idealist—a minister who sacrifices the health and welfare and finally the lives of his wife and child rather than violate his stern sense of duty to his starving parishioners. When Brand finally leads his congregation to the greater Church of Life high in the mountains, the people who cannot follow his arduous and painstaking route fall behind and abandon him. In the para-

Program for Ibsen's *Brand*

digmatic closing scene on the mountain "Ice Church," as Brand is about to be crushed by an avalanche, he calls out to God—and hears a voice saying "God is love."

Lugné-Poë's enactment of Brand was full of energy and power. He used just the right tonal combinations to portray a divinely inspired man. As Brand's character evolves during the course of the play, so, too, does Lugné-Poë's understanding of its mythic dimension. Isolated, aloof, even scornful at the outset, Brand remains incarcerated in his rigid view of life. His relationships and associations with others are remote—those of a person who feels contempt and not admiration for the pusillanimous members of his parish.

> Oh, I know you through and through,
> Dull souls and slovenly minds. Your prayers
> Have not the strength nor the agony to reach
> To Heaven—except to cry:
> Give us this day our daily bread!"

Slowly, Brand begins identifying with Christ in a kind of *imitatio Christi*: "I have dared to take upon myself/The salvation of Man." Ministering to the dying father who had killed his starving child, he grows in understanding. Later, he even confesses to Agnes what he would have formerly considered a timorous trait, and, therefore, an offensive quality: his dream of glory, his love of "wholeness" or completion, and his hatred of "halfness," which may be equated with weakness.

Brand's isolated and loveless childhood, revolving around a mother whom he feared and associated with darkness, colored his entire world. "What icy gust, what cold memory from childhood/Numbs me? Merciful God!" Mother and son are antagonistic, hostile, threatening forces. It is from her, and the whole polluted town of which she had always been a part—"this stifling pit"—from that Brand seeks to escape at the outset. When he decides to remain with his parishioners, he takes on an excoriating burden; he also, paradoxically, becomes his son's murderer. He had been warned by doctors that if he did not take his son to a warmer climate he would die. When he forces his wife to give up their dead son's little cap—her last memory of him—to a gypsy woman who needed it for warmth, he did so knowing she would die for lack of love. Unable to tolerate such 'weakness,' he forced her to prove her own spirituality by rising above material and earthly ties. Climbing up the mountain, his parishioners grow increasingly weary from the long trek and refuse to go further. Brand forges on, reaches the "Ice Church" hidden in the midst and hears voices break out as if from everywhere. He understands that he was misguided in his venture: human beings must never try to liken themselves to God. Before he dies, he hears his wife's voice and that of others—and he cries out in agony:

> Answer me, God, in the moment of death!
> If not by Will, how can Man be redeemed?

Lugné-Poë had infused such power and depth into this "crushing" role that some critics labeled it apocalyptic—unforgettable in scope and dimension. But there were others, like Lemaître, who stated that Lugné-Poë's psalmodying was "intolerable."[29]

*

Although Ibsen had become a kind of cult figure in France, many critics still did not appreciate what they termed his mystical vision of life. Lemaître, though conceding to Ibsen's genius and influence on contemporary French literature, referred to him as "the polar bear" and resented his popularity in a land with a plethora of dramatists of its own.[30] Sarcey and Daudet insisted upon being entertained when going to the theatre and not depressed and bored by what they viewed as Ibsen's constant probing and self-interrogation. The past relived, revised, and reviewed, was too morbid, too frightening, too tormenting.[31]

The Danish critic, George Brandes, lashed back. Lemaître had no right to discuss and vilify the works of a man whose language he did not speak, whose people he did not know, and whose culture was foreign to him. He took particular umbrage at the comparisons Lemaître forwarded between Ibsen's works and those of Georges Sand and Dumas fils, with the implication that the Norwegian playwright had helped himself lavishly to some of their themes. Ibsen defended himself, stating that he had never read the works of Sand and had used the plays of Dumas fils as models of what not to do in theatre. The literary debate ensued. Émile Faguet sided with Lemaître and Victor Basch with Brandes.

Whatever the altercations and vilifications, Lugné-Poë went on producing Ibsen's works: *Pillars of Society* (June 17, 1896); *Peer Gynt* (November 12, 1896); *Love's Comedy* (June 23, 1896); *John Gabriel Borkman* (November 9, 1897).

Ibsen: Peer Gynt

Peer Gynt, a dramatic poem for which Edvard Grieg composed the musical suite and Edvard Munch designed the program, is considered a visionary work. Ibsen was convinced that only Nordic people would understand the mythical intent of *Peer Gynt*—certainly not the French. Lugné-Poë was intent upon proving him wrong.

Abel Deval played Peer Gynt, the Norse folklore hero, whose boastful, capricious, fanciful, and irresponsible nature irritated so many in his entourage. An extraordinarily adventuresome life takes Peer to many a strange land, where he makes and loses a lot of money, saves his own life in a shipwreck by allowing another to drown, and confronts the Button Molder, who attempts to melt him in his ladle. Peer has always suffered from one great fear: a loss of identity. What identity? one may question. He really has none. In the end, however, Solveig, the maiden pure in heart, who has always loved him, saves him—though there were occasions when even she had been frightened by his boisterousness, his overpowering energy, and grotesque lies.

> I can turn myself into a troll!
> I'll come to your bedside tonight at midnight.
> If you hear something hissing and spitting
> Don't think it's the cat. It's me, my dear!

Lugné-Poë's mise-en-scène brought out the divisiveness in Peer's view of life: the opposition he felt so keenly between the real and the fantasy world, the actual and the ideal. "I shall succeed . . . in performing the play *in its entirety*," Lugné-Poë remarked, "in real sets for realistic scenes and in a single schematic decor for the philosophical scenes or those revolving around discussions."[32]

Deval emphasized Peer's intrinsic personality conflict by clever manipulation of his vocal tones and facial gestures—nuanced and subdued at times, and at others, overtly brash and aggressive. Léon Xanrof, the chansonnier, called him "superb" in the part: energetic and sensitive, fully able to bring

Münch's program for Ibsen's *Peer Gynt*

forth the scope of the character.[33] Because he played up Peer's worthlessness, egotism, weaknesses, and lack of commitment, when certain scenes called for warmth and loving tenderness, the contrast made them memorable. When Peer learns that his mother is dying, he returns to her hovel at the risk of his own life. He holds her in his arms and consoles her by conjuring up the past and all the experiences they had shared when he was a child. His voice, usually gruff, has become soft and caressing, dissimulating the real pain he now suffers. As he sits at the foot of her bed, his verbal vocalizations take on a variety of timbres and pace, creating an aerial climate of muted and undefined scope—until the end, when she dies with a smile on her face.

Solveig, portrayed by Suzanne Auclair, was delightful. Her voice, clear and mellifluous, endowed the stage happenings with a haunting and disquieting tone. Anitra's dance, performed by Jane Avril—famed dancer at the Divan Japonais and the Moulin Rouge, whom Toulouse-Lautrec immortalized in his lithographs—was a marvel. Her black hair adorned with peonies stood out stark against her pale skin. Her dance movements were accomplished with the brio, joy and grace for which she was known—and in perfect time with Grieg's music. Fouquier's reactions, nevertheless, were negative. She danced, he wrote, with "the contorsions of a rabbit who had just been struck in the kidneys." Lugné-Poë played Mr. Cotton, Solveig's father, with his usual expertise, and in a most realistic way, critics wrote. Not Catulle Mendès, however, who considered him a mediocre actor with a poor memory, who asked for a cherry brandy as if he were in a cabaret in Marseille.[34] The Old Man of the Mountain was enacted by a newcomer: the twenty-three year old secretary of the Théâtre de l'Oeuvre, Alfred Jarry (appearing under the name of Hemge), destined to make theatrical history in a not-too-distant future.

Negative criticism was always forthcoming. There were scenes, Sarcey, Fouquier, and Romain Coolus suggested, that Lugné-Poë failed to set forth clearly: Peer's visit to the trolls, for example. The demarcation line between dream and reality remained unclear. The same obscurantist reaction was echoed by Shaw regarding Peer's encounter with the Boyg. The stage was pitch dark and audiences heard only howling—" a strange voice squealing behind the scenes, a woman calling at intervals, and not a word that anyone could catch." Shaw maintained that Lugné-Poë had not really understood the fourth act in which the devoted and loving Solveig awaited Peer's return, while he, the wayward one, not only never thought of her, but already had his mind focused on his next adventure in Africa.[35]

Other mistakes were also evident. Peer, who wore a turban around his head and a worn dressing gown, looked like a prophet. Anitra's makeup was considered overly amateurish. Some of the sound effects were likewise wanting. The noise designed to portray an exploding yatch, effected by knocking over a chair back stage, did not give the wanted impression.

Nevertheless, audiences sat on the edge of their seats when the Button Molder, whose function it was in Norwegian lands to buy up old and broken silver buttons and recast them, informed Peer that his epitaph would read: "Here No One lies buried." That Peer was redeemed at the end of the play by Solveig's all-forgiving and consoling love was an example, Shaw remarked, of middle-class sentimentalism. And he added:

> M. Lugné-Poë, with all his realism, could no more help presenting the play sentimentally and sublimely than M. Lamoureux can help conducting the overture to *Tannhaüser* as if it were the 'Marseillaise'; but the universality of Ibsen makes his plays come home to all nations; and Peer Gynt is as good a Frenchman as he is a Norwegian, just as Dr. Stockmann is as intelligible in Bermondsy or Bournemouth as he is in his native town. Peer Gynt will finally smash anti-Ibsenism in Europe, because Peer is everybody's hero. He has the same effect on the imagination that Hamlet, Faust and Mozart's Don Juan have had.[36]

Despite the shortcomings of Lugné-Poë's production, Shaw saw it again in London, and remarked that it caught "more of the atmosphere of a poetic play with the most primitive arrangements than some of our managers succeeded in doing at a ruinous outlay."[37]

> Praise alone was accorded to Grieg's music for *Peer Gynt*. One has the feeling that Fate has just passed; one single fugued phrase is sufficient to illustrate Aase's sad destiny; one single phrase develops, intensifies, is repeated later on, suddenly stops, creating an atmosphere of strangeness and terror. The theme and its repetitions under various circumstances give rise to an atmosphere conducive to the disappearance of this world which is a soul . . .[38]

Ibsen: John Gabriel Borkman

Munch drew the illustration for *John Gabriel Borkman*, produced on Nov. 9, 1897, which featured the inflexible head of the dramatist set out above the backdrop of a maritime city, illuminated by the radiant rays of a lighthouse in the distance.

John Gabriel Borkman dramatizes the relationship between a father, Borkman, and his twenty-three year old son, Erhart. Aloof and restrained, Borkman was a man who had sacrificed love for ambition and expected his son to do likewise. Reintheim, the ancestral home, is used as a metaphor to convey the protagonists' psychological condition: stifingly hot within and icy cold without.

As in the case of other Ibsen plays, the past, which is decanted in slow potions to audiences, determines the present situation. We learn that Borkman, a miner's son, had dreamed of becoming a powerful capitalist by developing the mineral wealth of his area. To this end, he broke his engagement to Ella because Hinkel, the man whose help he depended upon, wanted to marry her. Borkman marries her sister instead. His financial rise was spectacular; so, too, was his downfall, for which Hinkel was responsible since he disclosed Borkman's misappropriation of bank funds. Hinkel never forgave Ella for refusing to marry him and blamed Borkman for his suffering. After Borkman's release from jail, he tries to convince his son Erhart to help him rebuild his fortune. The three parental figures—Borkman, his wife, and Ella—each pull Erhart in different ways. He rejects them all, opting for happiness and leaving his entourage with the girl he loves. Borkman, trying symbolically to recover the life of fulfillment and love that he has lost, walks up the mountain with Ella—seeking renewal.

> I shall go on, and on, and on. See if I can find my way back to freedom and life and humanity. Will you go with me, Ella?

But Ella knows better. Neither redemption nor fulfillment are for Borkman. He cannot return to the past nor right the destruction he has wrought.

> You have killed love in me. Do you understand what that means? The Bible speaks of a mysterious sin for which there is no forgiveness. I have never understood before what that could be. Now I do understand. The great sin for which there is no forgiveness is to murder love in a human soul . . .

When he dies of a heart attack, Ella's portentous statement made years earlier seemed to have been prophetic: "You will never ride triumphant into your cold kingdom."

Münch's program for Ibsen's *John Gabriel Borkman*

Edvard Munch's backdrop for *John Gabriel Borkman* depicted a powerful winter landscape: dark skies against white snows, the contrasting tonalities symbolizing the seering antagonisms implicit in the play.

Lugné-Poë's portrayal of Borkman received accolades from Faguet. No longer emphasizing the mystery or subtleties of his character, which left audiences in a state of confusion, Lugné-Poë played Borkman in realistic style, revealing his protagonist's chaotic inner motivations in sharp vocal, gestural, and facial intonations. As Sarcey wrote:

> Lugné-Poë injected color in the illuminated Borkman. Only at the end did he again indulge in his habitual detestable mystical chantings. We, therefore, were very pleased with the second and third acts."[39]

Lugné-Poë, who rarely committed himself verbally concerning his art, wrote Sarcey concerning his interpretation of Borkman.

> If I write to you, it's only to inform you that I am definitely breaking with my history of theatrical chantings: people have labeled me the precursor of this kind of intonation.
>
> No, no with all my strength! and my friends must confirm the fact that during rehearsals, I demand life, together with stylistic perfection, which is, in my mind, part of the comedian's art, so very different from the reality of the third-rate actor who plays for effects.
>
> Therefore, deprived of actors—the Oeuvre being ostracized by directors—I was forced to play the role of Borkman. Until the preview, I had interpreted it realistically and as a living being from one end of the play to the other. After the performance, Count Prozor said to me: *But no, everything is good except for the last act. Make it lyrical, make the Shakespearian in Borkman emerge: he is a dead man from the end of the fourth act.* I did just that at the opening; nothing more and even if I were not up to my part, I think that Count Prozor is right; the text is superhuman. It's understood—that a dead man is speaking.[40]

Style is important when creating a role. As are feeling and intuition, Lugné-Poë affirmed, thereby rejecting once again what he considered to be Antoine's lack of style in his cut-and-dried realistic portrayals. Lyricism, when called for, may be incorporated in a role, toned down or accentuated in keeping with the situation. There are no rigid rules to follow when breathing life into a character—except that of fulfilling the protagonist's potential.

Ibsen was delighted with Lugné-Poë's production which he did not see, but which he heard about in detail.[41] Not only had Lugné-Poë's vision of Ibsen's dramas deepened and broadened during the course of the years, but he better understood the complexities involved in the characters he portrayed. When first incarnating Ibsen's protagonists, he was so troubled by the existing ambiguities in the scheme of things that when he tried to point up emotion or underscore tension, he muddled his way through the very pain, jealousy, or rage he sought to protray. The spectators felt, understandably, excluded from the stage happenings and unable to experience the full impact of the drama.

*

Ibsen was not the only Scandinavian dramatist produced at the Théâtre de l'Oeuvre. Also offered was *Beyond Our Power* by Bjørnstjerne Bjørnson (1832-1910), writer and political leader, and director of the Ole Bull Theater in Bergen, succeeding his friend, Ibsen. Lugné-Poë had been warned by his friends that Parisian audiences would not be interested in the theological arguments revolving around Bjørnson's metaphysical and social drama. Still, he went ahead and produced *Beyond Our Power*; the play lagged. Some considered the happenings implausible; others were troubled and dismayed by the morbidity and depressing ambiguity enunciated by the protagonists and their theological and abstract arguments.

Lugné-Poë also turned to Strindberg.

Strindberg: The Creditors

The Creditors, another misogynic drama, confirmed Strindberg's views that women are takers and men givers; that neither possess free will; and that actions are determined in advance and in keeping with the specific personalities involved. Like Schopenhauer, Strindberg believed that man was a marionette with a built-in will to live, guided and compelled into activity by a puppeteer.

Tightly structured, *The Creditors* observed the classical unities of time, place, and action. In keeping with the drama's concision, the properties and accessories were reduced to a minimum. *The Creditors* revolves around Gustave, Tekla's first husband, a small-town teacher who seeks revenge upon Adolphe, a painter and her second husband. His reprisal consists in intellectual and psychological torture: he keeps reminding Tekla of how much she owes him.

The curtains part on a reading room in a resort hotel by the sea, where Tekla is sojourning with her second husband. Unbeknown to her, Gustave, traveling incognito, is also staying at this same hotel. We learn that Tekla's first marriage to Gustave had grown stale; she had become bored with what she considered his limited ways, his wishy-washy attitude, his intellectual paucity. Now, however, Gustave is wiser; experience has hardened him and he is determined to punish Tekla for the suffering she had caused him. Coldly, he thinks up a plan to bring the coquettish Tekla to his feet. Meanwhile, Tekla has again wrought her damage. Now that she has succeeded in crushing the sentimental Adolphe's spirit, she finds him weak and tiresome. On the other hand, she is taken with her new flame—Gustave—and exercises her wiles to conquer his affection. Gustave, who knows his Tekla, prepares himself for the 'masterful' retribution scene his plan calls for. He encourages the flighty vamp to declare her feelings and to accept a clandestine rendez-vous with him. When Adolphe, who was in an adjoining room and has heard the entire conversation, enters, Gustave unmasks himself. His plan has worked out perfectly. Casting a disdainful look upon the poor husband, then rejecting the unfaithful Tekla outright, he flaunts his completed vengeance.

The critics for the most part—even Sarcey—praised the direction and the acting for its exactitude and its clarity. One scene in particular caught the eye of many an observer: when the timorous Adolphe, seated in front of a clay figure he is in the process of modeling, complimenting himself for having met the fascinating Gustave, he does so with the naïveté of a newborn. Tekla, charming and intelligent, acted her role of the emancipated woman with intelligence and finesse. Accolades went to Rameau for his portrayal of the ironic, hard, sceptical and bitter Gustave. Beneath his studied, simple, and contained exterior, Rameau's gestures at times revealed the tragic pain Tekla had caused Gustave.

Strindberg, annoyed at the fact that his great enemy, Herman Bang, had helped direct his play, did not attend the performance.

*

As the years passed, Lugné-Poë who was becoming more and more involved in the actor's art, wrote the following insightful statement concerning this *métier.*

The comedian . . . must forget he is a comedian, and remember the first times when, as a child, he attended the theatre as a pious spectator, and reject in toto all the bad advice, and become ONE— whatever happens, with dangling arms, immobile gesture.

To become the living incarnation of heroes and epochs, he must forget the ridiculous science of composition, from operetta to naturalisms. An example: a piece of straw in his mouth, an unkempt beard, a handerkerchief hanging from his pocket no longer suffice to indicate a peasant. He must become the *actor,* the character, reconstructing by means of his talent or genius all the effects the author attempts between him and the spectator . . . he will understand that multiple gestures are odious only when he succeeds in giving shape to the abstraction he is incarnating. He must keep effects in abeyance and even abandon them, if he doesn't want to criminalize his art. His small finger, when observed by the spectator, must reveal its ambulatory nature which, if developed, is more powerful a gesture than any of Mounet's beautiful postures. The author sensed the circular movement of the arm, but to exaggerate such a gesture, would be to violate the soul and the work. The art of the true actor differs from what one usually sees, the way painting differs from sculpture.

Diction must not spring up willy nilly in the actor's voice. To be sought for is perfect harmony, without wranglings. During entire scenes, the actor will try to convey, to persuade his nerves to reveal the anguish his will instills in him; only via the moisture surrounding his eyes, does he impose a sense of religious respect. The leitmotif or tone will rise only by means of a harmonic entente between the wills of the author and the audience, intent upon shouting out their fears or hopes.

But let us confess, it's really part of Nature itself; and from the very outset, the hoped-for art.[42]

Chapter 7

A Scandal at the Théâtre de l'Oeuvre:
Alfred Jarry's *King Ubu*

When Lugné-Poë invited Alfred Jarry (1873-1907) to become secretary-general of the Théâtre de l'Oeuvre in 1896, replacing Adolphe Van Bever, the would-be dramatist accepted with perhaps the not-unconscious motive of having *King Ubu* eventually produced. Jarry fulfilled his letter-writing functions with great zeal, transmitting publicity and collecting articles glorifying the Théâtre de l'Oeuvre, and keeping creditors away.[1] When necessary, he also played bit parts—that of the Troll, for example, in Lugné-Poë's production of *Peer Gynt*.

In time, everyone associated with the Théâtre de l'Oeuvre grew accustomed to Jarry's incredible fantasy world and "strange" attire—usually a bizarre bicyclist's outfit. Jarry enjoyed entertaining friends with his outlandish antics and his colorful tales about "walking streets" and people who entered their apartments from the top rather than from the ground floors. Rachilde, co-editor of the *Mercure de France*, along with her husband, Valette, described Jarry as looking like a wild animal. "His face was pale, almost masklike, his nose short, his mouth incisive, his eyes black and singularly phosphorescent . . . at once stary and luminous, like those of night birds."

Jarry, the "Enfant Terrible of Symbolism," as he was sometimes called by his friends, radiated charm and kindliness, which endeared him to his large circle of friends. Jarry was an anarchist, an inpenitent, and a humorist à la Rabelais. From him came neither romantic sweetness nor beautiful plastic images, but rather mordant satires, cruel ironies, invectives, puns, neologisms, jokes, and riddles.

Jarry used to go to Mallarmé's famous weekly gatherings at his home on the rue de Rome. There, and elsewhere, he met other Symbolist writers, such as Henri de Régnier, Pierre Louys, and Paul Valéry. Like them, he tried to penetrate into that world beyond the rational, and to express his visions of it in brilliantly explosive and poetic terms.

Jarry also contributed articles to *La Revue Blanche, La Plume, L'Art Littéraire,* and others. He founded a review, *L'Ymagier,* together with the Symbolist critic, Rémy de Gourmont; and a magazine of prints, *Perhinderion,* (meaning pilgrimage, in the Breton dialect); authored *Minutes de Sable Memorial* (1894) and other strange works in the Symbolist tradition, such as *César Antéchrist* (1895), where exploding sensations are blended in a personal and original manner.

Jarry was searching for *truth* and *reality.* To do so required that he crush the constricting boundaries of "old-type reality"—that is, the rational world. The routine and pedestrian sphere of "appearance" with which the academic poets and painters of his day flooded the public held no magic for Jarry. Their truth could not act as a basis from which he could go on to discover that fathomless and exciting *other* world. Jarry was not trying to substitute one sphere of being for another. He was attempting to introduce a new way of looking at things, much as the Impressionist and Post-Impressionists had done before him.

Jarry sought to break through the facades of the world of "appearances" via *shock.* Such shock would cause a loss of equilibrium in readers and audiences and open up for them a new realm of fabulous color and dimension. To *shatter,* to *dislocate* the world as men knew it, and reach the *inner being* was Jarry's goal. Once the destructive act of breaking down and clearing away had been accomplished, the constructive side of this two-fold experience could begin. From within the psyche, the continuously flowing and glowing sensations would be released, creating altered visions and conceptions of the surrounding world.

King Ubu would, to a certain extent, illustrate his concepts. But first Lugné-Poë had to agree to the production of Jarry's strange brew. When Lugné-Poë expressed his reservations about the work, Rachilde interceded and convinced him to keep the promise he had made to Jarry when he accepted to work at the Théâtre de l'Oeuvre. He agreed. Rachilde also suggested that the *guignol* side of *King Ubu* should be underscored. Let it come across as a *drôlerie.* Lugné-Poë, convinced, followed her suggestion.

Jarry: King Ubu

King Ubu, which opened on December 10, 1896, rocked the Parisian theatrical world. A precursor of Dadaism, Surrealism, and Absurdism, Jarry's approach to people and to things was uninhibited, his humor biting, his imagination keen. Because his play revealed a rebellious attitude against what he considered to be stupidity, cowardliness, greed, and hypocrisy, it was thought of by many to be 'eccentric'—theatrical madness.

King Ubu was not a spur-of-the-moment work. The main character, Ubu, had had a long period of gestation. Indeed, he was not merely a figment of Jarry's imagination, but rather was modeled upon one of Jarry's former physics' teachers, Professor Hebert at the Lycée of Rennes. Professor Hebert, a pleasant but rather ineffective teacher, had always been the butt of his students' ridicule. Little attention was paid him during his lectures. His students talked throughout the class period, threw things at the black board, and satirized him mercilessly after school hours. The boys had nicknamed him Heb or Hebé and had written plays and stories entitled the "Adventures of Father Heb." Jarry's sister, Charlotte, and two of his friends, Henri and Charles Morin, had staged the plays they had written in Mme. Jarry's attic at Rennes. The actors, for the most part, performed as wooden marionettes. This way, they could, Jarry felt, best depict the protagonist's nature.

As the years passed, Père Heb became Père Ubu. And in the spring of 1896, Paul Fort, founder of the Théâtre des Arts, and contributor to the *Mercure de France*, began pressing Jarry to give him the play about which he had spoken for so long. Fort and two of his friends went to Jarry's room on Boulevard Saint-Germain and there demanded to see what was still handwritten in his school boy's notebooks. Jarry had subtitled his work "Prose drama in five acts restored in its entirety as it was performed at the Théâtre des Phynances in 1888"—that is, as it had been staged in Jarry's attic in Rennes. From these pages Father Ubu arose full-grown.

Jarry, unlike many of his contemporaries, did not write plays to please his audiences. He refused to write *down* or to write *up* to them. Those who did not understand or appreciate what he had in mind could leave the theatre or, as far as he was concerned, be forcibly ejected. The theatre, for Jarry, was neither a civic festival, nor a morality lesson, nor was it designed for relaxation. His was a theatre of *action* designed for an elite and not for the masses who respond to flashy decor, gaudy ballets, and obvious, accessible emotions. The spectator viewing a Jarry play cannot merely sit back and *take in*. Jarry's use of shock forces the spectator to become an active participant in the stage drama. As a result of this experience, the spectator may create and discover, or re-discover, his own feelings as they are projected onto the creatures on stage. Since these *active* spectators are bringing something of themselves into what is happening on stage, they are participating, according to Jarry, "in the realization of one of their creations." Jarry wrote in his "Dossiers acenonettes du collège de Pataphysique" that his theatre is "accessible only to that person who feels himself sufficiently virile to create life."[2]

Jarry had definite ideas concerning theatrical production. He considered sets "hybrid" because they were neither *really* "natural" nor *really* "artificial." Furthermore, the painter who creates decors must not impose his conceptions of the play through his sets onto the public. The artist is there only to suggest. The spectator must discover for himself the "hidden meanings" in the play. Decor should be *suggestive* and, therefore, far more effective than *trompe-l'oeil* sets, which Jarry labeled as "stupid."

Actors, declared Jarry, in "The Uselessness of Theatre in Theatre" (1896), should wear masks so that the "eternal quality" in the character would become evident. The masks Jarry had in mind would not resemble those used in Greek and Roman theatre, which did not represent character, but merely sadness or joy. Instead, Jarry wanted the mask to indicate specifically "the character of the person: the Miser, the Hesitant, the Avid. . . ." To make the drama on stage still more effective, the acting must by stylized, with few but meaningful gestures which would always underline the "universal" aspects of man. Jarry did not mean pantomime, which he considered conventional. The usual mime-language of the day was always the same. It had become "fatiguing" and "incomprehensible." Jarry sought "universal gesture." His actor, behaving like a marionette to express shock and surprise, for example, would step back violently and bump his head against the set. To underline the puppet-like nature of his actors, Jarry would have them speak in a perfunctory, almost detached tone, each actor thereby sounding as though "the mask itself were speaking."[3]

To underscore the mysterious and hidden meanings in a

Jarry's program for *King Ubu*

theatrical production, Jarry wanted lighting to assume the importance of a protagonist. The interplay of light and shadow should create vertical and horizontal strips of light, and a variety of moods and sensations reflecting the inner march of the characters' emotions.

Jarry stated his ideas concerning the way he would like to see *King Ubu* produced in a letter to Lugné-Poë (January 8, 1896).

> The main character, Ubu, would wear a mask . . .
>
> For the two equestrian scenes, a cardboard horse could be hung from the actors' neck as they used to do in old English theatre; all these details are in the spirit of the play because theatre then becomes a *guignol*.
>
> Only one set, or better still, one uniform backdrop would be used: doing away, thereby, with the raising and lowering of the curtains during a single act. A person dressed in a suitable manner would come on stage, as they do in puppet shows, and put up signs indicating where the scene is to take place. I am, you realize, certain that written signs are more "suggestive" than sets. No set or any kind of device could represent the "Polish Army on the march in the Ukraine."
>
> Crowds would be eliminated on stage: they are frequently useless in creating the desired atmosphere and hinder one's understanding of the work. Therefore, there should be only one soldier in the parade scene, one in the fighting scene when Ubu says: "What a horde of people, what a flight, etc."
>
> An "accent" or better still a special "voice" is to be adopted by the principal character.
>
> Costumes which have as little local color and historical significance as possible should be used (they better give the impression of something eternal): preferably modern costumes since the satire is modern and sordid ones, because the drama would then appear even more wretched and ghastly.[4]

The entire play was to be howlingly comic, comparable to the "macabre of an English clown" or the Medieval "dance of the Dead." Ubu, though humorous because of his grotesqueness, exaggerated clumsiness and cruelty, and his vocabulary consisting of vulgar, provocative, invented, assonanced, and rhymed words, was to be, in reality, a hideous and monstrous creation. He was to be the Satan who lived breathed, and grew in *everyman's* breast.

*

Firmin Gémier of the Odéon was chosen to portray Father Ubu; and Louise France, Mother Ubu. After accepting Lugné-

Poë's offer, Gémier had second thoughts. He believed that such an outlandish role might blight his reputation and, besides, he confessed to not knowing how to interpret the role. Lugné-Poë was adamant: he would not allow the comedian to change his mind.

Few realized on opening night the incredible experience in store for them. Before the curtain rose, a table covered with sack cloth was brought forth on stage. A short and slim man, dressed in a baggy black suit, with a billowy chiffon scarf tied around his neck, his face wearing the chalk pallor of a mask, stepped before the footlights. It was the author. He talked to the audience in his staccato voice for nearly ten minutes. First, he thanked those who had helped him bring his play to the stage, he then commented upon the puppet-like quality of his creatures. Finally, he described the locale of the play— Poland—which meant "Nowhere." He mentioned the cardboard horses, which Ubu and the Tsar would ride during their meeting. He conveyed his disappointment at not having an orchestra consisting of percussion instruments and a trombone, pianos and timpani.

Jarry then left the stage. The curtain rose to the accompaniment of music created for the play by Claude Terrasse, Bonnard's brother-in-law. The "perfect decor," to use Jarry's own words, became visible. A combination of talents was responsible for this incredible backdrop: Bonnard, Vuillard, Toulouse-Lautrec, Ranson, and Sérusier. It consisted of a modest fireplace of black marble decorated with clocks, which split in two and served as doors; and palm trees growing green at the foot of beds, so that little elephants perched on shelves could browse on them; views of the sea, woods, and snow-covered landscapes under blue skies and gallows. Placards were placed on stage which announced the various locations of the scenes as well as such events as "A Battle," inviting the audience to understand the crucial nature of the fight, but also enabling them to dispense with the many extras which would have to be present.

Ubu came forward. Grotesque, giant-like, the incarnation of the bloated bourgeois, wearing a grotesque mask with a nose like an elephant's trunk, he bellowed forth his one-word opening line: "Merdre" ("Shite"). The house went into bedlam. Never had such a word been uttered in a theatre. To make matters even worse, it seemed to have been directed at those in the audience. Fifteen minutes went by before the shocked and outraged audience could be silenced. They whistled, they booed, screamed, laughed, showed their firsts. Georges Courteline got up on a seat and screamed: "Don't you understand that the author is playing us for suckers."[5] Jean Lorrain walked out. Edmond Sée compared the chaos in the theatre to the turmoil taking place during the battle of *Hernani*. A scandal. The actors were stunned. What to do? To divert attention from the audience's frenzied outburst, Gémier began to dance a jig. He continued to do so for fifteen minutes until everyone calmed down and the play could continue.

The plot of *King Ubu* is simple. Ubu, greedy for gold and power, and spurred on by his wife's avarice, decides to become King of Poland. He kills and tortures anyone and everyone who prevents him from reaching his goal—and always without the slightest hesitation. After his brutalities have become excessive, he is driven out of Poland by the heir to the Polish throne.

After the word "Merdre" was again uttered by Ubu, as he strutted on stage in all of his grotesque crudity, pandemonium broke out anew. War had been declared between actor and spectator. The din slackened for a while, only to be heard moments later. By the end of the evening, Jarry had succeeded in alienating his audience. Everything in the play ran counter to the atmosphere and the temper of the age.

King Ubu was indeed a brutal caricature of the self-centered, crude, egotistical, cruel, often stupid human being. But Ubu and his wife were much more than mere satires leveled at society. They were the frightening images of what man's inner being or his soul might *really* be like. The spectators felt perhaps that they were watching their mirror images and they resented the savage aspects of themselves, which they saw before them in Ubu. As Catulle Mendès wrote, the audience looked upon itself as Ubu—a being composed of "eternal human imbecility, eternal viciousness, eternal gluttony, baseness of instinct which had assumed tyranical force."

King Ubu was *man* as Jarry saw him, exposed in all of his sordidness. The wooden-hearted beings on stage remained unfeeling and callous. Insults, cruelties, assaults, beatings, slayings, bloodshed—nothing seemed to provoke any kind of human response from any of the protagonists. There were no psychological probings, no evolution of character, no romantic climax or shattering suspense scene. Nor were women spared:

they were portrayed as gluttonous, greedy, vicious, and cruel, with a few exceptional humanitarians and dreamers.

In some respects, *King Ubu* is a modern version of the Adam and Eve myth. Jarry, a misogynist, set out to point up the harshness, selfishness, and greediness of womankind. Just as Eve had lured her husband Adam into eating the apple, so Mother Ubu entices her spouse Ubu to kill the King of Poland and wipe out his entire family. Eve painted a glowing picture of the power with which Adam would be invested; Mother Ubu informs her husband that if he goes through with her plan, he may have as much pork sausage as he wants, and even have an umbrella, a long cloak, and a hood for rainy weather. The ridiculousness and childishness of her husband's desires are overshadowed only by the ignominy of her own intentions. When Ubu finally agrees to murder, Mother Ubu utters the most devastating of all commentaries, pointing up Ubu's own unconscious feeling of worthlessness and emasculation: "now you have become a real man."

In addition to Ubu's vulgarity and stupidity, he is also a glutton. He guzzles the food his wife has prepared for their guests and wants to eat all the comestibles in sight. In Mother Ubu's inimitable manner, she threatens to tear his eyes out if he persists. To whet his appetite, she recites the menu which is made up of the most unusual delicacies—fit for a King and for a mouse.

Above all, King Ubu is greedy for gold. He savours it, touches it, thrills to it, and will go to any lengths to acquire it. His killings, plunderings, and brutalities unfold in ever-increasing speed and numbers. In a new version of the French Revolution's interlude referred to as the "Reign of Terror," Ubu, in his own humorous "décervelage scene," has the heads of three hundred nobles and five hundred magistrates cut off. The horror of such an act is so unbelievable that audiences and actors alike remain as detached as that "famous" or "infamous" character created by Charles Dickens in his *Tale of Two Cities*, Mme. Lafarge, who sat knitting as heads rolled off the guillotine.

To be as specific and realistic as possible, as well as *guignolesque*, Jarry had forty life-size wicker figures—clothed mannequins of sorts—act as stand-ins for the nobles, judges, and financiers to be slaughtered. Ubu could easily topple them into the pit below stage with his *crochet à phynances*. And they were ignominiously thrust down into the theatre's underground.

Satirizing the great hero that Ubu is not, who kills in the face of terrible odds, Jarry's protagonist begins to tremble and cower when he fears discovery. He decides to lay the blame for the plot to overthrow the King of Poland on his wife and Captain Bordure.

Is Ubu a humanitarian? Perhaps, since he believes the most humanitarian way of killing his enemy, the King of Poland, is to put some arsenic in his food. But no, Captain Bordure does not agree with him. He wants to split the King open from head to toe. After all, isn't everything fair in love and war?

Jarry also makes a mockery of dreams, visions, and pronouncements. The Queen of Poland has had a dream. She warns her husband not to march in the parade because he will be killed by Ubu and his men, just as, centuries earlier, Calpurnia had begged Julius Caesar not to go to the Senate on the Ides of March. Infuriated, the King snickers at her fears, in resentment of the accusations she has leveled at his friend and confidant, Ubu. As Caesar was killed, so too was the King of Poland.

In most conventional plays, the role of the hero is to unravel the plot and to see that right triumphs. Bougrelas, the Polish King's fourteen-year-old son, played by one of Jarry's long-haired, handsome boyfriends, is the dramatist's version of this character. Bougrelas is a modern Joan of Arc who hears voices—not in a field, but in a mountain cave. A great admirer of Shakespeare, Jarry has shadows emerge on stage and one of them proceeds to speak to him, as Hamlet's father had to his son. Bougrelas is informed that he has been appointed to avenge the entire royal family by striking down the villain. He is given a sword—under mysterious circumstances, as were his great prototypes Roland, Beowolf, Siegfried, Arthur, etc. The play ends with justice winning out. Ubu, his wife, and his henchmen sail back to "la douce France" and to their castle of Mondragon.

*

The poets and writers present on opening night, such as Arthur Symons, Jules Renard, W. B. Yeats, and Mallarmé, to mention a few, were intrigued by Jarry's originality. In Yeat's *Autobiography*, he described opening night, when the head-on actor-audience collision took place.

The players are supposed to be dolls, toys, marionettes, and now they are all hopping like wooden frogs, and I can see for myself that the chief personage, who is some kind of King, carries for a sceptre a brush of the kind that we use to clean a closet. Feeling bound to support the most spirited party, we have shouted for the play, but that night at the Hôtel Corneille I am very sad, for comedy, objectivity, had displayed its growing power once more. I say: "After Stéphane Mallarmé, after Paul Verlaine, after Gustave Moreau, after Puvis de Chavannes, after our own verse, after all our subtle colour and nervous rhythm, after the faint mixed tints of Conder, what more is possible? After us the Savage God.

Yeats' words were prophetic, expressing with perspicuity and, perhaps, a twinge of pathos, the end of one era and the birth of another.

The theatre shook on the night of the opening; the audience was hostile, reminiscent of the most beautiful days of Romanticism. It was, in all senses of the word, a battle of *Hernani*, among the new schools, decadents, symbolists, and the bourgeois critics incarnated in the self-satisfied ponderous and fat old Sarcey . . . Long-haired poets, dirty and grandiloquent esthetes, various other orders of new literati discussed, gesticulated, exchanged the latest gossip with the porters.

And the praise offered by Mallarmé in a letter to Jarry, was perhaps the most moving of all. He had attended,

. . . simply to admire *King Ubu* and to shake your hand, in keeping with the saying, better late . . . You made a prodigious character and his entourage stand forth, to which you applied a rare and durable hand glaze, in the manner of a sober. It enters the repertoire of high taste and it haunts me."[6]

Jacques Copeau, destined to become one of the great theatrical innovators of the twentieth-century, was only seventeen years old when he saw *King Ubu*. It made a tremendous impression upon him and he later declared, in *The Art of the Theatre*, that Jarry's school-boy drama was a masterpiece. This somber and incisive caricature of the cruel, avid being, who swallowed up everything that lay in his path and destroyed what he could not devour, was "a hundred percent theatre . . . pure theatre."

Although *King Ubu* was one of the great events at the Théâtre de l'Oeuvre, it left Lugné-Poë deeply in debt. "An artistic disaster," it had been his most successful failure.[7]

Chapter 8

Lugné-Poë's Eclecticism

Lugné-Poë's enthusiasm for theatre was eclectic. It ranged from past to present, far and wide—French, Scandianavian, British, Russian, German, as well as Sanskrit theatre. As he stated:

> The desire for liberty and harmony which permeates today's social body will find its needs fulfilled in the theatre by means of an art based on truth. In no way will it resemble today's theatrical habits and *only from a distance will it have anything in common with what one calls today dramatic art.*
>
> We try most forcefully to present works with broad meaning: in terms of thoughts, ideas, and without taking into consideration the theatrical structures these may necessitate. . . . Nor do we limit ourselves by seeking only to renew theatrical techniques; most of all we want to orient ourselves toward new and unexplored thought. . . . L'Oeuvre does not claim the title, "theatre next door" for nothing; and if another word could be substituted for the term "theatre," we would have chosen it. We want to perform works in which the idea alone will dominate . . . *we attach only slight importance to the material side of what one calls theatre* . . . . If brutal, rough theatrical work, written without any knowledge of theatrical rules, and in complete ignorance of what we call dramatic art, if this work probes or solves a serious social problem, if it furnishes us . . . with a new interpretation of a philosophical question, we will receive it with joy, forgetting willingly that it isn't theatre, and believing that one performs enough of these so-called plays under the thirty theatrical directors in Paris. We would like in some way to be a college, where different forms of thought and new concepts of the mind will be taught and preached.[1]

Shudraka: The Toy Cart

Lugné-Poë's production of the Sanskrit play, *The Toy Cart* (January 21, 1895) revealed his proclivity for both the esoteric and the eclectic. Written by the mythical king, Shudraka, supposedly between the first century B. C. and the first century A. D., *The Toy Cart*, as produced by Lugné-Poë at the Théâtre de l'Oeuvre, fulfilled a need in Parisian audiences for the different and the remote. Critics responded for the most part favorably to the "exquisitely sentimental and lyrical sequences"—particularly those which emphasized the purity of the child and the beauty of altruistic love.[2]

Many in the audience—particularly the Symbolists and Parnassians who had been students of Indian culture and philosophy—were familiar with the mysteries and marvels of this ancient land. Edouard Schuré published his synchretistic work, *Great Initiates* in 1889, in which he pointed up parallels between Hindu beliefs and contemporary spiritual views. So, too, had Leconte de Lisle, Michelet, Maeterlinck and countless other creative spirits gone back in time, probing long-forgotten eras, so as to broaden and deepen their views. What intrigued theatre people most intensely were the complex rules and conventions involved in Indian performing arts. These had been laid down by the legendary sage, Bharata (2nd B. C.), in a thirty-chapter work, *Natya Shastra (The Art of the Theatre)*. For the Hindu, theatre is a rite of passage which takes an individual from one state of being to another. The spectacle, therefore, is not to be considered merely a work of art, entertainment, or an object to be admired for its fine craftsmanship and expert character delineations, but rather as an experience to be absorbed and assimilated—one which gives its participants spiritual nourishment.

Partly historical and partly fictional, like other Sanskrit theatrical works, *The Toy Cart* fuses word, music, song, dance, action, and iconography. Unlike Western theatre, the aim of Sanskrit theatrical performance is to create in the spectator a feeling of *aesthetic delight (rasa)* expressed, not through words exclusively, but via suggestion and the combination of art forms. *Rasa* means "flavor" or "relish" and refers to a person's aesthetic taste and emotional sensitivity. An abstract transpersonal perception, *rasa* comes into being via symbols and audibility. What is crucial, then, in Sanskrit theatre is the evocation of *emotions* and not the story-line nor the characters. The protagonists are not considered real. They are prototypes, idealizations, portraying certain basic human feelings *(bhava)* as concretized in specific situations.

Symbolists, mystics, avant-gardistes, elitists and literati of all schools were understandably fascinated by *The Toy Cart*, and all for different reasons: either a genuine aesthetic and philo-

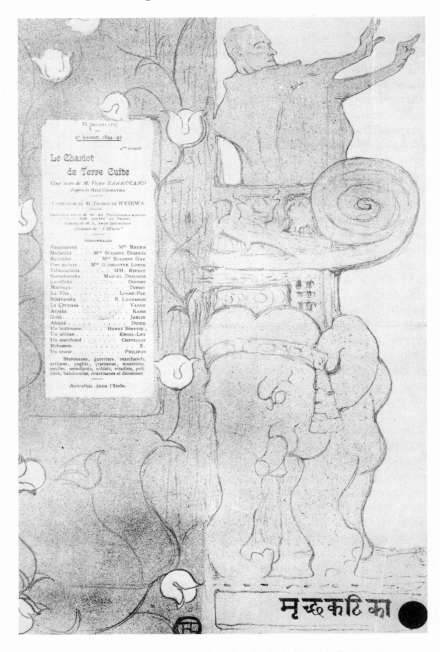

Toulouse-Lautrec's poster for Shudraka's *The Little Toy Cart*

sophical understanding of the play; or for political reasons, through identification of its theme with anarchical values; or for snob-appeal. After all, how many had seen Sanskrit theatre before?

The Toy Cart, a ten-act play involving adultery, dramatizes the story of a courtesan, Vasantasena, in love with a poor married Brahman, Charoudatta, who follows the passive path in life, so convinced is he that it is the way of the Gods. The evil prince Sansthanaka, continuously rejected by Vasantasena, strangles her and, believing her to be dead, leaves her. Because he is so powerful, he has Charoudatta condemned for the crime. Vasantasena arrives on the scene as the sentence is about to be carried out, thereby proving her beloved's innocence. He wills no evil and forgives his accuser.

Certain episodes were singled out for praise: when, in the third act, a child is seen crying because he only has a clay cart with which to play while another has one made of gold; when the beautiful young courtesan, Vasantanesa, seeing him so sad, is deeply moved and she takes off her magnificent jewels which she then places in his little chariot, transforming this vulgar object into a precious entity. So, too, may all things in the world of contingencies be elevated in value: destiny divests some in order to enrich others. The gentility and tenderness of the courtesan, as she makes her way most unobtrusively to the child, and his amazement as he sees the miracle occurring before his very eyes, was praised by the great majority of critics.[3]

The decors featuring Charoudatta's cabin, set in the middle of a somber countryside, impressed the critics for the *feelings* it generated. The still and silent atmosphere is interrupted by the sudden flight of Vasantasena, dressed in white tulle, attempting to escape the evil prince in hot pursuit, was praised for the verisimilitude of the actress' facial expressions and body movements.

Although the mob scene at the play's conclusion was directed with felicity, the restrained tone and pace of the trial scene heightened the extreme excitement to virtually unbearable levels. Problems did arise, nevertheless, with this very scene. Because of Lugné-Poë's tight finances, only lightweight flannel material bought on sale was used to costume the fifty actors on stage. That they were scantily dressed was an understatement. Each piece of material was cut into increasingly smaller strips, so that many of the actors did not have enough material to encircle their waists. It was decided, then, that these strips should be used to make turbans, thus symbolizing Hindu dress. Other bits of material and fabrics of all types, gathered here and there, were dyed ochre, then painted with red or yellow colors to give the impression of authenticity. Some actors were fortunate enough to be able to borrow costumes which they wore underneath this incredible creation; others used additional ornaments to cover up their bodies. The impression was one of divestiture or nudism, which distressed Lugné-Poë, since he feared negative reactions from his subscribers and guests. His solution: one of the actors, wearing a turban and a bit of cord knotted in the right place, stepped to the center of the footlights during intermission, sat down cross-legged, back to the audience, arms raised as in prayer during the entire time. Some in the audience laughed at the procedure; others understood.

All admired Henri de Toulouse-Lautrec's program cover for the *The Toy Cart*. It consisted of a sketch of Félix Fenéon, the anarchist and Symbolist art critic, and a drawing of a large elephant, so important an animal in Hindu culture. Above the animal stands a Brahman wearing a loose fitting garment, with arms outstretched. Outlined forms of flowers surround the square plaque on which the cast is listed, creating a mandala effect. Toulouse-Lautrec also designed the backdrop for the play. Unfortunately, its pastel colorations and luxurious tones were barely visible from the orchestra because of the extremely subdued lighting on stage.[4] In keeping with Hindu tradition, the decors were so sparse as to be virtually nonexistent. Since Hindu drama is suggestive, it needs only a few symbolic items to carry out the meaning and philosophical impact of the work. The toy cart, sculpted by Henry Cros, stood out as an exception to the rule.

Reactions to Lugné-Poë's production were mixed. Erik Satie, formerly a Rosicrucian who had severed his relations with this group in 1892 to found his own church (*The Metropolitan Church of Art of Jesus the Leader*, the purpose of which was to foster art, beauty, and morality), was offended by the production. He wrote Lugné-Poë a scathing letter in which he condemned him for having sinned against the higher values of art. The nudity he had seen on stage was virtually unacceptable. The author of an article in *La Plume*, seeking to quell the remonstrances, labeled the composer *"Erik Sottise."* Others, such as Romain Coolus, dramatic critic for *La Revue Blanche*, conveyed his gratitude to Lugné-Poë for the extraordinary beauty of the work produced, which proved once again the "jeunesse infléchissable" of this ancient drama.[5] Jules Lemaître's critique was positive: a masterpiece, he declared, and "nothing in Greek, English and French theatre appears to me to be superior to this Indian comedy."[6] Although the ramifications of the subtleties of Sanskrit theatre and culture escaped him, and he erroneously confused Dumas' and Hugo's depictions of the redeemed courtesan with Hindu metaphysis on the subject, he was impressed by the aesthetic message of the play. Silvain Lévi, the author of *Le Théâtre indien* (1890), was disturbed by the distortions made by Victor Barrucand, the play's adapter. Not sufficient stress was placed on the Hindu's disdain for the real world, considered an illusion; nor would Vasantasena, he suggested, ever feel intimately connected or related to society's untouchables, as she was purported to be in the French adaptation. Others, like Mallarmé and Gustave Kahn, commented on the beauty of the adaptation: its language was able to convey finesse and graciousness and also express so well the essential paradox of the courtesan, who not only humbles but impoverishes herself so as to become worthy of her lover, while still remaining a paradigm of sensuality.

The perverse, evil, cruel prince, and Suzanne Deprès, making her debut as Madanika, Vasantesana's charming slave, were praised for their characterizations. Others in the cast were also lauded for that outer-worldly quality they incorporated into their roles. Nevertheless, there were those critics—as always— who looked upon the stage play as incoherent. Sarcey was aghast at the crowd scene, declaring that this was the first time he had ever seen nude men on a Parisian stage. Others commented mirthfully on the conglomerate and their colorful turbans.

> There were many Russian scarves, Roumanian kerchiefs, Algerian bedcovers, Japanese dresses, some armor, a few rugs from the Place Clichy and even—everything comes here—some Indian shawls. This Indian crowd seems to have crossed space and time, pillaging, dressing in tawdry garments stolen from Carthage, Rome, Tokyo, Constantinople, Seville, Liberty, the thrift shop, the flea market and from Cairo Street during the last World's Fair. Our yellow skin was the only unifying force in the group; the synmthetic ochre coloring furnished by Lugné.[7]

Kalidasa: Shakuntala

Eleven months later, on Dec. 10, 1895, Lugné-Poë produced another Sanskrit drama, *Shakuntala*, by Kalidasa, who

Program for Kalidasa's *Shakuntala*

lived at some time between the fourth-century B. C. and the second-century A. D. A dramatic ritual, *Shakuntala* draws its viewers into a love sequence experienced first on an earthly plane and concluding in the supernal realm of blissful understanding and detachment. Drawn from the first section of the religious epic, the *Mahabahrata* (c. 200 B. C.), *Shakuntala* combines liturgical drama with the elegance and sensitivity of Sanskrit theatre.

The play opens as King Dushyanta, ruler of India, is hunting in a forest. Just as he is about to wound a stag, he comes upon a hermit who tells him that this animal is sacred. The King is given hospitality in the neighboring ashram. Its beautiful flowering plants and trees and its tamed animals set the tone for Shakuntala's entrance. It is through her, the daughter of a nymph and a mortal, and through the forces she represents, that the King will be able to fulfill his karma and experience heightened consciousness. The events which follow their meeting bring pain to both protagonists; but pain, like joy, is considered necessary for the spiritual ascesis leading to *moksa* or salvation.[8]

Shakuntala, portrayed by A. Meri, and Priyamvada, her friend, by Suzanne Deprès, earned success. Beautifully garbed in long white dresses, these actresses seemed part of and yet stood out from the fascinating Indian atmosphere Paul Ranson suffused in his decor. The musical score composed by Pierre de Bréville blended perfectly with the evolving events and the spiritual ascesis implicit in the drama. The prologue, in keeping with Sankrit theatrical custom which features the director of the troupe and one of his actresses who announce the program for the evening, was portrayed respectively by Lugné-Poë and Suzanne Deprès.

Although *Shakuntala* was not exactly unknown in Paris —having been performed at the Odéon in 1850, in an adaptation by Mery and Nerval; also adapted by Gautier and Reyer for the ballet at the Opera (1858); and evoked by Goethe in verse, Lugné-Poë's production both thrilled and pleased his viewers. It wafted them far from their habitual mundane world with its worries and problems into a world of enchantment—where the spiritual domain reigned supreme.

Wilde: Salome

In sharp contrast was Oscar Wilde's *Salome,* which premiered at the Théâtre de l'Oeuvre on Feb. 11, 1896. Incidental music by René Larde, a set by Sérusier and a lithograph for the program by Henri de Toulouse-Lautrec did much to draw notice to this work.   Since Lugné-Poë included a play by Romain Coolus, *Le Ménage Brésile*, on the same program, it is understandable that Lautrec's lithograph featured the author on one side, and opposite him, a sketch of Wilde, with Westminster Abbey and the Tower of London enveloped in fog. Appreciated by continental audiences perhaps more than by his compatriots, it is thought that, out of gratitude for his neighbors across the channel, he had written *Salome* (1891) in French rather than English.   The French edition bore but one illustration drawn by Felicien Rops; the English translation, by Lord Alfred Douglas, was adorned with a cover design and twelve illustrations by Aubrey Beardsley.

Wilde's notoriety was perhaps instrumental in part in filling the Théâtre de l'Oeuvre on opening night.   French literary circles had been verbally flagellating the British for their hypocrisy in charging Wilde with homosexuality under the Criminal Law Amendment, declaring him guilty, and imprisoning him for two years to hard labor.   Because of the publicity surrounding anything Wilde undertook, Lugné-Poë prepared his mise-en-scène and rehearsed his cast in secret for fear of arousing the ire of various groups.

Wilde's play concentrates on John the Baptist and Salome, the reviled erotic dancer who was the focal point of the saint's disgust.   So antipathetic a human being is Salome, that Wilde does not even describe her dance, leaving the appropriate undulations to the actress portraying the role.   Wilde's imagery in his dialogue and on stage, implicit in the complex lighting effects used by Lugné-Poë, underscores the intensity and virulence of the action.   A blood-red moon provides the atmosphere; it heightens the excitement engendered by the confrontation between Salome and John the Baptist.

Commented upon favorably by the critics was the scene in which John the Baptist, invisible to audiences since he was imprisoned in a cistern (under the floor boards in the theatre), uttered his pronouncements.   His voice, as though arising from the depths of the earth, sounded hollow and ghostly, lending added emphasis to his fearsome prognostications resounding throughout the theatre.   In slow and calculated tones, he tells of the evils and punishments awaiting the sensual and blood-lusting Herod and his family.   Repudiating the lascivious Salome,

Toulouse-Lautrec's poster for Wilde's *Salome*

John urges her to repent. Fascinated by his eyes—they are "like black holes burned by torches . . . like black caverns where dragons dwell . . . like black lakes troubled by fantastic moons"—she longs to kiss him. He refuses, unwilling to be sullied by her kind. After Salome's orgiastic dance, Herod, who has promised to fulfill her wish after its completion, is compelled to grant her John's head. Brought to her on a silver shield, Salome grabs her beloved's head and cries out: "Ah! thou wouldst not suffer me to kiss thy mouth, Jokanaan. Well! I will kiss it now. I will bite it with my teeth as one bites a ripe fruit. Yes, I will kiss thy mouth."

Difficulties arose with this last scene. Lugné-Poë, who had found an executioner and a suitable platter, could not, understandably, locate a bloody head. Finally, he went to the Musée Grévin, famed for its waxworks. The director lent him one, with the provision that he assume responsibility for it. Lugné-Poë agreed, unable to foresee that, during the dress rehearsal, when the executioner raised the head on the platter from beneath the floor boards to give to Salome, before she could embrace it, he suffered such stage fright that his arms began to tremble and the head fell and shattered. Although the pieces were glued together for the performance and no one noticed the cracked skull, Lugné-Poë had to pay steeply for the damage.

Still other problems faced Lugné-Poë. The Comédie-Parisienne, where the play was to be performed, was the only building remaining of a whole group that had been condemned and razed. Lugné-Poë requested permission to use it before it would be demolished and it was granted. So bad a state was it in, that the dressing rooms could not be used; as for the halls and passageways, they were so encumbered with falling plaster and debris that the cast and technicians could barely make their way through them. On opening night, Suzanne Deprès discovered to her horror that some of the costumes had for some strange reason caught fire. She started to put out the flames single-handedly and did so until Lugné-Poë as Herod, wearing his cardboard crown, noticed the conflagration. Then, he and the others began pouring water on the burning material, finally quenching the flames. Incredibly, no one in the audience even suspected the danger!

Salome earned Lugné-Poë great success. His portrayal of Herod, the cruel and sadistic, sex-driven monarch, portrayed in sober tones, was greeted with accolades as was Max Barbier's

Iokanaan, whose deep rich voice and sparse gestures enhanced his character's spiritual power and depth.

Line Munt as Salome was grave and serious in her gestures and measured in tone before working up to her frenzied excitement. Her paradoxically cold and passionate ways mesmerized young and old in the audience. The critic, Jean de Tinan, wrote: "This voice and this beauty filled me with the most frenetic emotions I have ever had."[9] Other critics, such as Fouquier, although admiring Salome's acting abilities, her expressive and lionesque vocal tones, considered her dancing second rate. Moreover, because the text itself is repetitious, the performers should not have spoken so slowly and solemnly—reverting to that psalmodyzing mystique they had used for the Ibsen productions.[10]

Wilde, moved by Lugné-Poë's production of his play, wrote about his reactions to a friend:

> It is something that at a time of disgrace and shame I should be still regarded as an artist. I wish I could feel more pleasure: but I seem dead to all emotions except those of anguish and despair. However, please let Lugné-Poë know that I am sensible of the honour he has done me. He is a poet himself.[11]

Lugné-Poë's *Salome* was the first of many productions of this play by other theatrical directors, and an opera at Dresden, on Sept. 9, 1905, by Richard Strauss.

Gogol: The Inspector General

Another innovative production at the Théâtre de l'Oeuvre: Nikolai Gogol's *The Inspector General* (Jan. 8, 1898). Lugné-Poë went to great lengths to see that every detail in this production was just right. He wanted no mishaps to mar the production. He read Prosper Merimée's remarkable translation of *The Inspector General* aloud so that his approach would be fresh and not encumbered with distortions.

The Inspector General, a five-act satire on the mores of government officials during the reign of Nicholas I, was difficult both to cast and direct. Gogol, like many an innovator, including Lugné-Poë himself, detested the cheap melodrama that had invaded the stages throughout Europe. A rejection of sensationalism is evident in a statement made by Gogol concerning theatre in general: "Only mediocrities desperately grab at the unusual . . . murder, fire, wild passion."[12] Gogol's realistic comedies, as they were called, were inspired by unsensational and mundane daily occurrences, which he used, together with highly stylized characterizations, to point up the stupidity, vulgarity, and corruption in daily existence.

The Inspector General revolves around a single event. Officials in a small town are warned that an Inspector General is coming to their town incognito to check up on them. Their terror has rendered them so senseless that they are convinced that Khlestakov, a small clerk from St. Petersburg who has been staying at the inn after having gambled his money away, is the anticipated Inspector General. The town officials, therefore, not only wine and dine him, but lend him money, hoping he will not report the corruption, bribery, and suffering taking place in their community. Khlestakov leaves before his identity is found out. But before doing so, he writes a letter, aware that the director of the post office, who always reads everyone's mail, will surely open this letter. He does so, and is shocked by its contents. Alarmed, he rushes to the other town dignitaries, gathered together to congratulate the governor on his clever handling of the Inspector General, and reads derogatory excerpts concerning each one. The utter surprise, shame and indignation of the corrupt functionaries reaches its climax when, suddenly, the real Inspector General arrives.

Since its inception, *The Inspector General* has proven to be a fascinating theatrical vehicle for actors and directors, including such greats as Meyerhold and Jouvet in the twentieth-century. As for the role of Khlestakov—a complex of arrogant and calculating traits, an imposter who knows how to take advantage of the cupidity of others though pusillanimous, conceited, and essentially stupid himself—it is a role most fine actors like to play. Lugné-Poë portrayed this universal type, displaying *real* talent, finesse and intelligence, wrote Bauer. Never excessive in his vocal tones or gestures, the mixture of measure and comedy was unforgettable.[13]

Gogol had taken great pains to warn directors and actors not to caricaturize the role of Khlestakov, the most difficult role in the play. Gogol had written the following as a guide to actors undertaking such a part:

> God forbid it be played with the usual farcicalness—as braggarts and theatrical scapegraces are played. He is simply stupid; he babbles only because he sees that they are disposed to listen; he lies because he had a hearty dinner and drank a considerable quantity of

wine. He is frivolous only when he approaches the ladies. The scene in which he starts lying at random should receive special attention. His every word, i. e., sentence or utterance, is a completely unexpected impromptu, and therefore should be expressed abruptly. One shouldn't lose sight of the fact that towards the end of the scene the wine begins to have an effect on him, little by little. But he absolutely should not totter on the chair; he should only turn red and express himself more unexpectedly and more and more loudly the further he goes. I am extremely worried about this role.[14]

Critics in general were satisfied with Lugné-Poë's Khlestakov and commented as they did on his nuanced, restrained, yet life like stance. Some even remarked that they had never thought Lugné-Poë capable of playing the part of this "featherbrained, haughty, spineless and yet flegmatic young man," and were impressed with the results.[15] Indeed, Lugné-Poë had never before played a comic role of such magnitude. His portrayal of Khlestakov gave him the opportunity of conveying his feelings concerning humankind's vanity, arrogance, and bent for deception. He accomplished his purpose with simplicity and with ease. When emotion or scenes of drunkenness were called for, his speech took on a staccato-like quality, and although his gestures seemed irrationally motivated and uncontrolled, they were studied. Each nuance assumed its rightful place and each displacement of his body followed a preconceived plan.

Gogol's need to destroy whatever illusion humankind may still harbor was well served by Lugné-Poë in the series of stage situations comprising *The Inspector General.* Perhaps he, too, like Gogol, had met Khlestakovs in real life—people so filled with feelings of self-importance that they thought the world revolved around them. Whatever the reasons, Lugné-Poë's portrayal of Khlestakov was remarkable!

*

Despite the Théâtre de l'Oeuvre's successes and Lugné-Poë's increasing fame, he was coming to the end of his tether. Lack of funds, deteriorating economic conditions, growing rivalry with theatres in general and with Antoine in particular (he had recently opened his Théâtre Antoine), had fatigued Lugné-Poë physically and emotionally. He felt drained and dejected and needed time to renew himself. In a letter to Saint Georges de Bouhélier, he wrote:

> I gave, gave until the time has come when I don't know what to do
> anymore. I know, I have taught people the techniques of working.
> Where has it gotten me . . . I am not living. My expenses are small,
> but the Oeuvre never gave me my yearly bread. Do you know some-
> thing: I'm especially tired of asking people for money. I've always
> outdone myself like a slave. Knocking at fifty doors, ringing a hun-
> dred door bells, I am always seen soliciting subscriptions.[16]

What depressed Lugné-Poë was not the time spent preparing for his productions, working with the actors and technicians, but the efforts expended trying to acquire funds. Moreover, the dearth of fine French playwrights also saddened him.
In a letter to Romain Rolland, Lugné-Poë spoke of his desire to
reorient the Théâtre de l'Oeuvre: he would produce more
Shakespeare in fresh and vital translations. His friend, the celebrated English critic Walter Pater, suggested he produce *Measure
for Measure*. And he did, at the Cirque d'Été, on Dec. 10, 1898.
Everything about the mise-en-scène was considered perfect: costumes and decors were historically accurate; likewise, the staging
and the acting received only praise. Lugné-Poë, however, had
made only one mistake and it was a big one—a blunder in judgment. Rather than taking the time to have the play retranslated,
he used Louis Ménard's error-filled work. Not only was it riddled with misconceptions, but its verse was dead, weighing
down the play rather than livening it up and divesting it of
Shakespeare's power, strength and genius. Lugné-Poë's *Measure
for Measure* was a betrayal, Shakespearians contended.

Still he was proud of his achievements and stated so in
the circular announcing his program for the Théâtre de
l'Oeuvre's sixth season.

> L'Oeuvre remains and will always be the only independent thea-
> tre; independent of everything and of everyone, without worrying
> about pleasing audiences and without thinking of attracting a
> crowd. Indifferent to receipts, it will not fear of going against the
> frequently oppressive majority opinion, as it always has done; and
> will consider it an honor to retain the title given to it, and also to
> its seniors, that of theatre of the avant-garde and of combat.[17]

Nevertheless, despite all of Lugné-Poë's good intentions
and his talent as actor and director, his theatre no longer enjoyed
the success it once had. Audiences and critics alike seemed to
have lost confidence in his cultural and aesthetic message.

Before closing the doors of the Théâtre de l'Oeuvre—on

June 21, 1899—he offered two more works to Parisian audiences: Diderot's *The Dialogue with the Maréchale* and Romain Rolland's *The Triumph of Reason*. Although the former cannot be considered theatre, but rather a discussion of ideas, it represented an approach to the performing arts which had always been dear to Lugné-Poë: a blend of philosophy and theatre. As for Rolland's work, it focussed on the assassinated Marat. Did Lugné-Poë identify with this revolutionary leader? Hadn't he also been murdered, in a way, by a now unfeeling and unresponsive public?

PART III

Jacques Copeau

The Théâtre du Vieux-Colombier

1913-1924

Chapter 9

Jacques Copeau (1879-1949)

Like Antoine and Lugné-Poë, Jacques Copeau also attempted a theatrical innovation. He, too, was energized by the fervor, excitement, and optimism of youth. Copeau had but one desire: to serve the dramatist, by bringing to the performance the purest, simplest, truest re-creation of the author's intent.

A spirit of *indignation* also infused Copeau's ire in his fight against commercial theatre, which he considered dominated by deception and hypocrisy.

> Unrestrained commercialism degrades our French stage more cynically each day and turns the cultivated public away from it. Most theatres are monopolized by a handful of entertainers in the pay of shameless tradesmen. There seems to be the same spirit of play-acting, speculation, and baseness everywhere. And even where great traditions should command a certain sense of decency, there still is bluffing, every type of overbidding, and all sorts of exhibitionism, living off an art, of which there was no longer any question that it is dying. Inertia, disorder, lack of discipline, ignorance and stupidity, disdain for the creator, hatred for beauty seem to be everywhere. The productions have become more and more insane and vain; critics have become more easily satisfied, and the public taste more and more misled. It is all this which arouses and revolts us.[1]

Dedicated to his art, and aescetic in his ways, Copeau's work habits were marked by passion.

*

Jacques Copeau was born in Paris. His mother, a bourgeoise from the provinces, and his father, in small industry, both loved theatre. Their small library of melodramas, particularly those of Dumas père, used to keep the young Copeau regaled for hours on end. When old enough, his parents took him to the Boulevard theatres on a regular basis.

As a student at the Lycée Condorcet, he dreamed of becoming an actor and went to the theatre as frequently as he could. He remembered with pleasure the time when his grandfather had played dominos at the café de la Porte Saint-Martin with the great Frédérick Lemaître, and had returned from the experience entranced. At seventeen, Copeau had a change of mind. He decided to become a dramatist. After his first play, *Morning Fog* (1896), was performed by his classmates at the Nouveau-Théâtre, he was thrilled to be introduced to Francisque Sarcey. Not only did the well-known critic of *Le Temps* congratulate him for having followed the tradition of the "well-made play," but also for having used Dumas fils as his model. When, the following day, the flattering account of Copeau's play appeared in the *Temps*, the budding playwright walked on air.

Nevertheless, Copeau had a hard road ahead. He decided to take a *licence* in letters and philosophy at the Sorbonne (1897-1898), thus preparing him for the École Normale Supérieure and then a teaching career. It seemed a more secure road at the time than acting. But after having begun his studies, they palled, and he spent the great bulk of his hours and meager sous going to the Théâtre Antoine and to Lugné-Poë's Oeuvre—the only oases in Paris where serious work was taking place in the theatre. An inveterate reader, Copeau knew well both classical and contemporary drama, novel, and poetry—most particularly, the works of Verlaine, Mallarmé, and Rimbaud.

Copeau's cherished fantasies of becoming a dramatist, and even of going to the École Normale Supérieure, vanished with his father's sudden death. He had to begin earning a living and went to Scandinavia where he gave French lessons, thereby combining travel with work. Nevertheless, the young Copeau still entertained thoughts of being an author. He was greatly encouraged by the fact that the magazine which favored symbolist and neo-classical writers, *The Hermitage*, published several articles by him which condemned the superficial pseudo-philosophical theatre of Paul Hervieu and praised André Gide's novel, *The Immoralist*.

Copeau, optimistic about his future, returned to Paris at the end of the year, in 1903, with a Scandinavian wife, Agnes Thompsen. He went to visit Gide, who had written him enthusiastically in Copenhagen, encouraging him to pursue a literary career. Such considerations, for the present at least, seemed out of the question since Copeau's family had asked him to take over the directorship of his father's foundry in the Ardennes. A man of duty, Copeau yielded, though to distance him from Paris and from the work he so loved was a great sacrifice for him. After two years, in 1905, the business failed and Copeau returned to the capital, determined, this time, to fulfill his bent.

He again sought out Gide who, impressed with Copeau's talents, introduced him to a young group of writers: Henri Ghéon, Jean Schlumberger, Jacques Rivière. Their forthrightness and dedication to art motivated Copeau in his struggle to carve out a path of his own. Gide, Georges de Porto-Riche, and Albert Besnard found him a position as salesman and exhibit director at Georges Petit's Gallery of Modern Art, where he remained for four years.

Copeau led a double life: working by day and writing by night for such magazines as *The Hermitage* and *La Revue d'Art Dramatique*. He spoke out boldly for theatrical reform, but also demanded that critics change their ways. He condemned the publication of superficial, conventional, one-sided, and deceitful reportages on theatrical performances. [A critic, he wrote most emphatically, must be courageous and not indulgent, audacious and not passive, sincere and not hypocritical, cultured, and *an artist in his own right.*] If he does not conform to these standards, he can be considered as frivolous and as much to blame for the aridity in theatre as are the producers of Boulevard plays.[2]

Copeau was given his big chance in 1907. Léon Blum gave up his column on drama criticism at the *Grande Revue* and its director, Jacques Rouché, asked Copeau to take it over. Such a position gave him the opportunity to reach out to the general public and inform them of the paucity of French dramatists and the banality and old-fashioned nature of the stage productions offered. Certainly, Copeau was not alone in deploring the situation: Romain Coolus and Romain Rolland, for example, also cried out against the outright mercantilism in contemporary theatre. What kind of plays were popular at the beginning of the century? Copeau questioned. Either those that cater to humankind's love of violence or the ultra-conventional comedies where marital difficulties or the like take precedence: *Sentier Street; The Honors of War; The Lady of the Louvre; The Queen of Roses*, and more of this ilk.

1909 is a date to remember because of the founding—by André Gide, Jean Schlumberger, André Ruyters, Henri Ghéon, and Copeau—of the *Nouvelle Revue Française*, which was destined to become one of the outstanding magazines of the century. Such a journal gave creative young people the needed exposure to express their innovative ideas and pursue, each one in his own way, his course in life.

Coupled with his work at the *Nouvelle Revue Française* was Jacques Rouché's invitation to Copeau to write a play for the Théâtre des Arts. Now that he was assured a full-time job in theatre, he was able not only to leave his post at the gallery, but also to rent a small house in the country, at Limon, near La Ferté-sous-Jouarre.

Copeau's first endeavor for the 1910-1911 season at the Théâtre des Arts was to consist of an adaptation of Dostoyevsky's *The Brothers Karamazov*. He asked Jean Croué, a young actor at the Comédie-Française, to help him write the stage play.

The Théâtre des Arts, a small theatre situated on the Boulevard des Batignolles, seated six hundred people, and, from the very first day of its founding, attracted some attention. Rouché was bent upon experimenting with his own theatrical ideas and drew to his aegis many fine young talents, such as Copeau, Louis Jouvet, and Charles Dullin. Rouché had been impressed by the rich decorations of Diaghilev's Ballet Russe, its orgy of color and its sensual dance rhythms and music, which had burst onto the Parisian scene.[3]

Rouché had outlined his own rather revolutionary ideas on the stage in his book, *Theatrical Art*. The mise-en-scène for a play, he wrote, "must neither distort it, nor embellish it excessively, but merely give just value to its main lines and the appropriate character of its beauty."[4] Convinced that stage sets should be highly decorative and not merely *trompe-l'oeil* concoctions, Rouché engaged the artist Durec to do the decors for his productions. Like the Duke of Saxe-Meiningen and Talma before him, he stressed the close harmony that must exist between costumes, decor, direction, and acting. Rather than jarring, they must be woven together in a harmonious pattern so as to make a unified impression.[5]

The atmosphere at the Théâtre des Arts was almost monkish in its sense of dedication to its work. The men and women associated with it were indifferent to everything but the theatre, and their capacity for selfless application was complete. They labored in every phase of the theatre, sometimes remaining in the small dim building until the early morning, working out some acting problem, or studying a text or decor.

The Brothers Karamazov was pronounced a success by Parisian critics, and although Copeau could have spent many years with Rouché, as well as long summers in the Limon adapting and writing plays for the Théâtre des Arts, he realized that were he to do so, he would begin to stagnate. He had to fend for himself, seek out young and talented playwrights and create his own style, his own mise-en-scènes, and an individualized acting technique which could reflect his very personal vision of the performing arts. To reconstruct theatrical art from the base up was his goal.

The old theatre Copeau rented and intended to refashion —the Théâtre de l'Athénée Saint-Germain—was situated on the Left Bank, on a street populated largely by artists, writers, poets, and students. The street had a fine but shadowy association with the theatre of the seventeenth-century. It was here, supposedly, that Molière, Racine, and La Fontaine used to call on Boileau. Thus, the Rue du Vieux-Colombier was of some historic importance, and despite Copeau's wrathful iconoclasm, it appealed to him. ⌐The theatre would, of course, be remodeled to accord with Copeau's conceptions. To attract audiences to a theatre in the backwash of Paris, he undercut the price of tickets at the Boulevard theatres; moreover, like his predecessors, Antoine and Lugné-Poë, he instituted a system of season subscriptions, attractive to those with artistic ideals and little money. By these maneuvers, he made his theatre the least expensive to attend in all of Paris. ⌋

Copeau was a man of great force and intelligence. Both traits revealed themselves plainly in the direct grip he took on any project. He had long been occupied with thoughts of the theatre and had formulated a system of ideas which, by virtue of his very dynamic nature, he sought to impose on his co-workers. In all of his articles written thus far—for the *Gaulois, Le Petit Journal, La Grande Revue, La Nouvelle Revue Française*—Copeau attacked with savage directness the debased state of the contemporary theatre in France. He was determined to change the trend with his founding of the Théâtre du Vieux-Colombier in 1913.

The new theatre was to be designed along simple classic lines. He would have none of the fustian of the Boulevard theatre, the heavy ornamentation, the gold plate, the roccoco cut-glass chandeliers. He would let in clean air where there had been an accumulation of dust, stuffy ideas, dimness and an intol-

erable stagnation.   In short, he would cleanse the commercial-
ized theatre of all that was hideous, cheap, and frustrating.

His theatre would be as simple in conception and as
harmonious as a Doric temple—at once functional, orderly, and
beautiful.   Copeau would embody in its construction all that he
had assimilated and felt he could use of the ideas of Gordon
Craig, Adolphe Appia, Constantin Stanislavski, Harley Granville-
Barker, and Vsevolod Meyerhold.   Light yellow wall panels,
green curtains draping back to the sides of the stage, and indirect
lighting, soothing to the eyes, would provide the interior decor-
ation for his new theatre. ⌈The stage would be bare to permit
direct contact between the audience and the actor.[6] ⌉

No detail was neglected. This was going to be a new kind
of theatre for Paris: functional without being mechanical, revolutionary without being sentimental. It would provide a more
appropriate backgound for plays both old and new; old plays
would be seen in fresh perspective, and new plays interpreted in
the light of the times.   The functional element would compre-
hend a new conception of the theatre, as something more than
theatre, with broader cultural outlook and social implications.   It
would be a unit, housing beside the theatre itself all of the
administrative offices, including a publicity service, and a store-
room for plays and manuscripts. The latter in itself was an innovation at times when manuscripts, unless specially solicited,
were carelessly handled; here, at least, they could be found
without difficulty when desired and would have the benefit of a
tomb. ⌈In the lobby, standing on a pedestal, was placed a bust of
Molière, symbol of dedication to an idea.⌉

Copeau's nimble and perceptive mind had already laid
down the course that the Théâtre du Vieux-Colombier was to
take. He would seek fresh techniques for achieving more powerful and suggestive visual and dramatic effects, while strictly
adhering to the import of the text. He would also try to make
finished and versatile actors out of unleavened human talent.
The potentialities of those who auditioned before Copeau, in the
spring of 1913, were generally discernible to him, though they
had often been overlooked by the blasé professional judges of the
commercial theatres. What he planned to do in his theatre was
to be as marked a departure from the commercial theatre's way
of functioning as was the departure of the Impressionists from
the stale formalistic painting that had preceded the great innovators.

Copeau's poster for the opening of the
Théâtre du Vieux-Colombier

Copeau hired ten actors, who were to constitute the core of his new efforts and were to develop under his tutelage, working together harmoniously for long hours, for days, for years. Blanche Albane had attracted Dullin's attention when she acted in *The Combat*, a play by her future husband, Georges Duhamel, at Rouché's Théâtre des Arts; Louis Jouvet had acted in Henri Ghéon's *Bread* at the Château d'Eau theatre; Charles Dullin had impressed all who saw him as Smerdiakov in *The Brothers Kara-mazov*; Roger Karl, in the role of Dimitri in the same play, also had performed at Jacques Rouché's Théâtre des Arts; Gina Barbieri had been praised five years earlier by Copeau in one of his theatrical criticisms; Jane Lory came directly from the Conservatoire to the Vieux-Colombier; Suzanne Bing, Cariffa, Armand Tallier, and Lucien Weber had all acted before. Together, these actors helped establish France's foremost modern theatrical venture before the First World War.

Copeau had very pointed ideas about what constituted an actor's physical and emotional equipment. Following the principles of Molière and the Elizabethans, he would try to develop the actor's every potential and to make him a thoroughly versatile individual, as skilled in physical exercises as with voice, body, and mask.

While the old Théâtre de l'Athénée Saint-Germain was being renovated in June of 1913 to become the Théâtre du Vieux-Colombier, Copeau took his troupe of ten actors to the lovely green countryside of Le Limon in the region of La Ferté-sous-Jouarre, about an hour away from Paris by train. They were settled in relative comfort at the homes of nearby farmers, unhampered by economic worries and in a position to devote themselves unremittingly to study and hard work. Copeau's group would rehearse out-of-doors every day, sometimes for five hours without interruption. For stage settings, he would turn to to nature—a group of trees, a bush, a field, He made every demand on his actors, striving to create vigorous and graceful bodies as physically adept as those of the Elizabethan actors, able to fight, run and perform any arduous leap that a play might require. They swam, fenced, and danced; their bodies became suppler and stronger. This working schedule was carried on in complete isolation for ten weeks. On September 1, 1913, the troupe, pronounced fit, prepared to return to Paris. The actors were masters of their bodies, of their voices, and of the various dramatic techniques which Copeau had taught them.[7]

Photograph of the Vieux-Colombier troupe at Le Limon

In a now famous statement, "An Essay on Dramatic Renovation," Copeau set down his ideas for the future Vieux-Colombier Théâtre.

The *Vieux-Colombier Théâtre* is open to all efforts, provided they reach a certain level and are of a certain quality. We mean: *dramatic* quality. Whatever may be our avowed preferences as critics and men of the theatre or our personal bent as writers, we do not represent a school whose entire prestige risks being called into question when the first blush of its novelty wears off. We do not bring a formula, nor are we convinced that the theatre of tomorrow will arise and develop from these beginnings. In this respect we differ from undertakings which have preceded us. All of them—we say this without minimizing the high merit of its director, André Antoine— were unconsciously rash enough to limit their field of activity within the narrow confines of a revolutionary program. We do not feel the need of a revolution. Our eyes are concentrated on too great models to feel such a need. We do not believe in the effectiveness of aesthetic formulas which are born and die every month among little groups, whose boldness is for the most part made up of ignorance. We do not know what the theatre of tomorrow will be. We proclaim nothing. But we pledge ourselves to react against all the worst features of the contemporary theatre. In founding the *Vieux-Colombier Théâtre,* we are preparing a place of refuge for future talents.

The Company

Even theatrical companies subsidized by the State are today suffering from a lack of guidance and discipline, from greediness for profit, and the absence of a common ideal. As for the Boulevard theatres, they belong to the great "stars" who force their directors to make ruinous expenditures, throw stage-productions out of balance, attract the audiences to themselves rather than to the play, and cheapen the playwright's talent by using their plays only as vehicles for their own stardom.

The last integrated company we saw in France was that of the *Théâtre Libre.* The members had a faith they all shared. And the director brilliantly exploited their common sentiments.

The *Vieux-Colombier Théâtre* in its turn brings together, under the direction of one man, a troupe of young, disinterested, and enthusiastic players whose ambition is to *serve* the art to which they have devoted themselves. To put an end to "ham-acting," to create for the actor a better atmosphere for his development as man and artist, to educate him, to inspire him with a sense of conscience, and to initiate him into the morality of his art—to that end our efforts will be stubbornly bent. We will always have in mind the perfecting of individual talents and their surbordination of the group. We will fight against routine procedures, against all professional distortions, against paralyzing overspecialization. Finally, we will do our best to renormalize these men and women whose calling it is to represent all human emotions and gestures. As much as we possibly can, we will bring them in contact with nature and life outside the theatre!

For two months now, the full company of the *Vieux-Colombier Théâtre* has been together and its work has begun. On July 1, it moved into its summer headquarters: in a tiny village in the Seine-et-Marne district, way out in the country. There, every day for five hours the members study the plays in the repertory under the guiding eye of its director. Two further hours are spent in the open, devoted to sight reading as exercises in mental alertness and voice training, to analyses of literary texts (plays, poems, fragments of classic prose), and to physical exercises. The advantages of this kind of training will not be fully appreciated until several years have passed. But already they are beginning to be felt.

Today, September 1, already knit together by two months of work in common and in command of a part of its repertory, the company is returning to Paris to rehearse for a month and a half more—on the stage, with costumes and stage-sets.[8]

Chapter 10

Productions at the Théâtre du Vieux-Colombier (1913-1914)

木 → The night of October 22, 1913, was to be memorable in the lives of all associated with Copeau. The Vieux-Colombier was inaugurating its first production. Roger Martin du Gard, whose novel, *Jean Barois*, had just been published, was in charge of the cloak room; Léon-Paul Fargue had handwritten the prospectus given to the audience as they walked in; Georges Duhamel was the prompter; Hélène (Mme. Roger Martin du Gard), who had created the costumes, worked until the last moment, sewing, cutting, adjusting.

Two plays had been selected: *A Woman Killed with Kindness*, in five acts, adapted by Jacques Copeau from the original of the Elizabethan Thomas Heywood, and Molière's *The Love Doctor*.

Heywood: A Woman Killed With Kindness

The Vieux-Colombier was filled to capacity and, of course, the actors were tense with expectation and excitement. When the green drapes were finally drawn back, the stage revealed a severely simple mise-en-scène, consisting of a table, two high-backed chairs, and a sun-gold background.

The Heywood play is, understandably, old in style and rather heavy in pace. Copeau had attempted to modernize it by omitting all unessential parts, giving it a clearer and more forceful dramatic line. But he still followed the general plan. It related the consequences of Mistress Frankford's (Blanche Albane) infidelity to her husband with his best friend, Wendoll (Jacques Copeau). Master Frankford (Roger Karl) seemed inclined to be lenient when he discovered his wife in a compromising situation with his friend, but he actually turned out to be a despot, dealing out the sort of kindness that kills. Heywood, like Shakespeare, was both an actor and an author, and he indulged in plots and counterplots. By cutting all Elizabethan excess, Copeau

tightened up the dramatic situation, but apparently not sufficiently. The play was performed only twenty-six times.

Copeau was not only uneasy playing the seducer, Wendoll, but his accoutrements also weighed him down. His wig
was overly large and cast a long shadow on his face; the felt hat
which he wore had such a large brim that it deadened and flat-
tened his features. Not only were few facial expressions visible,
but each time he greeted someone, he feared that the wig would
come off with the hat.[1] As a result, Copeau's gestures were awkward, his stance rather stiff, and his words difficult to understand.

Louis Jouvet, who had played a small part in Heywood's
play, that of Master Cranwell, had been engaged by Copeau not
merely as an actor but also in other capacities—as scene painter,
mechanic, manipulator of lights, and decorator. It was as a master of lighting effects, oddly enough, that Jouvet distinguished
himself in Copeau's troupe. His subtle manipulation of lights to
create a fitting atmosphere for the scenery was something new.

Restraint in stage setting was still novel at that time when
the stage was generally overstuffed with props to create the impression of verisimilitude. The simple stage sets created by Francis Jourdain for this production gave full scope to the audience's
imaginative participation. The only props, in the scene in which
Master Frankford and his servant surprise his wife in a
compromising situation, were an iron fence and dark blue
drapes. In the scene in which Mistress Frankford plays on a lute,
there was only a plain backdrop with a grayish-gold luminous
horizon above it. The costumes, designed by Valentine Rau,
belonged to the period; Copeau, as did previously the Duke of
Saxe-Meiningen, believed in historical accuracy in his mise-en-
scene.

Molière: The Love Doctor

The second play of the evening, a three-act impromptu,
The Love Doctor, written, rehearsed, and performed in five days
by Molière for Louis XIV, was performed by Copeau's troupe
with verve and abandon. The joy and humor of this marvelous
work, consisting of an hour of song, dance, and colorful improvisations, was emphasized by Copeau in his mise-en-scène and costuming. The performers, all wearing different-colored costumes
—brown, yellow, green, gray, purple—offered a feast for the eyes.
Outstanding for their inherent sense of the comic in this comedy

which ridicules quack doctors, ignorance, and pompous pretension, were Lucien Weber and Louis Jouvet. The latter, as Macroton, was overbearing and bombastic. Suggestive make-up was necessary to perfect this characterization, and Jouvet was as much a student of this art as he was of lighting. Macroton, a skeletal figure, was draped in a black robe. Large spectacles hung perilously from the tip of his nose. His prominent cheek-bones were smudged with grease, and his face was seamed with wrinkles.

After the performance, the entire cast was cheered. André Suarès wrote that Molière had never been so well served. "I am crazy about your two doctors, the fat one . . . and the other one, that tall stammering skeleton. I almost died laughing." Henri Ghéon, writing for the *Nouvelle Revue Française*, also expressed his delight. There were other, less indulgent critics: Paul Souday was annoyed because he liked to go to the theatre to be amused and Heywood's play was all but amusing. He considered the grey tones "monotonously sinister." Other critics were annoyed that an Elizabethan—and not even Shakespeare—had been chosen as opening fare for a new theatre.[2]

Excited and stimulated by their success—at least that of Molière's play—the actors remained in the theatre long after the audience had left, talking themselves out till the early morning, discussing future plans and conjuring up broad vistas of brilliant achievement.

*

Copeau was indefatigable. No sooner had the curtain rung down on this first night than he was discussing the fourteen other productions slated for his first season—an enormous undertaking for a newly-formed troupe. He knew, however, that the two months spent at Limon rehearsing, in addition to the zeal and dedication of the troupe, made them equal to the task.

Variety in his choice of plays guided Copeau. He would inject classical dramas with new life, contemporary and avant-garde plays with simplicity, and foreign dramas would be revitalized—either translated anew or re-adapted for the stage according to Copeau's vision of them. In keeping with the tradition started by Antoine and continued by Lugné-Poë, Copeau had also rejected the star system as well as the custom of using *ouvreuses* (ushers paid to accompany the public to their seats).

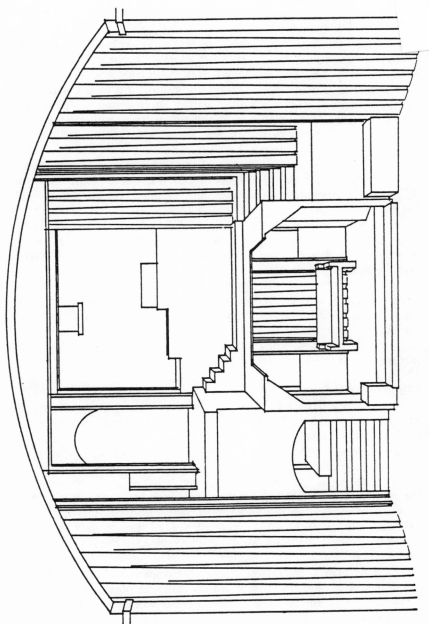

Stage design for the Vieux-Colombier stage, Paris

The troupe, by now superbly organized, spent the following days and weeks in hard work. It not only rehearsed many long hours, but made its own costumes and scenery. It functioned as a unit, all the members submitting to the same discipline and devoting themselves to the same ends. Copeau had never accepted "the middle of the road" attitude toward actors or dramatists, so characteristic of the Boulevard theatrical directors. For his second production, he chose a play by an unknown but interesing literary talent, who was a friend and one of the founding members of the *Nouvelle Revue Française*: Jean Schlumberger. His play, *The Louverné Sons*, opened on November 11, 1913.

Schlumberger was a keen analyist of character and expressed himself with simplicity and point. Two brothers are the principals of *The Louverné Sons*: one, Didier (Roger Karl) cruel and egotistical; the other, Alain (Charles Dullin), marked with the same defects, but who, with a growing awareness of himself, finally manages to overcome them. This somersault in character was made brilliantly plausible by the author's skill and understanding and actually is not foreign to human nature. Although superbly performed, with tensions nicely sustained and balanced throughout, it failed in effect.

Musset: Barberine

A week later, *Barberine*, a three-act comedy by Alfred de Musset, delighted audiences. It conjured up the Hungary of the Middle Ages, when King Mathius Corvin was at war with the Turks. When produced in 1882, *Barberine* had a characteristic excess of decor. Copeau, whose aim was integrity, reduced the mise-en-scène to the simplest: a chair, a table, and a cushion on the proscenium. The actor therefore had far more freedom to express himself, but the burden of projecting his character was without the support of a multiplicity of props, which might serve to conceal his inadequacies. It required a very subtle art to make this poetic fairytale effective.

The critics marveled at how Copeau had been able to inject a whole new dimension into a classical play. In the role of Ulasdislas, tall and stately, a man of the world whose seductive powers had already been the talk of the town, Jouvet enchanted audiences, as did the entire cast. Perhaps because Copeau gave Jouvet, whose abilities he so well understood and appreciated, greater liberty of action, he aroused jealousies among the other members of the troupe. Copeau was the first, perhaps, to realize that Jouvet had the potentialities of becoming a great specialist in Molière's roles, roles for which Jouvet had thought himself entirely inadequate.

As the lighting director, Jouvet varied his techniques to such an extent that in a single play they might run the gamut of the most pastel-like delicacy to the most brilliant and dazzling; or, as a piece of pure bravura, they might radiate from all sides of the stage, in all colors, cross, crisscross, and finally merge to produce a wonderfully soothing and harmonious atmosphere. His dawns and sunsets, moonrisings or settings, his hot mellow summer suns—all these were the products of Jouvet's fertile imagination and inventive resourcefulness. Once, when called upon to project the atmosphere of Spain in daylight, he turned on all the lights to the full and flooded the stage till it was as warm and rich as amber. Jouvet, always fascinated by the idiom of light, even designed special lamps, which he called *les Jouvets*.[3]

Since Copeau, like Appia, Antoine, and Lugné-Poë before him, had done away with the footlights, considering them to be too harsh in their effects, Jouvet was given free reign to indulge in creating all sorts of effects with color by clever manipulation of the electrical equipment. For instance, in the scene of Master Frankford's nocturnal return in *A Woman Killed with Kindness*, the lights were blocked by solid objects, producing shadows on the proscenium with a mysterious sculpturesque effect which aroused a sense of awe and dramatic involvement on the part of the spectators. In *The Love Doctor* , he filled the stage, as the Impressionists did their canvases, with splashes of bright light, creating a sense of unreserved delight—a clear utterance of joy and laughter.

Copeau, intent on setting new dimensions for the French theatre, was to give Paris the best in classical plays. He presented them with the contemporary point of view in mind. Though he was always keen for historical accuracy, he was contemporaneous in psychology; and he believed that the plays which had proved their worth in the past had also something to say to the present. With these principles in mind, he produced *The Miser* on November 18, 1913. Charles Dullin distinguished himself as Harpagon. His depth and understanding of the role of the avaricious being was rendered symbolically, as a universal and eternal type, present in all societies at all periods. But, as he lumbered about the stage, slowly, incisively, conserving what energies he had in the same manner as he secreted his ducats, critics then, and each time he performed this role during his entire career, lauded him for his unforgettable portrayal.

It was at this time, too, that Copeau instituted his *Poetic matinées:* a series of lectures, discussions, and readings of poems from all periods.   Both aesthetic and technical matters were broached, in this way broadening the understanding of the habitués of the Vieux-Colombier, as well as outsiders who were also invited to participate.   The contemporary poets, whose works were being read and discussed, were asked to attend, making the get-togethers that much more intimate and meaningful.

Meanwhile, Copeau's plans were being carried out: *Household Bread* by Jules Renard; *Fear of Beatings* by Georges Courteline; *La Jalousie du Barbouillé* by Molière; and Claudel's *The Exchange* were all performed.

Jouvet made his mark in Molière's one-act *La Jalousie du Barbouillé.*   It was exactly the right vehicle for him and he received resounding acclaim.   He played the role of the Doctor —the perfect pedant—often with pure grotesque and sometimes standard comic effects, while making blunt dramatic use of the course language and stinging insults that punctuate the play. The doctor's height was exaggerated, and he was in turn talkative, clownish, pompous, stiff, and self-righteous.   The audience responded in a way most rewarding to an actor, by not only relishing the characterization with pure fun and delight, but also by acknowledging its familiarity and unwittingly participating in the action on stage.[4]

Claudel: The Exchange

Claudel's *The Exchange* was to cause Copeau great problems.   It was perhaps this dramatist's poorest play, revolving around adultery, materialism, and death.   Claudel had been caught in the same trap that Georges Duhamel and Jean-Paul Sartre would be in later years.   A brief journey to the United States had encouraged these French writers to consider themselves experts in appraising the new world, materially as well as spiritually.   "The enslavement in which I found myself in America was very painful," Claudel wrote, "and I depicted myself in the traits of a lively young man who sells his woman to recover his freedom. . . it is I who am depicted in all these characters, the actress, the husband, the abandoned wife, the young savage and the calculating merchant."[5]

Louis Laine (Dullin), the young dreamer in *The Exchange*, and his wife, Martha, who is jealous of his creativity, live in a cabin by the sea, lent them by the materialistic Thomas Pollack Nageoire (Copeau) and his actress wife, Lechy Elbernon. While Nageoire attempts to seduce Martha, Lechy succeeds in steering Louis' emotions away from his wife and towards her. When Lechy is aware that he really wants to return to his wife, she provokes his death.

Although the plot of *The Exchange* is banal and contrived, the text may be looked upon as sequences of eruptions of colorful, rhythmic and searing images filled with brutalizing energy charges. Claudel's poetics are based on special breathing techniques and stylized gestures, which accentuate and prolong the dramatic moment. Just as brash sonorities are injected into the dialogue, so are periods of protracted *silences*, each accentuating the play's fearful and excoriating side.

Dullin, who had mastered Claudelien breathing techniques, appeared on stage sunburned, in an open bright red shirt and linen pants—as the incarnation of dream. As if he were a foreign element to this earth, he stood stark against the blueness of the sea, reminding the critic Claude-Roger Marx of a Gauguin painting. Underscoring the pauses after each period and comma, his lines sounded like incantations or litanies. His gestures spoke their own language as they replicated meaning, tone, rhythm, and image. His smile was tender; his voice at times disquieting, and tense.

> He was not made for happiness. His body never ceases being at the mercy of feeling, thought. A kind of inner fatality emanates from all of his creations.[6]

Although Roger Martin du Gard felt that Dullin played without conviction, Copeau, he thought, was "dazzling" in his portrayal of Nageoire. His garish yellow jacket, green tie, and grey sombrero, in the first act, in addition to his "unctuous and cooling voice, modulating the word dollar with force" was unforgettable. Equally impressive was Copeau's demeanor in the last act, appearing dressed in the reddish colorations of the Far West: a colossal, shiny, broad-rimmed top hat, a long black Macfarlan which hung down at right angles from his pointed shoulders, and two brilliant large diamonds most visible on his shirt front.

As for Guillaume Apollinaire, he remarked that Parisian

theatre was so poor that *The Exchange* was the only worthwhile play to see and that Claudel is "the only living dramatist."

What made *The Exchange* even more effective was Copeau's expert use of *silence*. To make the most, paradoxically, of emptiness, that is, to fill a void, is to allow the mind to wander prior to the birth of new antagonisms and dread. Copeau elaborated:

> The very essence of drama, is *silence*. The more powerful it is, the more rebellious, the more intense is the drama which attacks and tears it apart. Drama begins with silence; it also ends with it. It emerges from it only to revert back to it. Like a rupture, a fugitive awakening, it takes on the power of a discordant exclamation between two bordering silences. At the outset of a play, nothing *has been said yet*. At its conclusion, *there is nothing to say*. Everything has been consummated, all has been accomplished, *through the action*. Such is the meaning of tragic "purgation." Fulfillment does not happen with the word. And I sense a grave lesson to be learned in such silence without recall; such deadly silence which the great tragic dramatists had hovering over the stage as the plot was being *unraveled*.[7]

Despite the effort that was expended on Claudel's work, audiences remained unmoved and unappreciative of the drama itself. Copeau, however, was far from discouraged. He would perform another type of play, going back a few years. Although never really taken with naturalist or realistic drama, he decided to produce Becque's ironic satire, *The Merry-Go-Round*, which, according to the critic for *Le Mercure de France* (Maurice Boissard), he injected with new life. On the same program was a peasant farce by Roger Martin du Gard, *Father Leleu's Will*, in which Dullin won accolades for his astonishing portrayal of the cynical peasant about to die.

Dostoyevsky: The Brothers Karamazov

A revival of the Copeau and Croué adaptation of *The Brothers Karamazov*, first performed at the Théâtre des Arts, was to be next on the roster. Jacques Rivière had commented on the clarity and simplicity of the early stage adaptation back in 1911 and remained of the same opinion concerning Copeau's revival. No artifices were used to heighten the multiple episodes or point up the many harrowing events implicit in Dostoyevsky's tale. Because of Copeau's and Croué's "masterful intelligences" and profound knowledge of the theatre, feelings of dread and contrition seemed to flow forward naturally.

Copeau's production of Dostoyevsky's
The Brothers Karamazov

Rouché was gracious enough to lend Copeau the costumes and decors he had used. Copeau was Ivan; Paul Oettly, Dimitri; Jouvet, Feodor Pavlovitch Karamazov; the seductive Grouchenka was Valentine Tessier; Dullin, who once again astounded audiences with his incarnation of Smerdiakov, was "the deepest incarnation of the blood of Dostoyevsky."[8]

Copeau's mise-en-scène was ingenious. He used and manipulated the actors' stage positions to achieve the greatest effect. For example, a three-dimensional stage and three-dimensional actors peopling the proscenium underscored the solidity of the figures. The proximity between stage and audience also created an active undercurrent between them—as if the energy emanating from the stage happenings activated and inflamed the entire orchestra and theatre.

Dullin's performance of Smerdiakov stunned his audiences. Claudel was astounded by his character's "surprising relief."[9] Henri de Régnier considered Dullin's Smerdiakov memorable: he knew how to reveal all the nuances of character in the simplest of ways. And he predicted that "Dullin's name would be remembered. I would be greatly surprised if M. Dullin does not one day achieve an important place in the domain for which he is so brilliantly gifted."[10]

Dullin, however, did not just walk into the part. He confessed that it took great study, much thought and inner probing to understand the complex being he was going to incarnate.[11] Indeed, when first performing this role, in 1911, he felt he had not absorbed to his satisfaction Smerdiakov's many-sideness: he didn't *hear* him. Rehearsals were going badly, and he was discouraged. Suddenly, something happened. He felt a chill throughout his body:

> . . . for I had heard the voice I was searching for: false and mawkish, moaning and mysterious, a voice wreaking with flattery and capable of saying terrible things without blanching; a voice which made me shudder, as I turned around bruskly on my chair and pronounced the name—Smerdiakov.
> A strange looking person stood before me: immobile and stiff, as if he were awaiting orders or an invitation, bending low with deference and a touch of obsequiousness.
> It was he, Smerdiakov, holding a little grey hat in his hands. He was wearing one of those old-fashioned black velvet jackets, and pants with elephant feet, and polished boots.
> While his red and pudgy hand—a kitchen maid's hand—smoothed down his greasy hair, and he looked impudently about inspecting

the walls of my room, I glanced at him rapidly. His face wore the pallor of a castrato, thin and wrinkled, outrageously framed by two tufts of slightly dirty red hair. There was a little drop of saliva in the corner of his purplish lips which, maintaining its equilibrium at first, inevitably slipped down to his chin and from his chin on to his white—completely white—vest.[12]

Smerdiakov revealed himself—his being—to Dullin in this remarkable exchange between the actor and his double. Only after this meeting could Dullin take him into himself and give one of the most extraordinary performances French audiences had seen in many a year. Indeed, he portrayed Smerdiakov time and time again throughout his long acting career and always to rave criticisms.

Jouvet put so much zest into his characterization of Father Karamazov, and he had such a fine grasp and understanding of this debauched and decrepit sinner, that he made him odious, and lascivious, winning high praise for his performance. As he walked about on stage, at times bent, at other moments straight, sneering and leering, he looked like a Rodin sculpture. Form had invaded the stage—an architectural construct more real than even the reality of his expression could convey.

Jouvet's makeup consisted of a long white beard, a mustache, and a wig. He wore a smoking jacket. In one scene, when the father is disputing with his sons, he leans forward in his mahogany chair and looks blearily across the table, his hands clutching the chair's arms, his face wearing an expression of such cynical amorality that the critic, Matei Roussou, labeled him "a terrific cynic, a guzzler, a drunkard . . . and in spite of this, one perceives, now and then, a mystical flash in him, like a bit of blue sky amid the gray of the clouds."[13]

Copeau conveyed Ivan's madness through bodily movements. His torso stood out in all of its loneliness upon a stark stage. Nervous, fidgety, nodding his head, looking furtively about, appealing directly to his audiences, he enticed them to share in his anguished madness. By way of suggestion and insinuation, he modulated his gestures, his stage-play, and his intonations. Copeau's Ivan was perhaps best described by Harold Clurman, the American director, who saw him years later performing the same role.

There is something incisive, precise in his play; the character's mystery is not expressed in any blurred or vague manner, but on the contrary, by a style which is at once austere and direct. There is something almost formidable in Copeau's lucidity.

Although Ivan is a highly emotional person, the portrait Copeau draws of him is severe and acidulous. Even in his mad scene in the last act, where he achieves great power, Copeau's emotions remain vigorous and always dominated by the mind. His play is always contained, tempered with reflection and without aridity, efficacity without artifice, intensity without violence.

Technically, Copeau perfects the remarkable exactitude and relief he gives his portrait, not by his admirable power of concentration, but by his diction whose purity and precision is unequaled. Copeau's language, nevertheless, retains its clarity, and its acute sense of rhythm which also rules his play; which is one of the greatest gifts of the metteur-en-scène.[14]

The lighting for *The Brothers Karamazov* was so expertly conceived and carried out that it, too, became personified. Tones of slate-grey permeated the stage, turning slowly into green, blue and violet, slowly, ponderously when needed, or frighteningly, when terror, doubt, and hatred raged.

Praise greeted Copeau and his troupe for the expertise of their performances and the uniqueness of the mise-en-scène. Elated by the sucess of the first season, the company left on March 23, 1914 for England, to regale their friends across the channel with a French fare. They succeeded, and returned to Paris to set to work on a new production of Shakespeare's *Twelfth Night*.

Shakespeare: Twelfth Night

Twelfth Night was produced at a critical juncture in the life of the Théâtre du Vieux-Colombier. Its fortunes up to this point had wavered and its finances were insecure; it had never quite firmly established itself. Individual actors, like Dullin and Jouvet, had had outstanding successes but the troupe as a whole, in comparison to the Boulevard theatres, had not achieved any remarkable success. Copeau, fundamentally a practical man, realized that the future of his theatre was at stake, to the extent that its very life might hang on the success or failure of *Twelfth Night*. He put more energy and planning than ever into this production.

Twelfth Night opened on May 22, 1914. There was much confusion at the last moment, some of it vastly amusing—for instance, the sight of Duncan Grant, the English painter, bespattered from head to foot with paint, rushing madly after the actors, with brush in hand, adding finishing touches to the already extraordinarily conceived costumes.

Translated by Thomas, *Twelfth Night* was a mélange of poetry, wit, sentiment, drama, and farce. The actors succeeded magnificently in re-creating the Shakespearian spirit, generous in its use of color, poetry, highflown hyperbole, and magnificent impudence. They enjoyed speaking the famous Elizabethan lines, ran the gamut of blitheness, from exquisite delicacy to emphatic bluntness and sometimes tortured rhetoric.

Copeau's scenic arrangement for *Twelfth Night* was arresting. The play was enacted on three different levels and with seem-ingly infinite perspectives. A balcony, a stage, a trap door, not only facilitated the rapid entrances and exits of the characters, but allowed them every now and then to peer in—their silhouettes evoking laughter or mystery—in the strangest and most humorous of ways. Such activity also served to create designs in space, further enhanced by the special lighting effects used throughout the performance. These at times gave the impression of floating and fantastic figures entering and withdrawing from the stage happenings; it also played up the actors' multiple movements, grimaces, and capers.[15]

Although Copeau had little confidence in musical interludes in theatre, believing they detracted rather than enhanced the textual material, the eight musical sequences introduced into *Twelfth Night* answered a specific need. At the very outset of the play, for example, when silence pervaded, violins began playing as the Duke of Illyria (Tallier), in love with Olivia, entered the stage.

> If music be the food of love, play on;
> Give me excess of it, that, surfeiting
> The appetite may sicken, and so die.
> That strain again! it had a dying fall:
> O! it came o'er my ear like the sweet sound
> That breathes upon a bank of violets,
> Stealing and giving odour. Enough! no more:
> 'Tis not so sweet now as it was before.

Then, followed by his courtiers, the Duke of Illyria stepped into the shadows, left stage, as Viola stepped into attenuated light, right stage, draped in veiled rose tones, and holding a palm in her hand. In keeping with the stage happenings was the interplay of the voices. The serious, grave, and melancholy tones of the Duke's words faded into the background, as a clear, well-timbred woman's voice softly imposed itself on the picture.   An instant later, guided by the Captain who had rescued her from a sinking ship, Viola followed the Duke's path toward the left. Only at the completion of these two scenes, which serve to prolong the musical sequence, does the curtain part, revealing a brilliantly lit stage, ready for the burst of activity which the play calls for.[16]

Olivia, who is in mourning for her brother, will not even receive the Duke's emissary.   Such aloofness elicits further excitement on his part.   Nor is her prolonged mourning looked upon favorably by her riotous uncle, Sir Toby Belch (Romain Bouquet).   As for Sir Andrew Aguecheek, a foolish but affluent knight whom Sir Toby has advanced as a candidate for his niece's hand, he is considered in a positive manner.   Sir Andrew is aware that defeat is his, but Toby persuades him to remain a month longer.   And so the plot thickens, with comic situations drawn from the *commedia dell'arte* and the *commedia erudita*.

The scenes between Sir Toby and Sir Andrew were unforgettable for their humor and their satiric intent.   Jouvet, the skinny, gawky, absurd Aguecheek, was as ludicrous as his seventeenth-century counterpart, Gaultier-Garguille.   He was "the puppet on lead-strings of tragedy" par excellence.   So amusing was he that Copeau wrote:

> That one over there, whom we see from behind walking backwards, his hand on the hilt of his sword, his sleeve flowing, his arched leg in a flame colored stocking and his head crowned with an azure-colored top hat in which two rose-colored wings have been inserted, that is Sir Andrew Aguecheek, master Jouvet in person. Jouvet perhaps has never acted a comic role with more savory naïveté, more delicacy or more poetry.[17]

As for Sir Toby, whose costumes emphasized his girth, he bounded forth on stage.   He was the reincarnation of Gros Guillaume. When Fabien (Antoine Cariffa), perhaps the modern Turlupin, joined the two clowns, as they pranced, danced, and finally fell over each other, bedlam broke loose in the audience.

> Sir Toby: I could marry this wench for this device.
> Sir Andrew: So could I too.

Copeau's production of Shakespeare's *Twelfth Night*

Sir T: And ask no other dowry with her but such another jest.
Sir A: Nor I neither.
Fabian: Here comes my noble gull-catcher.
    (Re-enter Maria. They prostrate themselves before her.)
Sir T: Wilt thou set thy foot o' my neck?
Sir A: Or o' mine either?
Sir T: Shall I play my freedom at tray-trip, and become thy bond slave?
Sir: I' faith, or I either?

As usual, there was little scenery for the play. Olivia's round room, where most of the action took place, had blue walls, a green semicircular bench, two flowering bushes, and a staircase. When the scene changed to the Duke Orsino's palace, the background consisted of pink drapes. When the action took place out of doors, the color of the drapes changed to indicate the passing from twilight to dawn. The drapes, on which the lights poured their luminous tints, produced a varied and enriching atmosphere. In each scene the lighting was altered, thus projecting a variety of stimulating colors and spotlighting the actors.

After a charming little clown drew the curtains at the finale, all the actors came on stage: Maria on the arm of Toby, the clown on Fabien's shoulders, the Countess with Sebastien, the Duke with Viola; then followed Andrew Aguecheek, Malvolio, the Captain of the Guards, and the ladies-in-waiting. They all stood together on the proscenium, which glittered with the colors of the rainbow: reds, greens, yellows and blues. The colors, together with the simpler lighting effects, created a strikingly brilliant impression.[18]

Twelfth Night was acclaimed by the critics as the Vieux-Colombier's most outstanding production, which glowed in one's memory with a procession of unforgettable images. As Claude Roger-Marx wrote:

> The simplification of the stage sets adapted at the Vieux-Colombier, the frequent use of draperies, gives free reign to dreaming. As for the interpretation, it reveals a comprehension of the work, an understanding which governs the studying and distribution of the roles. Let us admire the fact that, having sprung from a literary group, this theatre remains in such direct contact with life.[19]

The writer René Boylesve had never seen Shakespeare so well served: "I cried and I laughed, in sum, my reactions ran the gamut of emotions, a reaction a real spectacle should provoke."[20]

The English critic and man of the theatre, Granville-Barker, who was also present, was "surprised to discover that the French actors perform Shakespeare better than ours usually do." As for Claude Debussy, he marveled at the *livingness* of the production. He felt as if Shakespeare himself were going to come out and take a bow at the conclusion of the play. It reminded Duncan Grant of Watteau's painting, *Embarkment for the Island of Cythera*. The violinist, Pierre Lalo, commented on Shakespeare's "sublime poetry, fantasy and buffoonery" and the "marvelous intelligence and unity" of the production. The novelist, Henry Bordeaux, remarked that it "began with a sigh and ended with a song."[21]

More important was the fact that Shakespeare, disfigured for so many centuries by the French—because of poor translations, adaptations, and an incomplete understanding of the meaning of the English bard's words—had, thanks to Copeau and his troupe, been restored to greatness. One must not be afraid, Copeau suggested, "to return to our stage its primitive expression . . . the austere mise-en-scène always the rule during its great periods."[22]

*

The performers of the Vieux-Colombier were just beginning to create their ideal and to live their dream of revivifying the masters of the past and injecting life into contemporary dramatists. And Copeau warned them that theirs would be a life of *sacrifice* and *dedication.*

> If the actor is an artist, he is, of all artists, the one who the most sacrifices himself to the ministry he exercises. He can give nothing but himself, not in effigy, but in body and soul, and without intermediary. He is at once subject and object, beginning and end, matter and instrument; his creation is himself.
> Herein lies the mystery: that a human being can think of himself and look upon himself as the raw matter from which art is to be born; act on himself like as if upon an instrument with which one must identify, while still seeing oneself as separated from it; and, at the same time act and be what one is acting, natural man and marionette.[23]

Chapter 11

The Vieux-Colombier: The War
1914-1917

The year was 1914, and the shadow of what seemed inevitable war lengthened. The Archduke Francis Ferdinand, heir-presumptive to the throne of Austria-Hungary, and his wife were assassinated in Sarajevo on June 28. When war broke out in August, 1914, all the able-bodied men in Copeau's troupe were called upon to serve their country.

Copeau went into the auxiliary forces; Dullin, an infantry-man, was sent to Lorraine and Jouvet to the front. Other members of the troupe were scattered over the war area.

During those years of destruction, sadness, and despair, Copeau never lost contact with Jouvet or with Dullin. Lodged in dirty and wet barracks, often exposed to danger, they managed to correspond frequently. In their letters, they discussed such matters as a new school of acting which Copeau had, for a long time, very much at heart. He wrote:

> Since our method bears on the very nature and character of individuals who have already been molded by previous influences, we do not doubt that it will encounter strong resistance. Hence, in this respect, we should like to go much further in our reforms. This involves creating not only the theatre but—side by side with it and in the same framework—a real *school for actors*. Admission would be free and we would enroll, on the one hand, very young people and even children, and on the other hand, men and women who have a love and instinct for the theatre but who have not yet compromised this instinct by defective methods or professional routine. Such a group of new talents would later constitute the greatness of our undertaking. From among them we would get, in the first years, actors capable of playing bit-parts and a number of trained walk-ons who felt at home on the stage—far superior to those who are generally used.[1]

Copeau was brimming with new ideas even during this

repressive and turbulent period. Most of all, he wanted to open a school in which he could mold talented young children of high-school age and make genuine actors of them—actors without the faults and routine accretions of those trained in the commercial theatres. His school would feature a well-rounded and extremely ambitious program: courses in speech, the history of drama, physical education, the architecture and construction of theatres, singing, reading, the well-known analysis of the text, and the dancing advocated by Hippolyte Clairon.

Such was Copeau's plan. At the base of the structure would stand human beings, disciplined men and women, who, when graduated, would feed his theatre with constantly new and productive talents. In this way, the Vieux-Colombier would never become ossified or lack fresh human material or bold minds to throw new light on classical or modern plays.

Copeau was convinced that the new school he had in mind could seed and stimulate the progress of the modern theatre. After his demobilization, Copeau visited Gordon Craig, the son of Ellen Terry and an internationally famous scenic designer. Craig had founded a school in Florence in 1913, which was forced to close in 1914. However, he continued to live in Florence, adumbrating plans for a new school to be founded when the war ended. It was his tenet, and one supported by Copeau, that actors must absorb all that there is to be known about the theatre: carpentry, costume-making, lighting, drawing, and so forth. Craig and Copeau talked at great length about trends in the theatre and possibilities for future developments in stage settings. Copeau learned from Craig, who called for a poetic, suggestive, beautiful, and imaginative rather than a concrete and realistic theatre. In his *On the Art of the Theatre*, Craig wrote:

> The actor looks upon life as a photo-machine looks upon life; and he attempts to make a picture to rival a photograph. He never dreams of his art as being an art such for instance as music. He tries to reproduce nature; he seldom thinks to invent with the aid of nature, and he never dreams of *creating*. As I have said, the best he can do when he wants to catch and convey the poetry of a kiss, the heat of a fight, or the calm of death, is to copy slavishly, photographically . . . he kisses . . . he fights . . . he lies back and mimics death . . . and when you think of it, is not all this dreadfully stupid? Is it not a poor art and a poor cleverness, which cannot convey the spirit and essence of an idea to an audience, but can only show an artless copy, a fascimile of the thing itself. This is to be an

> Imitator not an Artist. This is to claim kinship with the Ventriloquist.[2]

Copeau did not accept Craig's ground for disposing of the unpredictable human actor in favor of predictable marionettes. The English theorist stated:

> Do away with the real tree, do away with the reality of delivery, do away with the reality of action, and you tend toward the doing away with the actor. This is what must come to pass in time, and I like to see the managers supporting the idea already. Do away with the actor, and you do away with the means by which a debased stage realism is produced and flourishes. No longer would there be a living figure to confuse us into connecting actuality and art; no longer a living figure in which the weakness and tremors of the flesh were perceptible.
>
> The actor must go, and in his place comes the inanimate figure —the uber-marionette we may call him, until he has won for himself a better name. Much has been written about the puppet—or marionette. There are some excellent volumes upon him, and he has also inspired several works of art. Today in his least happy period many people have come to regard him as rather a superior doll— and to think he has developed from the doll. This is incorrect. He is a descendant of the stone images of the old Temples—he is today a rather degenerate form of a God.[3]

Soon after Copeau's return to France, in October, 1915, Craig visited him, sharing more of his ideas with the French director, offering him the use of his *Screens* for his productions and a marvelously exciting lighting system which not only did away with footlights, but with batten lights (herse).

Copeau was soon on his way to Geneva to meet Émile Jaques-Dalcroze (1865-1950), the inventor of Eurythmics. Dalcroze's philosophy was based on the firm belief that rhythmic dancing should be taught to actors to enable them to coordinate their bodily movements with their speech. He also believed that every gesture, facial nuance, rhythmic device, must serve to exteriorize an inner voice. The actor must listen to this invisible world, see it, translate its message into plastic images, mobile moods, and spatial compositions. Copeau consulted Dalcroze on the best methods of organizing rhythmical dancing classes. Most of what Copeau heard was not new to him, but these associations helped to convince him more than ever of the necessity of establishing a school of theatre on the broad basis he had contemplated.

Jaques-Dalcroze introduced Copeau to Adolphe Appia (1862-1928), the Swiss theorist of modern decor and lighting and great Wagnerite, who put much stress on the affinities that must exist between music and dialogue. In *Music and Stage Setting* (1899), he wrote:

> The loftiest expression of the Eternal in Man can only be reborn and forever renew itself in the lap of Music. In return Music demands that we have implicit faith in her. . . . In order to express the inner reality underlying all phenomena the poet renounces any attempt to reproduce their fortuitous aspects and once this act of renunciation has taken place the complete work of art arises. . . . Then Wagner appeared. At the same time that his music-dramas revealed a purely expressive form of art, they also confirmed, what we had hitherto dimly sensed, the omnipontent power of music. . . .
> Music and music alone can co-ordinate all the elements of scenic presentation into a completely harmonious whole in a way which is utterly beyond the capacity of our unaided imagination. Without music the possibility of such harmony does not exist and therefore cannot be discovered. . . . [4]

Innovative as well were Appia's complex ideas concerning the use and manipulation of lights during the theatrical happening. He was convinced that light and shade, as handled by Rembrandt, Piranesi, and Daumier, could also become operational in the performing arts, fusing stage, scenery, and actor into a single power.

> Light is the most important plastic medium on the stage . . . without its unifying power our eyes would be able to perceive what objects were but not what they expressed. . . . What can give us this sublime unity which is capable of uplifting us? Light! . . . Light and light alone, quite apart from its subsidiary importance in illuminating a dark stage, has the greatest plastic power, for it is subject to a minimum of conventions and so is able to reveal vividly in its most expressive form the eternally fluctuating appearance of a phenomenal world. [5]

Since the actor is three-dimensional, Appia argued, the background, which reflects, adds and suggests so much of what the actor does, should be the same. In keeping with this thought, he wanted structured sets which could be combined into various planes, extending into space in a variety of forms and shapes. [6] When lights of all colors and combinations would be focused on them, their images and outlines would be continuously altering, creating sequences of hauntingly imaginative effects.

> The mobile (spot-light) apparatus will be utilized to create plastic light and its mechanical perfection will have to be made the object of the most careful study. In conjunction with the more or less stationary flood-lighting apparatus, screens of varying degrees of opacity will be used; their purpose will be to soften the over-sharp definition of light thrown by lamps on parts of the setting or on actors in close proximity to any particular light-source. But the major portion of the spot-lighting apparatus will be used to break up light and diversify its direction in every way possible. These lamps will be . . . of the greatest importance in maintaining the expressive effect of the total stage picture.[7]

Once back in Paris, in November 1915, Copeau coordinated his efforts with those of Suzanne Bing, an outstanding actress in his troupe who had worked on the school project during his absence. They were now in a position to open the school within the month, starting with a dozen pupils, boys and girls, under the age of twenty. Using elements of the theories he had learned from Craig, Jaques-Dalcroze, and Appia, he trained the student-actor to use *his or her body*. As such, the initial work centered on a special kind of class work: the imitation of animal sounds, and the assuming of shapes of trees, benches, and other inanimate objects, in order to make their bodies supple and adaptable for any theatrical purpose. Varied improvisations, rhythmic attitudes, and the use of masks were part of the training.

Copeau was tremendously ambitious. Not only were acting techniques revisioned, but everyone connected with his small theatrical enterprise—the machinists, the accessorists, electricians—had to bring fresh attitudes and new ways of viewing their work. Copeau was not a utopist or a dreamer, he assured Jouvet in a letter to Jouvet of Aug. 25, 1915, but rather a realist able to work with and face beings and things. He wanted to endow his actors with *style*. He was *uncompromising* in his attitude, as was another theatrical innovator whose work Copeau admired: Harley Granville-Barker (1877-1946), the English actor who attempted to perform Shakespeare in a manner approximating Elizabethan theatre conditions. In his "The Heritage of the Actor," he dealt with the difficulties facing directors at the turn of the century, with its dearth of drama and lack of exciting poetry for actors. According to Granville-Barker, the actor is empowered to adopt "the speech and action of the author's imagining, to elucidate the character in the terms of his own personality, when that gives the thing that apparent spontaneity of life which is the drama's peculiar virtue. . . ." In his *The Exemplary Theatre*, Granville-Barker also suggested—and Copeau agreed—that the student-actor should not be given lead or difficult parts prematurely.

For Copeau, theatre was sacred. It consisted of religious rituals which could be firmed through training. Each element, "from gymnastics to the notion of inner rhythm, to music, to dance, to masked mime, to speech, to elementary dramatic forms, to conscious play, to scenic invention, to poetry," was significant in creating the *whole* actor. As psyche and body must work harmoniously, so must the disparate parts of the acting technique. To achieve this goal requires study, practice, sensitivity, and understanding—and a master of ceremonies endowed with superior knowledge!

Molière was Copeau's reigning deity and his great inspiration. *The Love Doctor*, *The Miser*, *La Jalousie du Barbouillé*, were all given during the first season; *The Rogueries of Scapin*, *The Doctor in Spite of Himself*, *The Misanthrope*, in addition to repeat performances, were offered from 1917-1919. Molière seemed to answer most all of Copeau's theatrical needs: "elasticity, detente, movement, diversity, constant preoccupation with stage play . . . naïveté."[8] Copeau wanted to revivify Molière, render that marvelous "savor and taste" which had disappeared from his works through heavy, static, cumbersome offerings which French directors churned out since that time. To Molière's texts, which Copeau respected as he did the Scriptures, he would add what he had learned about music, pantomime, stage play, improvisation, rhythm, and dance. Words would no longer have to be committed to memory, learned as an intellectual exercise; they would flow forth from the actor's mouth, spontaneously and naturally—without artifice and with that wonderful *livingness* which existed whenever Molière performed and directed his own works. Copeau remarked:

> You say that a comedian enters into his role, that he puts himself into a character's skin. It seems that this is not exactly so. It is the character that approaches the comedian, who asks of him everything he needs, who replaces him in his skin. The comedian does all he can to free that inner terrain.
>
> To neither really envision nor understand the character one is to portray is sufficient to be able to become that being. To possess it does not mean one can endow it with life. One must be possessed by it.[9]

For Copeau, a fusion takes place between the interpreter and the character he is incarnating—the actor and that *other*. Behind the *persona* or mask, even the bare face, the actor feels or intuits the reality of his character, is commanded by it, and therefore obeys its dictates.   As the performer enters into another world, he assumes new responsibilities. In so doing, he sacrifices the domain of reality (worry, malaise, pain, suffering) or he "is delivered by it." A comedian must know his character so deeply and so extensively that even if something goes wrong with the lighting, accessories, costumes, or a lapsus or some other unfortunate situation occurs, he can continue without detaching or separating himself from his character. He is still master of it, submissive to it—and giving of it.[10]

A comedian must experience a sense of repose, calm, relaxation and silence in order to be able to bring forth the character's *right expression*.   He must rid himself of all false *attitudes*, preconceived *grimaces* and other tics.   To be *sincere* in one's creation is to allow the character to penetrate and enter into one's being in his or her way. To read the text out loud before even working out one's portrayal is to understand better the author's intent.   To remain humble, to submit oneself to the meaning, words, freshness of the creator is "to pick the words in all of their freshness" and "to add nothing except the involutary emotion experienced in their discovery."[11]

Once the comedian has experienced *calmness* and benefits from an *inner silence* he is better able "to listen, answer, remain immobile, begin a gesture, develop it, return to immobility and silence, with all the nuances and demi-nuances these actions entail."   To remain immobile on stage is difficult.   Many performers are simply unable to use this *prolongation of attitude*, this *silence* as a means of broadening and deepening a character; rather, they try to fill it with all sorts of facial gestures, bits of conversation, and really grotesque movements.   The result: the actor indulges in a panoply of excessive antics, thinking that these are natural means of fleshing out his incarnation. . He is unaware of the fact that "immobility, like silence, is expressive." It is a distillation of an inner climate, in which mysterious feelings take shape, activated to some final end. Only when one is immobile can gestures take root, develop, continue, progress in meaning, sign, and attitude—be true and beautiful.[12]

Improvisation, an intrinsic element in Copeau's school, would encourage his actors to invent *modern* characters, endowed with passions, faults, and ridiculous moral and social traits, and to costume them as well. The Intellectual (doctor, philosopher, professor, etc.); the Representative (deputy, minister, merchant, etc.); the Adolescent (the child, the school boy, the lover, the artist, the soldier, the idealist, etc.)—each character would belong to the actor and would become his private *property* which he would nourish by means of his own feelings, observations, and life experience. In this manner, Copeau would build a *confrérie* of *farceurs* who would play together, improvising, acting, singing, performing acrobatic stunts as they did in Molière's time. Copeau would divest the stage of all decors, using the performers' bodies, facial expressions, gestures, as accessories for the most part.

*

The war was still going on and during those black years the French government wanted to send an Ambassador of the Arts to the United States to introduce both French culture and the new theatrical methods to the American people. This, the government hoped, would strengthen the bonds of sympathy between the two nations. The French Ministry of Fine Arts sent Copeau to New York as France's unofficial cultural ambassador of good will on January 20, 1917. He delivered six lectures at the Little Theatre, the effect of which was that Otto Kahn invited Copeau to bring his troupe to the United States. That same year most of Copeau's cast had been demobilized at his request. Copeau had asked the Ministry of Fine Arts for their release so that they could participate in the cultural project and insure its success.

New York at this period had a large French colony, with a number of French musical and theatrical artists in it: Jacques Thibaud, the violonist; Robert Casadesus, the pianist; the Capet quartet; the inimitable *diseuse*, Yvette Guilbert, sang her songs and ballads before enthusiastic audiences and Pierre Monteux, the conductor, was in the ascendant. Because so many New Yorkers had such deep feelings for France—their ally friend since Lafayette's day—Copeau's troupe virtually took New York by storm. Aside from plays by Becque, Mérimée, Curel, Marivaux, Courteline, Port-Riche, Marivaux, Beaumarchais, Bernstein, Dumas, Ibsen, Rostand, Vigny, Maeterlinck, it was Shakespeare's *Twelfth Night* and Molière's *The Rogueries of*

Scapin, La Jalousie du Barbouillé, The Love Doctor, The Miser, The Doctor In Spite of Himself, and *The Misanthrope* that won the Vieux-Colombier troupe its highest praise. Copeau was right when he said that Molière would put his acting company on the map.

Molière: The Rogueries Of Scapin

The Rogueries of Scapin (1671), a prose comedy by Molière, takes place in Naples. Scapin (Copeau), is valet to Léandre, the son of Seignor Géronte (Jouvet). He is imaginative, intrepid, and lithe in every way. Léandre falls in love with Zerbinette, a gypsy supposedly, but really the daughter of Argante; she had been kidnapped by gypsies when a child. Her brother Octave falls in love with Hyacinthe, whom he supposes to be the daughter of the wealthy Hyacinthe Pandolphe of Tarentum, but who, it is later learned, is the daughter of Géronte and, so, sister of Léandre. The gypsies demand large sums for the ransom of Zerbinette, and Octave requires money for his marriage with Hyacinthe. Scapin, the rogue, obtains the sums from the two fathers, lying and cheating all the way. At the conclusion, he is brought to the wedding banquet on a litter, his head bound—almost dead. He begs for forgiveness, obtains it, then leaps up from the litter to join the banqueters.

Copeau's stage consisted of a gray desert; the only piece of scenery was a small platform-like structure. After much thought on the subject, both Copeau and Jouvet had decided in 1917 to construct an apparatus which was most unusual in conception: a small platform, consisting of four large squares of wood, abutted by five staircases, with four steps in each; and three cubes, which, when assembled, served as a bench between the two front staircases. Copeau wrote:

> The stage is already action, it gives material form to the action, and when the stage is occupied by the actors, when it is penetrated by action incarnate—then the stage itself disappears.[13]

When the curtains are drawn for *The Rogueries of Scapin,* audiences see a bare stage with the platform structure described above in the center; and, in the rear, a semicircular orange velvet curtain. Nothing more is on stage. When in Act II the agitated Argante, father of Octave and Zerbinette, appears on the proscenium, gripping his hat with one hand and with the other wiping his face free of perspiration, he makes his way in

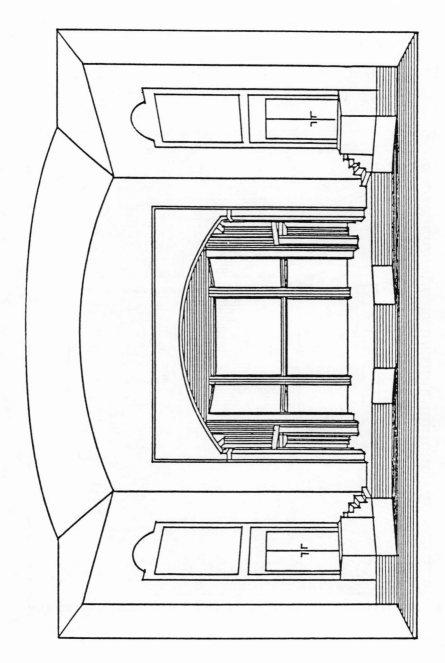

Stage design for the Vieux-Colombier, New York

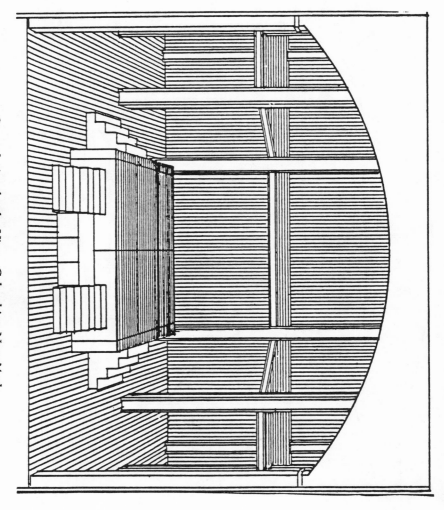

Stage design for the Vieux-Colombier, New York

arabesques around the wooden construct.   In direct contrast, Louis Jouvet, as Géronte, calm, takes short steps and holds a parasol over his head.   In Copeau's production, Géronte did not carry the traditional cane, but a parasol, which constituted an interesting innovation in itself.   Copeau and Jouvet thought that the parasol could more fittingly express the crotchets of his character; it also had the realistic function of protecting him from the torrid Neapolitan sun.   Here is psychological suggestiveness derived from the use of a single object.   In the course of the play Jouvet opens the parasol, closes it, strikes the ground with it, drags it behind him, and eventually uses it as a weapon, all of which is pantomimic and its significance is easily grasped by the audience.   Such postures, body movements, silhouettes, and the varied forms these images created on the proscenium, stood out in sharp relief on the bare platform.   Like sculptures in space, such motifs worked powerfully on the viewer' imagination and feelings.

Jouvet, as the *vieil os* Géronte, was physically decrepit and a victim of contending emotions—avarice, terror, rage, and humiliation. Jouvet gave all these feelings full scope and made excellent use of his almost vocal parasol, rendering the characterization with admirable breadth and humor.   The repeated cry "What the devil was he doing there?" was delivered with mounting force, yet with an infinite variety of comic overtones.

As Scapin, Copeau sought to emphasize the improvisational nature of this Italian dramatic form, as well as its violence and its cruelties.   A highly versatile and physically taxing part, Copeau brought out Scapin's turbulence, dynamism, and seemingly endlessly refreshing store of energy and imagination.   He was movement incarnate, cascading motility, leaping here and there, with long and lithe strides, stopping but for seconds—just enough time to think up new tricks, new deceits, acrobatic stunts, and rogueries, thereby accomplishing his ends in the most theatrically perfect way possible.   Rhythm is implicit in motility: it gives it its impetus, its variety, its comedy.   Scapin incorporated the spirit of mischief and ridicule in Molière.   He was robust and clever, youthful and racy—the opposite of Géronte in every respect.

After the second curtain call, a bust of Molière was brought on stage on a pedestal.   Then, silence.   Suddenly, the sound of Syrinx broke forth and a dancer, representing the satyric drama of antiquity, burst forth on the avant-scène and danced frantically, expressing joy, youth, and love. When he recognized Molière, he began dancing for him, with tenderness, moving closer and closer to the bust. Raising the flute he carried on him to his lips, he breathed into it, whereupon there emerged a kind of prolonged cry: wordless chorus-type singing emanating from backstage. The dance pursued its course for a bit, after which the evening concluded with a burst of laughter.[14]

The continual contrapuntal interplay between the characters in *The Rogueries of Scapin* was modeled on *commedia dell'arte* style. The actors made use of their entire bodies—face, hands, feet, voice—seeking through complex miming techniques to interpret the play as Molière himself might have done, with dancing, high spirits and light-footed comedy. Not one line of *The Rogueries of Scapin* was declaimed, as it still was at the Conservatoire; nothing about the interpretation was stilted; the words flowed naturally and with consummate artistry.[15]

Unfortunately, many in the audience were conditioned to their own traditional theatre, with its variety in stage sets and flat characterizations. Arthur Hornblow wrote that any actor could do as well as the French troupe if similarly trained in dancing and the like. Louis Defoe maintained that the play was merely a strenuous, turbulent farce, and an inadequate proof of the troupe's merits as artists or innovators. The grand qualities of the play were lost on the American critics, surfeited as they were by the harsh and glittering obviousness of American theatre. The pure spirit of comedy, playing upon passions and foibles of simple human beings, could not hold them; it seemed not only superficial, but unsophisticated—surprising, coming from the French. Copeau was disheartened, for the play that had delighted Parisian audiences was considered a cheap piece of buffoonery in America.[16]

Molière: The Doctor In Spite Of Himself

Copeau did not worship Molière as a classic who lived in some remote past era. He treated him as a contemporary and an intimate, and Molière had a way of kindling Copeau and bringing out the best in him as a director and actor. Each Molière play was examined anew every time it was performed and thought out from a fresh point of view. The characters, alive always, imposed themselves on Copeau's acute sensibilities. *The Doctor in Spite of Himself* (1666) was no exception. Audiences, witnessing the farcical theme and acute satire of the medical profession dear to Molière's heart since he had been so poorly treated by the doctors of his time, guffawed. The antics they saw on stage were so overtly humorous that some laughed to the point of tears.

Jouvet, who portrayed the lead, Sganarelle, the peasant conned into playing a doctor, was as striking in his demeanor on stage as the best of Daumier's caricatures. He pranced and mimicked; he was truculent as he gave vivid form and symmetry to his portrayal.

Copeau and Jouvet saw Sganarelle as a rude woodcutter with a heavy red beard, even though Martine, his wife, described him as being "a man with a large black beard." In addition to the red beard, he wore a mustache, with a trim unknown in the seventeenth-century. But this departure from historical accuracy went unnoticed by American critics.

In Act I, scene 6, Sganarelle is seated on a log, drinking and singing. Géronte's valet and steward approach him; standing on either side of him, they bow obsequiously and respectfully raise their hats. But Sganarelle pays no heed to them. At the finale of the scene, Sganarelle-Jouvet, half drunk, red-faced, and holding a bottle in his hand, falls over backwards, his legs flying straight up so that his face, with its flaming red beard, is framed between his long legs. Here Jouvet yields completely to the spirit of clowning. In his interpretation, he ran the gamut of emotions from light drama to comedy and outright farce; and his characterization was so completely integrated that it was constantly recognizable, human, vital, and vastly entertaining.

Under Copeau's direction and sensitive artistry, the cast once again wove the action into a living design, which, in turn, made for delightful and colorful visual impressions. High humor and abounding spirit served as Copeau's guide. *The Doctor in Spite of Himself* was declared a triumph by critics. The consultation scene in particular was singled out for praise: Sganarelle is called upon to cure a seemingly love-sick young girl; he slips into a virtual verbal frenzy as he speaks his well-known pseudoerudite lines, quoting mock-Aristotle with all the seriousness of a pedantic doctor of the time, bowing, scraping, and then demanding all the respect—and *money*—due such a wise and *great* physician.

Molière: The Misanthrope

The Misanthrope (1666) centers around Alceste, who has

vowed to say and act with complete candor and no longer obey the hypocritical conventions which govern human relations. During the course of the drama, he is pursued by the outwardly prudish Arsinoë; is unable to accept the real affection of the gentle and loving Eliante; and is in love with the sharp-tongued and arrogant coquette Célimène, the epitome—although he is unaware of it—of everything he despises. The loss of a law suit encourages Alceste to withdraw to the country where he will live far from the madding crowd. When he asks Célimène to join him and spend the rest of her days withdrawn from the frivolous life she leads in Paris, she refuses. Bitter and disillusioned, Alceste leaves.

The Misanthrope, a drama about incompatibility, not only satirizes an egotistic, self-satisfied, and hypocritical group of people, but also discredits the extremist attitude of a man who cannot adapt to the ways of others and rejects any life style that does not meet his demands. Extremes invite ridicule, and Molière, in his inimitable way, underscored the lengths to which pseudo-virtue will go to achieve its seeming end.

Copeau did not treat The Misanthrope as a highly didactic play or as a tragedy (as had been the custom throughout the nineteenth-century) but as a comedy—the way Molière had performed it. Nor did he have Alceste discourse at length on his philosophy of life, as actors of the Comédie-Française were wont to do. On the contrary, Alceste was portrayed as quite normal and understandably human. Although deeply introverted and unable to find a common denominator with people in general, suffering and pained each time he considered that purity and integrity had been violated, the extremes to which he carried his beliefs underscored the pathetic humor of the situation.

Copeau who played the complex figure of Alceste, a character so many have analyzed in countless volumes on Molière, revealed his foibles progressively throughout the play in successive illuminations of facets of the misanthrope's prismatic being. Although Alceste does not appear in every scene—he is hardly on stage in the third act—he is the focus of attention, since everything that happens in the play is related to him. For example, when Molière, in Acts One and Two, explores some of the notions and consequences of Alceste's point of view, he prepares the spectators for the hallucinating figure around whom the drama pivots. He also sets the stage to test Alceste's theories, orchestrating each in turn, encouraging the protagonist to do battle with them in salon society—and faulting all the while.

Copeau's subdued and controlled gestures, the slow and crystal clarity of his speech, the varied rhythms he injected into the dramatic edifice which is Alceste, fascinated the viewers. Copeau's unforgettable countenance—his eyes cast down or sometimes looking to the side, attempting to assimilate in small doses the pathos of his situation—was startling. Although at first glance Alceste seems a tragic figure, as mentioned previously, his role is rich in comic material: not only because of the protagonist's exaggerated ideas, but because of his petulance, his self-centeredness, and also because in certain ways he is just like the others. Alceste, as the rest of humanity, wants to be appreciated: "Je veux qu'on me distingue."

Like Alceste, Arsinoë also says what she means, but does so with spite and ire: "in all encounters / Let the depth of our hearts be evident in what we say." Sincerity can be a brutalizing force; it can pain others and emphasize unpleasantness, as Philinte (Jouvet), the spokesman for a reasonable way, suggested from the very outset. To speak the truth can be searing, but also irritating, remarked the beauty, Célimène: if everyone spoke the truth one would surely destroy an individual's self-esteem. The idealist Alceste, then, turns out to be a fop, and a pedant—an aspect of his personality which Copeau brought out only too clearly in his stage play. His narrow view and uncompromising nature are enunciated in halting as well as brusk vocal intonations, at a clipped pace, followed by protracted silences. His facial expressions and subtle body language paralleled his speech patterns, thereby creating the sought-for unified effect.

Just as Copeau had rid his proscenium of the clutter of nineteenth-century decors and accessories, so he divested his character of the multiple tics and refinements which countless performers had attached to this role. It was Copeau's custom, when creating a mise-en-scène or a portrayal, to go back to the sources—in this case, to Molière and the actors and technicians who had left written records of the performances. Only then could he begin to build his characters, endowing each with a soul of his own. Copeau achieved his end because he vowed, in the real sense of the word, to pursue an *austere* course, to perform on *a poor stage*, devoid of accoutrements, thereby permitting freedom for the nourishment of the objective/subjective actor and his double.

> A pure spirit, a spirit of fantasy and imagination, the free comic
> spirit of our fathers that we have weighted down with so many
> literary intentions and cerebral refinements, can breathe with life
> only on a bare stage.[17]

Copeau had stated this same idea most clearly in 1917:

> To give up the *idea* of decors.
> The barer the stage, the more can action give birth to its won-
> ders. The greater the austerity and rigidity, the freer the play of
> the imagination.
> It is on material constraint that spiritual freedom builds itself.
> The actor must realize everything, extract everything from him-
> self, on this arid stage.
> The comedian's problem—his play, the intimate *movements*
> intrinsic to the work performed, the purity of his interpretation—is
> thus posed in all of its amplity.
> *A bare stage and real comedians.*[18]

The fact that Copeau did not treat Molière as some relic
from a remote past, but rather as a contemporary and an intimate, gave new life to the seventeenth-century drama-
tist/actor/director, while also helping the twentieth-century
man of the theatre to give the best of himself and his troupe.
Their fresh and spirited approach to Molière reinforced the
sound classical style of the play while also underscoring its vitality and humanity.

Molière: The Miser

Copeau looked upon *The Miser* (1668) as a scenic unit—as
a "dance" revolving around one character, the rest of the cast setting off the protagonist in his or her own way.[19]

Although the miser is a stock character, the butt of ridicule since ancient times, the love of money is not essentially a
humorous trait. On the contrary, it is a vice which seems not to
appeal to audiences. Even Molière's *The Miser*, enacted in a
mood of banter and with satiric intent as well, was only performed eighteen times during the dramatist's lifetime. How did
Molière's Harpagon, differ, then, from Plautus's miser in
Aulularia, a good-humored stage concoction replete with gags,
puns, and confusion resulting from a variety of tricks played on
unsuspecting individuals? Or Ben Jonson's *Volpone*, which
sought to expose and shame the man obsessed with gold and to
debase this kind of creature by rendering him perverse and
ludicrous?

Molière's miser, Harpagon, as played by Dullin, does not merely amass gold for the pleasure of it. He sees it, perhaps unconsciously, as a guarantee against old age, impotence and death. Gold, for Harpagon, becomes a vehicle for a type of Faustian renewal and gratification of lustful desires. His avarice has so perverted him that it becomes the motivating force for all of his acts and the cause of his own dishonesty, as well as that of his children and servants.

Dullin, as had Molière before him, presents his audiences with a monomaniac—a man whose life revolves around an *idée fixe*. His actions, in this regard, are automatic and predictable. Nevertheless, his obsessions motivate him to act in strange ways, forcing him into the most comic of circumstances and situations. Stiff and uncompromising, Dullin's gestures and facial expressions, reserved and bound to his one-sided view of life, were humorous. As Bergson remarked, comedy emerges more from "rigidity than from ugliness."

Just as Molière knew how to *transpose* real life beings onto the stage, so, too, did Dullin. He incarnated Alceste intermittently for the rest of his career. Audiences always flocked to his interpretation of a character which he had made his own. Like Molière, Dullin knew how to make the most of small scenes or minor actions, using them to the fullest to accentuate Harpagon's one-sided nature, in real *commedia dell'arte* style. "Show me your hands," Harpagon tells his servant. And when he does so, and the miser realizes that no money is hidden within the palm of the hand, he stupidly says: "And the other." At another time, when Harpagon thinks he is being robbed, he bellows "Who is there? Stop," as he grabs his own arm. "Ah! It is I! My mind must be troubled. I don't know what I am doing, where I am." This episode certainly has farce-like ramifications. However, it also reveals Harpagon so deeply immersed in his obsession that he has lost all contact with the outer world. His mental powers, now virtually destroyed, emphasize his intractable and unchangeable nature.

Because Dullin had absorbed the vitality and ingenuity of the *commedia dell'arte* style, he was able to endow this obsessive, lunatic type with depth and pathos as well as with humor. Not that Dullin moved around the stage with alacrity; on the contrary, his gestures and pace were stilled, reserved, as if he were conserving not merely his gold, but the very essence of the life force. As Harpagon's fixation grew in force and dimension, so, too, did Dullin's plastic image of this being take on greater force and dimension. The consensus: the portrayal was "unforgettable."[20]

Dullin/Harpagon, incapable of human love, had transferred his entire emotional world onto money, which fed his every need: "He loves money more than reputation, honor and virtue." Only when experiencing extreme distress does his abject hardness vanish, and love emerge, albeit his love for money. "Alas, my poor money, my poor money, my dear friend, they have deprived me of you; and since you have been taken from me, I have lost my support, my consolation, my joy; all is finished for me and I want nothing more to do with the world." As long as Harpagon's complex was fed, as long as it dominated his pattern of existence, all continued on its regular course. When, however, he yields to sexual impulse, when he decides the world is his and the demonical power-urge takes hold of him, his realm disintegrates: his money vanishes and his plans to marry a young girl are dispelled. Yet, despite his own fundamental egotism—cruelty, one might say—Harpagon has children who love him and seek his love in return.[21]

Mérimée: The Carriage of the Holy Sacrament

Prosper Mérimée's *The Carriage of the Holy Sacrament*, produced on December 5, 1917, met with a "rare triumph." Under Copeau's baton, Mérimée's work, always considered unplayable, was brought to life with a never-before-seen freshness, liveliness, and excitement. In this short play, Jouvet acted unforgettably the part of the unctuous Archbishop of Lima, and designed and constructed the sets and created the lighting effects.

The play takes place in the eighteenth-century. The scene, the office of the Viceroy of Lima. Don Andres de Ribera, the Viceroy (Copeau), is completely infatuated with his mistress, the coquettish Périchole (Lucienne Bogaërt). The play reveals her strength and his weakness.

The costumes were colorful. It was interesting to observe that the characters appeared on stage in the order of the intensity of the colors of their costumes: that is, the first person to walk upon the proscenium, the Viceroy's secretary, wears brownish-yellow. The Viceroy himself appears next in a golden brocaded costume which seems to glitter under the lights; then La Périchole with her green, pink, and yellow dress and her Spanish mantilla. Later, the Archbishop comes on stage wearing his violet robes, skull cap, and white lace surplice. Standing in sharp contrast are the other clergymen, all in dusty black robes. A bright lemon-yellow light floods the stage and re-creates the atmosphere of Peru. The scenery, sparse as usual, consisted of four bright green plants surrounding the desk of the Viceroy. A drape, stained with a medley of bright colors, served as an exit-entrance.[22]

Copeau deftly underscored the unity existing among the Peruvian atmosphere, the colors of the costumes, the dialogue, and the actors' play to such an extent that the entire production, critics remarked, formed a cohesive whole. *The Carriage of the Holy Sacrament* was a feast for the eyes and an enchantment for audiences in New York, and in subsequent productions, in Paris and on tour.

*

World War I was over and the Vieux-Colombier returned to Paris in 1919. Now the troupe comprised a mature group of actors who had had the satisfaction of seeing their contributions to the theatre accepted in foreign lands. Despite some incomprehension and misunderstandings, the body of critics writing in New York newspapers and magazines realized that this French theatre had in some ways been wonderful and had sown the seeds of sound theatrical principles in American soil. In Paris again, they were more highly esteemed than ever. They had become a focal point of attraction for many of the finest writers, painters, musicians, and actors in Europe, and were to continue to thrive in this friendly atmosphere, with results beneficial to all concerned with the arts.

Chapter 12

Productions at the Théâtre du Vieux-Colombier
(1919-1924)

Once back in Paris, Copeau again made structural changes
in his theatre. Bare as usual, the stage now extended far forward.
A balcony was built in the rear, supported by four columns
which, whenever necessary, could be concealed by a drape. It
had three exits. On either side of the stage stood two towers, four
in all, each with a door, a staircase, and a window. A removable
platform on a slightly lower level reached to the front of the
stage. This construct provided for an extension of the stage and
could be used when necessary for the action; it also offered additional exits and entrances. The stage itself was constructed of
removable cement blocks.

The Vieux-Colombier troupe once again felt the excitement of opening night, on February 10, 1920, but how different
this opening was from the first in 1913. The actors were now
trained to the peak of perfection. The troupe was still intact,
with one exception: Dullin had broken with Copeau in New
York. The actors established an emotional rapport with their
audiences, which gave them a fuller sense of appreciation and
sympathetic collaboration. So here there existed a rare *esprit de
corps*. It would be considered almost indiscreet on the part of
friends of the troupe to single out one actor for special praise and
to put him above the others because it would disturb the atmosphere of equality, dedication, and craftsmanship that prevailed.

Shakespeare: The Winter's Tale
With *The Winter's Tale* (1611), the Théâtre du Vieux-
Colombier reached another dimension in its growth and depth.
Copeau loved Shakespeare as he did Molière, and read his plays
year in and year out. Never since Elizabethan times had the
theatre offered scripts comparable to Shakespeare's, which afford-
ed actors infinite possibilities to express passion, poetry, wit, and

to move with grace and beauty. Never since then had the actor had such freedom of movement on the stage, while audiences participated in the action with imaginative abandon. The Elizabethans had enlarged the forestage around which the audience sat, and therefore the audience had multiple contact with the players. The Italians, during the Renaissance, did the opposite, pushing the stage back behind a proscenium arch, reducing the playing area, and thus limiting the actor's freedom of movement. Copeau observed that since a restricted stage area had become the tradition, there had been scant opportunity for the actors to fully express the richness called for by the text. The advantages that depth and perspective could yield, richly magnifying the play's effectiveness, were lost. The result was a hampering of dramatic illusion. In Copeau's theatre, on the contrary, the action whirled all about the spectators, establishing a close contact with them and increasing communication.

For the production of *The Winter's Tale*, sets were made which would permit the action to flare up on one part of the stage, subside, and flare up at another, thus giving the audience a sense of rapid and busy sequence. Part of the stage would be illuminated wherever a scene was being enacted; drapes, behind which the company would be shifting sets for the following scene, covered the rest. The footlights had been done away with; the border of the stage was painted gray; the floor was of cement. All this produced an austere impression—the kind Copeau had meant when referring to a "poor theatre." Yet, the stage had the dignity and awesome nature of early Greek temples. There were only two exits on the stage—a walk-out through the garden and another in the rear. The stage itself was subdivided in the rear, to the right a door, to the left a staircase. The crowds, when called for, stood on the stairs, making for a superb mass impression. For instance, in the scene in which the queen is judged, the people gathered about on the stairs, producing the effect of a highly solemn assembly. There were a few props—a bed, some chairs made of lightly colored cubes, a throne, also made of cubes in a pyramid-like structure, and the staircase.

The costumes, designed by Fauconnet shortly before he died, were sober in line but beautiful in texture and fresh and lively in color. When the lights shone upon them, they assumed an exquisite fairy-like quality, charging the atmosphere with fantasy. A delicate and subtle suffusion of light made the scene of the Queen's vigil at the castle of Leotes extraordinarily effective. In this scene, the Queen's ladies in-waiting were chatting on the side of the stage under dim lantern lights; on the other side, the Queen was caressing her son. Because of the inspired lighting arrangement, the groups were harmoniously composed and not set apart; they were emotionally related and in fluid contact. The scene recalls the almost formal complementary poses in medieval sculptures. Lighting, as now used, was not only a force that pictorially enhanced the action and suffused the atmosphere to make just the appropriate dream-background, but it also added a subtle spiritual aura to the action. It made situations more emphatic or intangible or highly suggestive. The lighting fleshed out the characters' emotions, heightening or diminishing them as the case might be, or setting them into bolder relief by the manipulation of lights. The production was a masterpiece of stagecraft and direction.

In spite of all the love and devotion Copeau and his troupe gave *The Winter's Tale*, the Parisians remained indifferent. They were not impressed by the bareness of the grey walls, by the cement and the few decors. Some Shakespearian specialists considered it an affront to the master. Henri Ghéon did not care for the production as a whole, but he did highly commend the mise-en-scène and the acting.

> Before these ardent and docile young people, surrounded by a few older members whose experience is known to us all, one has the impression of disciplined spontaneity, of joyous rivalry, of a marvelously diverse source of energy which asks only to come to the fore, in brief, of an almost boundless reservoir for the author who might want to work with them.[1]

André Suarès was delighted with the production and the troupe's "loving and absolute submission to great poetic works." As for Antoine, he was impressed by the sincerity of this artistic enclave and felt that all interested in the furthering of theatre should support its work. Copeau, however, was disappointed and stunned to learn of the audiences' indifferent or negative reactions to a play which he had worked on with such love and care and which he considered "a marvel."[2]

*

Having decided, upon his return from New York, to remodel the forestage by projecting it out into the audience,

Copeau thereby eliminated some of the orchestra seats, cutting out the sales of 200 seats. Although the theatre was most frequently filled to capacity, the receipts could not cover expenses. Either the theatre would have to be enlarged or it would lose money on every performance, no matter how successful. A deficit of 116,000 francs was declared on July 17, 1920.

Reactions to this state of affairs soon set in. Copeau had always depended on gifts and donations in the past and he had almost always succeeded in obtaining them. Many members of the troupe were dissatisfied with this insecurity, which seemed to be chronic with the Vieux-Colombier, and they wanted to stabilize the situation. But Copeau fought off all arguments for commercializing his theatre; he was afraid that his freedom might be curtailed and jeopardized in some manner.

*

Copeau also turned his attention at this juncture to the reopening of his school of acting which he had had to close before his New York tour. He finally reopened the school in the fall of 1920, on the same basis as in the past. However, since he lacked space in his theatre to house so large an undertaking, he set up the school at 9 Rue du Cherche-Midi. Its program was to train students from the ages of fourteen to twenty in a broad group of subjects related directly or indirectly to the stage, such as diction, stage setting, makeup, physical education, the history of drama, play analysis, poetic and realistic techniques, and so forth. Frequently, writers and others famous in the arts were invited to lecture there. Jules Romains, the dramatist and novelist, became the director of the school and Mlle Marie-Hélène Copeau (now Marie-Hélène Dasté), its secretary. The school had probably the most brilliant and best-equipped teaching staff in France at the time.

Copeau taught a course on the history of the theatre, its religious origins, its scope, its development through Greek drama, with special stress on the tragedies of Aeschylus, Sophocles, and Euripides. Satire and the comedies of Aristophanes were taught as well. He also gave lessons in dance, improvisation, impromptu dialogue, pantomine, on how to arouse dramatic instinct, spontaneity, and inventiveness in the adolescent.

Jules Romains taught the techniques of poetry, prosody, and both ancient and contemporary versification. George Chenevière delved into analyses and practical exercises related to prosody in general, from ancient to modern times. Romain Bouquet taught courses in diction, in stage play, in the mise-en-scène. Music, solfeggio and singing, both solo and choral, were taught by Mme. Jane Bathori. Physical education, hygiene, breathing, and body tone were part of the program, as well as geometry, drawing, modeling, painting, and working with wood, leather, and cardboard.

Louis Jouvet gave courses on the theory of theatrical architecture; on Greek theatre in general; and on the relationship between audience and actor, orchestra and stage, stage and audience. Problems revolving around acoustics, visibility, lighting, were also studied. Jouvet was also technical advisor to those giving workshops in the practical study of stage material, geometric drawings, modeling, painting, working in wood, leather, cardboard, cutting and sewing. This studio work permitted the greatest latitude for the initiative and spontaneous taste of the student. Games, group walks to the museums, monuments, and gardens also entered into Copeau's plans.

The Vieux-Colombier ateliers were very simple, with an overall artisan-like atmosphere. The smooth functioning of the organization rested squarely on the shoulders of the directors of the workshops, strikingly similar to medieval guilds. The students were respected, never driven, and rarely given to excess; and a spirit of cooperation unified them. Each student pursued his work with untrammelled spirit under the sympathetic but vigilant eye of the *Patron*.

Copeau wanted to instill in his students a respect for manual labor, intellectual curiosity, and moral and spiritual honesty. He also believed that an artist could not develop into a fully rounded comedian with the ability to present the salient facets of a character unless he were intimate with every function of the theatre, such as lighting, scenic design, and the rest. In this, he agreed with Gordon Craig. The neophyte must, of course, learn how to use his body, hands, feet, and face to be able to project the integrated character across to the audience. His muscles must become flexible with constant use in such tasks as constructing scenery or in some work involving bodily activity connected with the theatre, which demands physical as well as mental effort; and above all, he must have a genuine delight in and love for all he does in the theatre. Without pleasure as a driving force, everything is done in a halfhearted way, and thus falls short of full realization.

The importance of a close rapport between the *lieu drama-tique*, where the action takes place, and the *lieu théâtral*, from which the action is followed, is imperative. Copeau's two sea-sons in New York had brought this home to him: the relation-ship had often been lacking, to the eventual detriment of the production. Stress upon this rapport was taught at the Vieux-Colombier and new vistas were constantly searched out. The classes almost always ended with an exchange of ideas between student and teacher, arousing the curiosity of the students to an even higher pitch.

The curriculum lasted approximately three years. The stu-dents who successfully passed the final examination had to per-form with the Vieux-Colombier group for another three years. They were given a modest salary, and forbidden to act with any other troupe. After that, they were free to go on their own and branch out as they pleased, or, if very gifted, they might be invi-ted to stay on with the Vieux-Colombier.

Copeau was deeply moved when his school became a real-ity; he vowed never to give up his theatrical ideal, never to allow his future to be marred through compromise, never to "enrich a group of capitalists or fatten a tribe of functionaries."[3] Originality and creativity were his bywords.

> I would like to *lock up every book*, and prevent you from using them. . . . You would be allowed to look at only graphic documents. Past learning, would be broached by *Me*, who would digest it, clar-ify it, and would transmit it to you little by little, *completely fresh, completely new*, pêle-mêle, with still unpublished personal findings. *No reconstruction*. Creation. Life.[4]

What was of import to Copeau and to his followers was to discover the text's inner and inter-action—its line, color, tone, and rhythm. Theatre was to be not representational, in the fash-ion of an Antoine or of a Stanislavsky, but suggestive, nuanced. Its aim was to create the "image of reality" and not "the reality of the image."[5] What Copeau sought to eternalize was "the actor moving about on a surface"—creating, thereby, a visual feast for the spectators.

The dramatist/poet is the comedian's guide, argued Copeau.

> The poet alone is the real source and life of all drama, as Aeschylus was for Greek drama; and the metteur en scène must capture the

spirit of that primitive unity in drama and incorporate its rhythm into the work. There must be full and complete coordination.[6]

Unlike Craig and Reinhardt, Copeau considered the director not the master of the stage happenings, but the poet's stage assistant.

> His (director) virtues are sincerity, modesty, maturity, reflexion, eclecticism; he does not invent ideas, he finds them anew! His role is to translate the author, to read the text, to experience its inspiration, to possess it, as the musician sight reads notes, sings them in key.[7]

Interestingly, Copeau attributed the decadence of play writing to the increased use of stage decorations and materials of all sorts. To rely upon accoutrements instead of the genius of a dramatist is to create *literary* works.[8]

*

In addition to the school and his writings on theory, Copeau was also producing play after play: *The Death of Sparta* by Jean Schlumberger, interesting because it reverted to the form of the *décor simultané*, which had been popular in the Middle Ages; revivals such as *The Doctor In Spite of Himself*, *The Enchanted Goblet* by La Fontaine and Champmeslé, *Phocas the Gardener* by Émile Mazaud, *The Carriage of the Holy Sacrament* by Merimée, *Love, The Golden Book* by Tolstoy, *Mr. Trouhadec Overcome with Debauchery* as well as *Crommedeyre-le-Vieil* by Romains, *Saul* and *King Candaule* by Gide, *Le Paquebot Tenacity* and *Michel Auclair* by Vildrac, and others.

Tours throughout France and foreign lands were arranged for Copeau and his troupe. Audiences were intrigued with his new methods and approach to theatre: the *bare stage*, the *poor theatre*, the spirit of *purity, austerity* and *dedication*, the sincerity and naturalness with which the actor absorbs his character. The Vieux-Colombier was not only well known; it had become stylish—a conversation piece! Alexander Woolcott remarked that nothing in Paris was as fascinating as the programs given at the Vieux-Colombier. Despite the high praise and the success Copeau's endeavors enjoyed, empty coffers awaited him. If he were to pursue his work, his friends told him, he would have to stop *philosophizing*. To which Copeau replied unequivocally:

What I call *living*, is to affirm one's nature, to follow one's spiritual destiny. Outside of this path, I find death. It is toward death that you drive us, if you urge us to follow a false route; if you do not respect our thought above all else; if you only know how to see material powers when in reality, the spirit has created everything; if you want to *exploit the idea of the Vieux-Colombier* before it has reached maturity, before the Vieux-Colombier has accomplished its *deed.*[9]

Copeau was intransigeant. He refused to plan for his future since that would encroach upon his freedom. "I would rather live day by day, as a beggar." Soon, Jouvet, Romains, and others left the Vieux-Colombier troupe, ready to carve out their own paths as actors, director, dramatists and novelists. The Vieux-Colombier Théâtre closed its doors at the end of the 1924 season, but Copeau did not cease being a man of the theatre. He retired to Bourgogne, where he established his school. His disciples, "les Copiaux," formed their own group without Copeau, and toured under the name of the "Company of Fifteen." From 1931 to 1933, they performed at the Vieux-Colombier, then travelled for several years. Although Copeau refused to take part in theatrical enterprises in Paris, he was associated from 1936 on with the Comédie-Française and directed its programs from 1939 to 1940. Considered undesirable by the Germans and by the Vichy government, Copeau withdrew once again to Bourgogne until his demise.

*

"We work day and night, without respite, looking ahead as our ideal grew," Copeau wrote when first founding the Vieux-Colombier Théâtre. He was not mistaken. The great theatrical reformer that he was had been the nourishing force and the catalyst for what is most innovative in twentieth-century theatrical direction, acting, and stage architecture.

Conclusion

The Reign of the Theatrical Director.   *French Theatre 1887-1924* has attempted to bring to light some aspects of the productions and performances of three great theatrical innovators: André Antoine and his Théâtre Libre, Lugné-Poë and his Théâtre de l'Oeuvre, and Jacques Copeau and his Théâtre du Vieux-Colombier.

The talents, energies, and drive of these three directors brought fresh and vital works to the stage while also injecting new life into classical texts.   Plays by foreign authors—Ibsen, Strindberg, Tolstoy, Hauptmann, Gogol, Wilde, Poe, and more—were accepted for production by Antoine, Lugné-Poë, and Copeau, lending an international flavor to their endeavors. Painters, such as Vuillard, Bonnard, Toulouse-Lautrec, Forain, Signac, and Munch, were invited to create backdrops and sets, bringing greater artistry to their productions.

Just as Antoine, Lugné-Poë, and Copeau had been hostile to Boulevard commercialism, so they shed the fustian and decadent ways of old theatre.   They created a community spirit between all segments of the dramatic arts. In so doing, new relationships were established between cast and director, working together within a truthful, simple and meaningful scenic architecture. So, too, was there a rapprochement between performers and spectators.

Young and untried dramatists were given a chance to see their works produced; actors and actresses with talent, but with little or no previous experience, were also offered the opportunity to perform in these "laboratory" theatres.   An esprit de corps reigned at the Théâtre Libre, the Théâtre de l'Oeuvre, and the Théâtre du Vieux-Colombier.

Prior to the advent of Antoine, Lugné-Poë, and Copeau, few directors had ever been given the opportunity to imprint their stamp on productions. The choice of plays to be performed became their responsibility, as did the casting, costuming, lighting, decors, and mise-en-scène. Directing, as they practiced this art, became a stunning outlet for their talents.

Is it any wonder, then, that Paris tingled with excitement; that a new generation of actors learned and benefitted from the revolutionary transformations effected by Antoine, Lugné-Poë, and Copeau? Men of the theatre, such as Louis Jouvet, Charles Dullin, Georges and Ludmilla Pitoëff, Gaston Baty, Antonin Artaud, Roger Blin, Jean-Louis Barrault, Jean Vilar, and so many more, were instrumental in bringing dramatic art to new heights.

The role of the theatrical director not only became noteworthy in France, but throughout the world: Max Reinhardt, Edwin Piscator, Gordon Craig, Harley Granville-Barker, Adolphe Appia, Konstantin Stanislavsky, Vladimir Nemirovich-Danchenko, Nikolai Evreinov, Vsevolod Meyerhold, Alexander Tairov, and more, revealed their creative artistry in multiple ways.

Antoine, Lugné-Poë, and Copeau were ground-breakers. Recoiling from drawing up fixed rules to which actors or playwrights would be forced to adhere, they preferred to be guided by their sensibilities and, as far as humanly possible, with a mind devoid of personal, literary, or historical preconceptions. They relied on experience to assess the rhythms of the dialogue and the structure of the play. Nor did they hesitate to follow the dictates of intuition, if need be, for they realized that the truths of the theatre are not always rational truths. To explore, to experiment, and to create was their way as it had been the path taken since earliest times.

It may be said that Antoine, Lugné-Poë, and Copeau not only enhanced the director's role, but also renewed, recast, and reorganized French theatre. The poem written about the three well-known seventeenth-century *farceurs*—Gros-Guillaume, Turlupin, and Gaultier-Garguille—who transformed their art from roving comics and mountebanks to established professional actors, is also applicable to the founders of the Théâtre Libre, the Théâtre de l'Oeuvre, and the Théâtre du Vieux-Colombier:

> How magnificent is this stage,
> How inventive are these actors!

List of Productions and First Performances
at the Théâtre Libre

1887

March 30: *Mademoiselle Pomme (Miss Apple)*. Comedy-farce in one act in prose by Edmond Duranty and Paul Alexis.

Un Préfet (The Prefect). Drama in one act in prose by Arthur Byl.

Jacques Damour. Play in one act in prose from a short story by Émile Zola, adapted for the stage by Léon Hennique.

La Cocarde (The Vain One). Comedy in one act in prose by Jules Vidal.

May 30: *La Nuit Bergamasque (Night of the Bergamasque)*. Comedy in three acts in verse by Émile Bergerat.

En Famille (In the Family). Play in one act in prose by Oscar Méténier.

1878-1888

October 11: *Soeur Philomène (Sister Philomène)*. Play in two acts in prose from a Goncourt novel, adapted for the stage by Arthur Byl and Jules Vidal.

L'Évasion (The Escape). Drama in one act by Villiers de l'Isle-Adam.

November 11: *Belle Petite (Little Beauty)*. Comedy in one act in prose by André Corneau.

La Femme de Tabarin (Tabarin's Wife). Tragi-parade in one act in prose by Catulle Mendès.

Esther Brandès. Play in three acts in prose by Léon Hennique.

December 23: *La Sérénade (The Serenade)*.   Three-act comedy in prose by Jean Jullien.

Le Baiser (The Kiss). Comedy in one act in verse by Théodore de Banville, with music by Paul Vidal.

Tout pour l'Honneur (All For Honor's Sake).   Drama in one act from *Captain Burle* by Emile Zola, adapted for the stage by Henry Céard.

February 10: *La Puissance des Ténèbres (The Power of Darkness)*. Drama in six acts in prose by Leo Tolstoy. Translation by Pavlovsky and Méténier.

March 23: *La Pelote (The Pin Cushion)*. Comedy in three acts in prose by Paul Bonnetain and Lucien Descaves.

Pierrot Assassin de sa Femme (Pierrot His Wife's Assassin).   Pantomine in one act by Paul Margueritte with music by Paul Vidal.

Les Quarts d'Heure (The Quarter of an Hours).   Two tableaux in prose: In the month of May II. Among Brothers. By Gustave Guiches and Henri Lavedan.

April 17: *Le Pain du Péché (The Bread of Sin)*. Drama in two acts and four tableaux in verse from Aubanel, by Paul Arène.

Matapan. Comedy in three acts in verse by Emile Moreau.

June 15: *La Prose (The Prose)*. Comedy in three acts in prose by Gaston Salandri.

Monsieur Lamblin. Comedy in one act in prose by Georges Ancey.

La Fin du Lucie Pellegrin (Lucie Pellegrin's End).   Comedy in one act in prose by Paul Alexis.

1888-1889

October 19: *Les Bouchers (The Butchers)*.   Drama in one act in verse by Fernand Icres.

Chevalerie Rustique (Rustic Chivalry).   Play in one act in prose by Giovanni Verga. Translated by Paul Salanges.

L'Amante du Christ (Christ's Lover).   Mystery in one act in verse by Rodolphe Darzens.

November 5: *Rolande*. Play in five acts in prose by Louis de Gramont.

December 10: *La Chance de Françoise (Françoise's Luck)*. Comedy in one act in prose by Porto-Riche.

La Mort du Duc d'Enghien (The Death of the Duke of Enghien). Drama in three tableaux in prose by Léon Hennique.

Le Cor fleuri (The Flowered Horn).   Fairytale in one act in verse by Ephraim Mikhaël.

January 15: *La Reine Fiamette (Queen Fiametta)*.   Drama in six acts in verse by Catulle Mendès. Music by Paul Vidal.

January 31: *Les Résignés (The Resigned)*.   Play in three acts in prose by Henry Céard.

L'Echéance (The Day of Reckoning).   Play in one act in prose by Jean Jullien.

March 19: *La Patrie en Danger (The Nation in Danger)*.   Drama in five acts by E. and J. de Goncourt.

May 2: *L'Ancien (The Former)*.   Drama in one act in verse by Léon Cladel.

Madeleine. Drama in three acts in prose by Émile Zola.

Les Inséparables (The Inseparables).   Comedy in three acts in prose by Georges Ancey.

May 3l: *Le Comte Witold.*   Play in three acts in prose by Stanislas Rzewuski.

Le Coeur Révélateur.   Play in one act, adapted from Poe's *Tell-Tale Heart*, by Ernest Laumann, from the translation by Charles Baudelaire.

La Casserole (The Pot).   Play in one act in prose by Oscar Méténier.

1889-1890

October 21: *Dans le Guignol (In the Guignol).*   Prologue in one act in prose by Jean Aicard.

Le Père Lebonnard (Father Lebonnard).   Play in four acts in verse by Jean Aicard.

November 27: *Au Temps de la Ballade (In Ballad Time).*   Play in one act in verse by Georges Bois.

L'École des Veufs (School for Widowers).   Comedy in five acts in prose by Georges Ancey.

January 10: *Le Pain d'autrui (The Bread of Others).*   Drama in two acts in prose by Ivan Turgenev. Translated by Armand Ephraim and Willy Schutz.

En Détresse (In Distress).   Play in one act in prose by Henry Fèvre.

February 25: *Les Frères Zemgano (The Brothers Zemgano).*   Play in three acts in prose by E. de Goncourt. Adapted for the stage by Paul Alexis and Oscar Méténier.

Deux Tourtereaux (Two Turtle Doves).   Play in one act in prose by Paul Ginisty and Jules Guérin.

March 21: *Ménages d'artistes (Artists' Ménages).*   Play in three acts in prose by Eugène Brieux.

Le Maître (The Master). Study of peasantry in three tableaux by Jean Jullien.

May 2: *Jacques Bouchard*. Play in one act in prose by Pierre Wolff.

Une Nouvelle école (A New School). Play in one act in prose by Louis Mullem.

La Tante Léontine (Aunt Leontine). Comedy in three acts in prose by Maurice Boniface and Édouard Bodin.

May 30: *Les Revenants (Ghosts)*. Drama in three acts by Henrik Ibsen. Translated by Rodolphe Darzens.

La Pêche (Fishing). Play in one act in prose by Henry Céard.

June 13: *Myrane*. Dramatic study in three acts in prose by Émile Bergerat.

Les Chapons (The Capons). Play in one act in prose by Lucien Descaves and Georges Darien.

1890-1891

October 29: *L'Honneur (The Honor)*. Comedy in three acts in prose by Henry Fèvre.

L'Amant de sa femme (The Wife's Lover). Parisian scenes by Aurélien Scholl.

La Belle Opération (The Fine Operation). Play in one act in prose by Julien Sermet.

December 25: *La Fille Elisa (Elisa, the Whore)*. Play in three acts in prose by E. de Goncourt. Adapted for the stage by Jean Ajalbert.

Conte de Noël (Christmas Story). Modern mystery in two tableaux in prose by Auguste Linert.

February 26: *La Meule (The Haystack)*. Play in four acts in prose by Georges Lecomte.

Jeune Bremier (Leading Man). Play in one act in prose by Paul Ginisty.

April 27: *Le Canard Sauvage (The Wild Duck).* Play by Henrik Ibsen. Translated by Armand Ephraim and Th. Lindenlaub.

May 26: *Nell Horn.* Drama in four acts and six tableaux in prose by J.-H. Rosny.

June 8: *Leurs filles (Their Daughters).* Play in two acts in prose by Pierre Wolff.

Les Fourches caudines (The Caudine Forks). Drama in one act in prose by Maurice Le Corbeiller.

Lidoire. Play in one act in prose by Georges Courteline.

July 6: *Coeurs Simples (Simple Hearts).* Play in one act in prose by Sutter Laumann.

Le Pendu (The Hanged). Play in one act in prose by Eugène Bourgeois.

Dans le Rêve (In The Dream). Comedy drama in one act in prose by Louis Mullem.

1891-1892

October 24: *Le Père Goriot.* Play in five acts in prose by Balzac. Adapted for the stage by Adolphe Tarabant.

November 30: *La Rançon (The Ransom).* Comedy in three acts in prose by Gaston Salandri.

L'Abbé Pierre (Father Pierre). Play in one act in prose by Marcel Prévost.

Un Beau soir (One Fine Evening). Comedy in one act in verse by Maurice Vaucaire.

December 21: *La Dupe (The Dupe).* Play in five acts in prose by Georges Ancey.

Son Petit Coeur (The Little Heart). Play in one act in verse by Louis Marsolleau.

February 2: *L'Envers d'une sainte (The Other Side of a Saint)*. Play in three acts in prose by François de Curel.

Blanchette. Play in three acts in prose by Eugène Brieux.

March 7: *L'Étoile Rouge (The Red Star)*. Play in three acts in prose by Henry Fèvre.

Seul (Alone). Play in two acts in prose by Albert Guinon.

April 29: *Simone*. Play in three acts in prose by Louis de Gramont.

Les Maris de leurs filles (Their Daughters' Husbands). Play in three acts in prose by Pierre Wolff.

June 8: *La Fin du Vieux temps (The End of the Old Days)*. Play in three acts in prose by Paul Anthelme.

June 27: *Péché d'amour (Love's Sin)*. Play in one act in prose by Michel Carré and Georges Loiseau.

Les Fenêtres (The Windows). Play in three acts in prose by Jules Perrin and Claude Couturier.

Mélie. Play in one act in prose by Jean Reibrach. Adapted for the stage by Georges Docquois.

1892-1893

November 3: *Le Grappin (The Grapnel)*. Comedy in three acts in prose by Gaston Salandri.

L'Affranchie (The Emancipated). Comedy in three acts in prose by Maurice Biollay.

November 29: *Les Fossiles (The Fossils)*. Play in four acts in prose by François de Curel.

January 16: *Le Ménage Brésile.* Play in one act in prose by Romain Coolus.

Mademoiselle Julie (Miss Julie). Tragedy in one act in prose by Auguste Strindberg. Translated by Charles de Casanove.

A Bas le progrès (Down With Progress). Satire in one act in prose by Edmond de Goncourt.

February 15: *Le Devoir (The Duty).* Play in four acts in prose by Louis Bruyerre.

March 27: *Mirages.* Drama in five acts in prose by Georges Lecomte.

April 27: *Valet de coeur (The Heart Valet).* Comedy in three acts in prose by Maurice Vaucaire.

May 29: *Les Tisserands (The Weavers).* Drama in five acts in prose by Gerhart Hauptmann. Translated by Jean Thorel.

June 12: *Ahasvere (Ahasuerus).* Drama in one act in prose by Herman Heijermans.

Mariage d'argent (Moneyed Mariage). Play in one act in prose by Eugène Bourgeois.

La Belle au Bois rêvant (Dreaming Beauty). Comedy in one act in verse by Fernand Mazade.

1893-1894

November 8: *Une Faillite (A Failure).* Play in four acts in prose by Bjørnstjerne Bjørnson. Adapted for the stage by Shurmann and Jacques Lemaire.

Le Poète et le financier (The Poet and the Financier). Play in one act in verse by Maurice Vaucaire.

December 26: *L'Inquiétude (The Worry).* Play in three acts in prose by Jules Perrin and Claude Couturier.

Amants éternels (Eternal Lovers).   Pantomime in three tableaux by André Corneau and H. Gerbault. Music by André Messager.

February 1: *L'Assomption de Hannele Mattern (The Assumption of Hannele Mattern).*   Dream poem in two parts by Gerhart Hauptmann. Translated by Jean Thorel. Music by Marschalk.

En l'attendant (Waiting for Him).   Comedy in one act in prose by Léon Roux.

February 23: *Une Journée parlementaire (A Day in Parliament).* Comedy in three acts in prose by Maurice Barrès.

April 25: *Le Missionnaire (The Missionary).*   Theatrical novel in five tableaux by Marcel Luguet.

List of Productions and First Performances at the
Théâtre de l'Oeuvre

1893-1894

May 17: *Pelléas and Mélisande.* Lyrical drama in five acts by Maurice Maeterlinck. Bouffes-Parisiens.

October 6: *Rosmersholm.* Drama in four acts by Henrik Ibsen. Translated by Count Prozor. Bouffes du Nord.

November 8: *An Enemy of the People.* Drama in five acts by Henrik Ibsen. Translated by Ad. Chennevière and H. Johansen. Bouffes du Nord.

December 13: *Ames solitaires (Solitary Souls).* Play in five acts by Gerhart Hauptmann. Translated by Alexandre Cohen. Bouffes du Nord.

February 13: *L'Araignée de cristal (The Crystal Cobweb).* One-act play in prose by Mme. Rachilde. Bouffes du Nord.

Beyond Human Power. I. Play in two acts by Bjørnstjerne Bjørnson. Translated by Count Prozor.

February 27: *Une Nuit d'avril à Ceos (An April Night at Chios).* One act in prose by Gabriel Trarieux. Bouffes du Nord.

L'Image (The Image). Play in three acts by Maurice Beaubourg.

April 3: *The Master Builder.* Drama in three acts by Henrik Ibsen. Translated by Count Prozor. Bouffes du Nord.

May 24: *La Belle au Bois dormant (Sleeping Beauty).* Fairy-drama in three acts by Henry Bataille and Robert d'Humières. Nouveau-Théâtre.

June 21: *Frères (Brothers)*. Drama in one act by Herman Bang. Translated by Viscount de Colleville and Fritz de Zepelin. Comédie-Parisienne.

La Gardienne (The Guardian). Poem by Henri de Régnier.

The Creditor. Tragi-comedy in one act in prose by August Strindberg. Translated by Georges Loiseau. Comédie-Parisienne.

1894-1895

November 6: *'Tis a Pity She's a Whore*. Drama in five acts by John Ford. Translated by Maurice Maeterlinck. Nouveau-Théâtre.

November 27: *La Vie muette (The Mute Life)*. Drama in four acts by Maurice Beaubourg. Nouveau-Théâtre.

December 13: *The Father*. Tragedy in three acts by August Strindberg. Translated by Georges Loiseau. Nouveau-Théâtre.

December 26: *An Enemy of the People*. Drama in five acts by Henrik Ibsen. Translated by Ad. Chennevière and H. Johansen. Nouveau-Théâtre.

January 22: *Le Chariot de Terre Cuite (The Toy Cart)*. Sanskrit drama in five acts attributed to Soudraka. Adapted by Victor Barrucand. Nouveau-Théâtre.

March 15: *La Scène (The Scene)*. Play in one act by André Lebey. Nouveau-Théâtre.

La Vérité dans le vin ou les Désagréments de la Galanterie. (Truth in Wine or the Troubles of Gallantry). Comedy in one act by Charles Collé.

Intérieur (Interior). Drama in one act by Maurice Maeterlinck.

Les Pieds Nickelés (Nickeled Feet). Comedy in one act by Tristan Bernard.

May 8: *L'Ecole de l'idéal (The School of the Ideal).* Play in three acts in verse by Paul Verola. Menus-Plaisirs.

Little Eyolf. Play in three acts by Henrik Ibsen. Translated by Count Prozor.

May 28: *Le Volant (The Steering Wheel).* Play in three acts by Judith Cladel. Menus-Plaisirs.

June 8: *Carmosine.* Comedy in three acts by Alfred de Musset.

June 22: *Brand.* Play in five acts by Henrik Ibsen. Translated by Count Prozor. Nouveau-Théâtre.

1895-1896

November 8: *Venice Preserv'd.* Play in five acts by Thomas Otway. Translated by Gyl Pené. Comédie-Parisienne.

December 16: *L'Anneau de Cakuntala (Shakuntala).* Heroic comedy in five acts and seven tableaux by Kalidasa. Adapted from the Hindu by A.-Ferdinand Herold. Comédie-Parisienne.

January 6: *Une Mère (A Mother).* Drama in three acts by Ellin Ameen. Translated by Count Prozor. Comédie-Parisienne.

Brocéliande. One act in verse by Jean Lorrain.

Les flaireurs (The Sniffers). Symbol in three acts by Charles van Lerberghe.

Des mots! des mots! (Words! Words!). One act in verse by Charles Quinel and René Dubreuil.

February 11: *Raphaël.* Play in three acts by Romain Coolus. Comédie-Parisienne.

Salome. Drama in one act by Oscar Wilde.

March 17. *Heraklea.* Drama in verse in three acts by Auguste Villeroy. Nouveau-Théâtre.

April 22: *La Fleur Palan enlevée (The Purloined Palan Flower)*. One act adapted from the Chinese by Jules Arène. Nouveau-Théâtre.

L'Errante (The Wanderer). Dramatic poem by Pierre Quillard.

La Dernière Croisade (The Last Crusade). Comedy in three acts by Maxime Gray.

May 6: *La Lépreuse. (The Leper)*. Legendary tragedy in three acts by Henry Bataille. Comédie-Parisienne.

May 20: *La Grande Galeoto (The Great Galeoto)*. Drama in three acts in verse preceded by a dialogue in prose by José Echegaray. (Mme. Ruth Rattazzi, Editor of *La Revue Internationale*.)

May 29: *Le Tandem*. Comedy in two acts by Léo Trezenik and Pierrou Soulaine. Nouveau-Théâtre.

La Brebis (The Sheep). Comedy in two acts by Edmond Sée.

June 17: *Pillars of Society*. Play in four acts by Henrik Ibsen. Translated by Bertrand and Ern. de Nevers. Nouveau-Théâtre.

1896-1897

November 12: *Peer Gynt*. Dramatic poem in five acts by Henrik Ibsen. Translated by Count Prozor. Nouveau-Théâtre.

December 10: *Ubu Roi ou les Polonais (King Ubu)*. Drama in five acts in prose by Alfred Jarry. Nouveau-Théâtre.

January 16: *La Motte de terre (The Clod of Earth)*. One act by Louis Dumur. Nouveau-Théâtre.

Beyond Human Power. I. Play in two acts by Bjørnstjerne Bjørnson. Translated by Alfred Jarry.

January 26: *Beyond Human Power*. II. Play in four acts by Bjørnstjerne Bjørnson. Translated by August Monnier and Littmanson. Nouveau-Théâtre.

March 5: *La Cloche Engloutie (The Sunken Bell)*. Dramatic tale in five acts by Gerhart Hauptmann. Translated by A.-Ferdinand Herold. Nouveau-Théâtre.

May 8: *Ton Sang (Your Blood)*. Contemporary tragedy in four acts by Henry Bataille. Nouveau-Théâtre.

May 15: *Le Fils de l'abbesse (The Abbess's Daughter)*. Thesis in three acts and four tableaux by Ambroise Herdey. Nouveau-Théâtre.

Le Fardeau de la liberté (The Weight of Liberty). Comedy in one act by Tristan Bernard.

June 23: *Love's Comedy*. Play in three acts by Henrik Ibsen. Translated by Viscount de Colleville and Fritz de Zepelin. Nouveau-Théâtre.

November 9: *John Gabriel Borkman*. Drama in four acts by Henrik Ibsen. Translated by Count Prozor. Nouveau-Théâtre.

January 8: *Le Revizor (The Inspector General)*. Play in five acts by Nikolas V. Gogol. Translated by Count Prozor. Nouveau-Théâtre.

January 22: *Rosmersholm*. Drama in four acts by Henrik Ibsen. Translated by Count Prozor.

Le Gage (The Wager). Play in one act by Frantz Jourdain.

February 18: *L'échelle (The Ladder)*. Social play in three tableaux by Gustave van Zype. Nouveau-Théâtre.

Le Balcon (The Balcony). Play in three acts by Gunnar Heiberg. Translated by Count Prozor.

May 3: *Aert*. Play in three acts by Romain Rolland. Nouveau-Théâtre.

May 18: *Morituri ou les Loups (Morituri or the Wolves)*. Play in three acts by Romain Rolland (pseud. Saint-Just). Nouveau-Théâtre.

June 20: *La Victoire (The Victory)*.   Tragedy in five acts by Saint-Georges de Bouhelier. Bouffes-Parisiens.

June 25: *The Master Builder*.   Drama in three acts by Henrik Ibsen. Translated by Count Prozor. Bouffes-Parisiens.

1898-1899

December 10: *Measure for Measure*.   Comedy in five acts by William Shakespeare. Translated by Louis Ménard. Cirque d'Eté.

February 9: *Noblesse de la terre (The Nobles of the Earth)*.   Play in four acts by Maurice de Faramond. Renaissance.

February 18: *An Enemy of the People*.   Drama in five acts by Henrik Ibsen.   Translated by Ad. Chennevière and H. Johansen. Renaissance.

May 18: *Fausta*. Play in four acts in verse with a prologue by Paul Sonnies. Nouveau-Théâtre.

June 6: *Le Joug (The Yoke)*.   Play in three acts by Lucien Mayrargue. Nouveau-Théâtre.

June 21: *Entretien d'un Philosophe avec la Maréchale (The Dialogue with the Maréchale)*. By Denis Diderot. Bouffes-Parisiens.

Le Triomphe de la Raison (The Triumph of Reason).   Play in three acts by Romain Rolland.

List of Productions and First Performances at
The Théâtre du Vieux-Colombier

1913-1914

October 22: *Une Femme Tuée par la douceur (A Woman Killed With Kindness)* by Thomas Heywood. *L'Amour Médecin (The Love Doctor)* by Molière.

November 11: *Les Fils Louverné (The Louverné Sons)* by Jean Schlumberger. *Barberine* by Alfred de Musset.

November 23: *Daisy* by Tristan Bernard. *L'Avare (The Miser)* by Molière.

November 24: *Pain de ménage (Family's Bread)* by Jules Renard. *Peur des coups (Fear of Beatings)* by Georges Courteline.

November 29: *Jeu de Robin et de Marion* by Rutebeuf.

December 22: *Farce du Savetier enragé (The Farce of the Enraged Shoemaker).*

January 1: *La Jalousie du Barbouillé* by Molière.

January 15: *L'Échange (The Exchange)* by Claudel.

February 9: *Le Testament du Père Leleu (Father Leleu's Will)* by Roger Martin du Gard. *La Navette (The Merry-Go-Round)* by Henri Becque.

March 10: *Les Frères Karamazov (The Brother's Karamazov)* by Dostoyevsky. Adapted by Jacques Copeau and Jean Croué.

April 25: *Eau de vie (Brandy)* by Henri Ghéon.

May 22: *Nuit des Rois (Twelfth Night)* by William Shakespeare.

1917-1918
New York

November 27: *Impromptu du Vieux-Colombier* by Jacques Copeau. *Fourberies de Scapin (The Rogueries of Scapin)* by Molière.

December 5: *Navette (The Merry-Go-Round)* by Henri Becque. *La Jalousie du Barbouillé* by Molière. *Le Carrosse du Saint-Sacrement (The Carriage of the Holy Sacrament)* by Prosper Mérimée.

December 11: *Barberine* by Alfred de Musset. *Pain de Ménage (Household Bread)* by Jules Renard.

December 25: *La Nuit des Rois (Twelfth Night)* by William Shakespeare.

January 8: *Nouvelle Idole (The New Idol)* by François de Curel.

January 23: *Frères Karamazov (The Brothers Karamazov)* by Dostoyevsky. Adapted by Jacques Copeau and Jean Croué.

January 31: *Surprise de l'amour (The Surprise of Love)* by Marivaux.

February 6: *La Traversée (The Crossing)* by Auguste Villeroy. *Poil de Carotte (Carrot Head)* by Jules Renard.

February 20: *Mauvais Bergers (Bad Shepherds)* by Octave Mirbeau.

March 5: *Petite Marquise (Little Marquise)* by Meilhac and Halévy. *L'Amour Médecin (The Love Doctor)* by Molière.

March 19: *L'Avare (The Miser)* by Molière.

April 2: *Paix chez soi (Peace at Home)* by Georges Courteline. *Testament du Père Leleu (Father Leleu's Will)* by Roger Martin du Gard.

April 2: *Chance de Françoise (Françoise's Luck)* by Georges de Porto-Riche.

1918-1919
New York

October 14: *Secret* by Henri Bernstein.

October 21: *Le Mariage de Figaro (The Marriage of Figaro)* by Beaumarchais.

October 28: *Blanchette* by Brieux.

November 4: *Georgette Lemeunier* by Maurice Donnay.

November 11: *Crainquebille* by Anatole France. *Voile du Bonheur (Happiness's Veil)* by Georges Clemenceau.

November 18: *La Femme de Claude (Claude's Wife)* by Alexandre Dumas.

November 25: *Le Médecin malgré lui (Doctor in Spite of Himself)* by Molière. *Gringoire* by Théodore de Banville.

December 2: *Rosmersholm* by Henrik Ibsen.

December 9: *Le Gendre de M. Poirier (M. Poirier's Son-in-Law)* by Emile Augier and Jules Sandeau.

December 16: *Les Caprices de Marianne (The Follies of Marianne)* by Alfred de Musset. *Le Fardeau de la Liberté (The Weight of Freedom)* by Tristan Bernard.

December 23: *Romanesques* by Edmond Rostand. *La Jalousie du Barbouillé* by Molière.

December 30: *Boubouroche* by Georges Courteline. *L'Énigme (The Enigma)* by Paul Hervieu.

January 6: *L'Avare (The Miser)* by Molière.

January 13: *Chatterton* by Alfred de Vigny.

January 20: *Frères Karamazov (The Brothers Karamazov)* by Dostoyevsky. Adapted by Jacques Copeau and Jean Croué.

January 27: *Le Menteur (The Liar)* by Pierre Corneille.

February 3: *L'Ami Fritz (Friend Fritz)* by Émile Erckmann and Alexandre Chatrian.

February 10: *Pelléas et Mélisande* by Maurice Maeterlinck.

February 17: *Washington* by Percy MacKaye.

February 24: *La Nuit des Rois (Twelfth Night)* by William Shakespeare.

March 3: *La Veine (Luck)* by Alfred Capus.

March 17: *Le Misanthrope (The Misanthrope)* by Molière.

1919-1920

February 10: *Le Conte d'hiver (The Winter's Tale)* by William Shakespeare.

March 5: *Le Paquebot Tenacity* by Charles Vildrac. *Le Carrosse du Saint-Sacrement (The Carriage of the Holy Sacrament)* by Prosper Mérimée.

April 10: *Oeuvres des athlètes (Atheletes' Works)* by Georges Duhamel.

April 27: *Les Fourberies de Scapin (The Rogueries of Scapin)* by Molière.

May 27: *Crommedeyre-le-Vieil* by Jules Romains.

July 1: *Phocas le Jardinier (Phocas the Gardener)* by Francis Viélé-Griffin. *Folle Journée (The Mad Day)* by Émile Mazaud. *La Coupe enchantée (The Enchanted Goblet)* by Lafontaine and Champmeslé.

1920-1921

October 15: *Le Médecin Malgré lui (The Doctor in Spite of Himself)* by Molière.

October 17: *Folle Journée (The Mad Day)* by Émile Mazaud.

October 19: *La Coupe enchantée (The Enchanted Goblet)* by La Fontaine and Champmeslé. *Pain de ménage (Household Bread)* by Jules Renard.

October 27: *La Surprise de l'Amour (The Surprise of Love)* by Marivaux. *La Jalousie du Barbouillé* by Molière.

November 5: *Phocas le Jardinier (Phocas the Gardener)* by Francis Viélé-Griffin.

November 29: *Le Paquebot Tenacity* by Charles Vildrac. *Le Carrosse du Saint-Sacrement (The Carriage of the Holy Sacrament)* by Prosper Mérimée.

December 22: *La Nuit des Rois (Twelfth Night)* by William Shakespeare.

December 29: *Les Fourberies de Scapin (The Rogueries of Scapin)* by Molière.

January 24: *Le Pauvre sous l'Escalier (The Poor Man Under the Stair Case)* by Henri Ghéon.

March 23: *La Mort de Sparte (Death of Sparta)* by Jean Schlumberger.

April 15: *Oncle Vania (Uncle Vania)* by Anton Chekhov.

May 13: *La Dauphine* by François Porché.

May 27: *L'Amour médecin (The Love Doctor)* by Molière. *Un Caprice (A Caprice)* by Alfred de Musset. *Le Testament du Père Leleu (Father Leleu's Will)* by Roger Martin du Gard.

1921-1922

October 15: *Au Petit Bonheur (Chance)* by Anatole France. *La Fraude (The Fraud)* by Louis Fallens.

October 26: *Le Mariage de Figaro (The Marriage of Figaro)* by Beaumarchais.

October 29: *Testament du Père Leleu (Father Leleu's Will)* by Roger Martin du Gard.

November 3: *La Navette (The Merry-Go-Round)* by Henri Becque.

November 6: *Le Caprice (The Caprice)* by Alfred de Musset.

November 30: *Les Frères Karamazov (The Brothers Karamazov)* by Dostoyevsky. Adapted by Jacques Copeau and Jean Croué.

December 5: *La Nuit des Rois (Twelfth Night)* by William Shakespeare.

December 19: *Crommedeyre-le-Vieil* by Jules Romains.

January 6: *Le Médecin malgré lui (The Doctor in Spite of Himself)* by Molière. *Pain de menage (Household Bread)* by Jules Renard.

January 25: *Le Misanthrope (The Misanthrope)* by Molière.

February 26: *La Jalousie du Barbouillé* by Molière.

March 7: *Amour livre d'Or (Love's Golden Book)* by Leo Tolstoy. *Mort joyeuse* (Happy Death) by Evreinov.

March 11: *L'Avare (The Miser)* by Molière.

March 13: *La Coupe enchantée (The Enchanted Cup)* by La Fontaine and Champmeslé.

April 10: *Le Paquebot Tenacity* by Charles Vildrac.

April 21: *Plaisirs du hasard (Chance Pleasures)* by René Benjamin.

June 6: *Saul* by André Gide.

1922-1923

October 14: *Le Mariage de Figaro (The Marriage of Figaro)* by Beaumarchais.

October 15: *Le Carrosse du Saint-Sacrement (The Carriage of the Holy Sacrament)* by Prosper Mérimée. *Le Paquebot Tenacity* by Charles Vildrac.

October 16: *Un Caprice (A Caprice)* by Alfred de Musset. *Le Testament du Père Leleu (Father Leleu's Will)* by Roger Martin du Gard. *Pain de Ménage (Household Bread)* by Jules Renard.

October 25: *Sophie Arnould* by Gabriel Nigond. *Pie Borgne* by René Benjamin. *Belle Haguenau* by Jean Variot.

November 15: *Le Menteur (The Liar)* by Pierre Corneille. *Maître Pathelin (Master Pathelin)*.

November 22: *Les Plaisirs du Hasard (Chance Pleasures)* by René Benjamin.

December 6: *Le Misanthrope (The Misanthrope)* by Molière.

December 14: *La Nuit des Rois (Twelfth Night)* by William Shakespeare.

December 21: *Michel Auclair* by Charles Vildrac.

January 27: *Sganarelle* by Molière. *Hyménée (Marriage)* by Gogol.

February 2: *Princesse Turandot* by Carlo Gozzi.

March 8: *Le Prologue improvisé (Improvised Prologue)* by Jacques Copeau. *Le Médecin malgré lui (The Doctor in Spite of*

Himself) by Molière.   *Un Caprice (A Caprice)* by Alfred de Musset.

March 22: *Le Misanthrope (The Misanthrope)* by Molière.   *La Coupe Enchantée (The Enchanted Goblet)* by La Fontaine and Champmeslé.

March 28: *Dardamelle* by Émile Mazaud.

April 4: *Folle Journée (Mad Day)* by Émile Mazaud.

May 15: *Bastos le Hardi (Bastos the Bold)* by Régis and de Veynes.

1923-1924

October 31: *L'Imbécile (The Imbecile)* by Pierre Bost.   *La Locandiera* by Carlo Goldoni.

November 8: *Bastos le Hardi (Bastos the Bold)* by Régis and de Veynes.

November 21: *Le Testament du Père Leleu (Father Leleu's Testament)* by Roger Martin du Gard.   *Pierre Borgne* by René Benjamin. *Folle Journée (Mad Day)* by Emile Mazaud.

December 18: *La Maison natale (Native House)* by Jacques Copeau.

January 3: *Le Misanthrope (The Misanthrope)* by Molière.

February 14: *Il faut que chacun soit à sa place (Each One Must Be in Place)* by René Benjamin.

April 3: *Le Paquebot Tenacity* by Charles Vildrac.   *Le Carrosse du Saint-Sacrement (The Carriage of the Holy Sacrament)* by Prosper Mérimée.

Notes

Notes: Introduction

[1] F. Sarcey, *Quarante ans de théâtre.* VII. "Les Surprises du divorce" by Alexandre Bisson, p. 277.

[2] Émile Zola, *Le Roman expérimental*, pp. 114-15.

Notes: Chapter 1

[1] Francis Prunier, *Le Théâtre Libre d'Antoine.* I, p. 20.

[2] Bettina Knapp, *Émile Zola*, p. 30.

[3] Prunier, *Les Luttes d'Antoine*, p. 48.

[4] Matei Roussou, *André Antoine*, p. 58.

[5] Samuel Montefiore Waxman, *Antoine and the Théâtre Libre*, p. 151.

Notes: Chapter 2

[1] André Antoine, *André Antoine's "Memories of the Théâtre-Libre."* Translated by Marvin A. Carlson. p. 81.

[2] Ibid., p. 84.

[3] Ibid.

[4] Ibid.

[5] Samuel M. Waxman, *Antoine and the Théâtre Libre*, p. 97.

[6] Matei Roussou, *André Antoine*, p. 73.

[7] Francis Prunier, *Théâtre Libre d'Antoine. Les Luttes d'Antoine*, p. 78.

[8] G. Renory, *La Réforme*, January 11, 1888.

[9] Roussou, p. 69.

[10] Antoine, p. 19.

[11] Ibid., p. 21.

[12] Roussou, p. 73.

[13] Antoine, p. 84.
[14] Prunier, p. 268.
[15] Ibid.
[16] Antoine, p. 27.
[17] Roussou, p. 92.
[18] Antoine, p. 47.
[19] Auguste Vitu, *Figaro*, October 12, 1887.
[20] Antoine, p. 106.
[21] Ibid., p. 43.
[22] Prunier, p. 144.
[23] Antoine, p. 56.
[24] Waxman, p. 179.
[25] Oscar Méténier, *L'Indépendence de l'Est*. November 20, 1887.
[26] Roussou, pp. 116, 169.
[27] Waxman, p. 58.
[28] Toby Cole and Helen K. Chinoy, *Actors on Acting*. Translated by Joseph M. Bernstein, pp. 217-222.
[29] Eugène Brieux, *Théâtre Complet*, I. p. vi.
[30] Waxman, p. 175.
[31] Ibid., p. 142.
[32] Antoine, p. 159.
[33] Ibid, p. 196.
[34] François de Curel, *Théâtre Complet*. II, p. 15.
[35] Ibid. Translated by Waxman, p. 158.
[36] Ibid. Translated by Waxman, p. 171.
[37] Curel, II, p. 142.
[38] Antoine, p. 210.

Notes: Chapter 3

[1] *André Antoine's "Memories of the Théâtre Libre."* Translated by Marvin A. Carlson., p. 61.
[2] J. Simmons, *Leo Tolstoy*, p. 538.
[3] Francis Prunier, *Théâtre Libre d'Antoine*. *Le Répertoire étranger*, p. 30.
[4] Ibid., p. 37.
[5] Henry Bauer, *L' Echo de Paris*. February 12, 1888.
[6] Henrik Ibsen, *Four Major Plays*, p. xiv.
[7] Antoine, p. 123.
[8] Prunier, p. 82.
[9] Antoine, p. 139.
[10] Samuel M. Waxman, *Antoine and the Théâtre Libre*. pp. 115-116.
[11] Antoine, p. 140.
[12] Ibsen, p. ixi.
[13] Ibid., p. xxviii.

[14] Waxman, p. 145.

[15] *The Goncourt Journals*, IV, p. 83.

[16] August Strindberg, *Seven Plays*. Translated by Arcid Paulson, p. 5.

[17] Ibid. Preface to *Miss Julie*, p. 66.

[18] Ibid., p. 71.

[19] Ibid, p. 72.

[20] Ibid., 74.

[21] Ibid., p. 73.

[22] Ibid., p. 75.

[23] Ibid.

[24] Antoine, p. 217.

[25] Gerhardt Hauptmann, *The Weavers*. Translated by Mary Morison, p. 117.

[26] Ibid., p. 131.

[27] Antoine, p. 219.

[28] Ibid.

[29] Waxman, p. 51.

Notes: Chapter 4

[1] *La Plume*, August 6, 1893.

[2] Gertrude R. Jaspers, *Adventures in the Theatre*, p. 2.

[3] Jacques Robichez, *Le Symbolisme au théâtre*, p. 58.

[4] Ibid., p. 115.

[5] Aurélien Lugné-Poë, *Le Sot du tremplin*, p. 200.

[6] Jaspers, p. 49.

[7] Ibid., p. 52.

[8] Bettina L. Knapp, *Maurice Maeterlinck*, pp. 41ff.

[9] *La Revue d'Art Dramatique*, May 15, 1891.

[10] J. Jullien, *Feuilleton de Paris*, May 22, 1893.

[11] Jaspers, p. 59.

[12] Knapp, p. 51.

[13] Robichez, p. 128.

[14] Jaspers, p. 61.

[15] Robichez, p. 132.

[16] *La Revue d'Art Dramatique*, Jan. 1, 1892.

[17] Jaspers, pp. 71-72.

Notes: Chapter 5

[1] Aurélien Lugné-Poë, *Parade*, p. 231.

[2] Croze, *La Plume*, 4 année, 1892, p. 310.

[3] Jacques Robichez, *Le Symbolisme au théâtre*, p. 164.   Letters from Maeterlinck to Lugné-Poë.

[4] *L'Echo de Paris*, May 9, 1893.

[5] *Encyclopédie du théâtre contemporain*, p. 50.

[6] J. Huret, "Conversation avec M. Maurice Maeterlinck," *Figaro*, May 17, 1892.

[7] Bettina L. Knapp, *Maurice Maeterlinck*, pp. 67-76.

[8] Françisque Sarcey, *Le Temps*, May 22, 1893.

[9] Octave Mirbeau, *L'Echo de Paris*, May 9, 1893.

[10] Jean Jullien, *Feuilleton de Paris*, May 22, 1893.

[11] Gertrude R. Jaspers, *Adventure in the Theatre*, p. 109.

[12] *La Plume*, 5 année, 1, 1893, p. 379.

[13] John Henderson, *The First Avant-Garde (1887-1894)*, p. 225.

[14] Albert Samain, *Mercure de France*, X, 1894, p. 361.

[15] Jaspers, pp. 145-147.

[16] Lugné-Poë, *Journal des Débats*, June 24, 1894.

[17] Aurélien Lugné-Poë, *Le Sot du tremplin*, p. 44.

[18] Ibid., p. 41.

[19] Robichez, p. 74.   Unpublished letter to Jullien, 1893, n.d.

[20] Knapp, p. 83.

Notes: Chapter 6

[1] David Thomas, *Henrik Ibsen*, vii, p. 449.

[2] Michael Meyer, *Ibsen*, p. 700.

[3] Ibid.

[4] Lugné-Poë, "Souvenirs sur Henrik Ibsen," *La Revue Hebdomadaire*, 37 année. Numero 3, 1928.

[5] *La Réserve.* September 27, 1893.

[6] Adolphe Brisson, *L'Estafette.* October 8, 1893.

[7] Alfred Valette, *Le Mercure de France.* IX, 1893.

[8] Marcel Bailliot. *La Plume*, 5 année, 1893.

[9] Meyer, p. 719.

[10] Ibid.

[11] Ibid.

[12] Ibid., p. 713.

[13] Gertrude R. Jaspers, *Adventure in the Theatre*, p. 127.

[14] *La Justice.* May 31, 1892.

[15] Jacques Robichez, *Le Symbolisme au théâtre*, p. 267.

[16] Meyer, p. 715.

[17] Ibid., p. 716.

[18] Robichez, p. 249.   From Maeterlinck's "Le Tragique quotidien" in *Le trésor des humbles*, p. 164.

[19] Ibid.

[20] Ibid.

[21] *Journal*, May 9, 1895.

[22] Robichez, p. 279.   From Just Bing, *Morgenbladet.* May 13, 1895.

[23] Ibid.

[24] Dorothy Knowles, *La Réaction idéaliste au théâtre depuis 1890*, p. 188.

[25] Meyer, p. 728.

[26] Jaspers, p. 167.   From Count Prozor's preface to Berteval, *Le Théâtre d'Ibsen.*

[27] R. H. Sherard, *The Humanitarian.* January, 1897.

[28] James Hurt, *Cataline's Dream*, p. 38.

[29] Ibid., p. 56.

[30] Jules Lemaître, *Les Contemporains*, VI, pp. 225-270.

[31] Léon Daudet, *L'Entre-deux guerres*, p. 198.   Francisque Sarcey, *Quarante ans de théâtre*, VIII, p. 338.

[32] Robichez, "Lettre inédite de Lugné-Poë au Comte Prozor."

[33] Léon Xanrof, *Paris.* Paris. December 14, 1896.

[34] Catulle Mendès, *Journal.* December 16, 1896.

[35] Meyer, p. 543.   From G. B. Shaw, "Peer Gynt in Paris," *The Saturday Review*, LXXXII, 1896.

[36] Ibid., p. 743.

[37] Jaspers, p. 220.

[38] *Le Mercure de France*, XIII, 1895, p. 124.

[39] *Le Temps.* November 22, 1897.

[40] Robichez, p. 437.   Unpublished letter from Ibsen to Count Prozor. December 5, 1897.

[41] Lugné-Poë, "A Propos de l'inutilité du théâtre au théâtre," *Mercure de France.* October, 1896.

[42] Ibid.

Notes: Chapter 7

[1] Noel Arnaud, *Alfred Jarry*, p. 221.

[2] Alfred Jarry, *Tout Ubu*, p. 149.

[3] Ibid., p. 204.

[4] Ibid., p. 113.

[5] Lugné-Poë, *La Parade*, p. 177.

[6] Arnaud, p. 239.

[7] Lugné-Poë, *Acrobaties*, p. 181.

Notes: Chapter 8

[1] *Le Journal.* November 10, 1896. *L'Eclair.* November 17, 1896.

[2] *Rappel.* January 29, 1895.

[3] *République.* January 21, 1895.

[4] A. Ferdinand Herold, *Le Mercure de France.* XIII, 1895.

[5] *La Revue Blanche.* 8, 1895, p. 186.

[6] Jules Lemaître, *Impressions de théâtre.* IX, p. 27.

[7] Jacques Robichez, *Le Symbolisme au théâtre,* p. 313.

[8] Bettina L. Knapp, *Theatre and Alchemy,* p. 220.

[9] Vervourt, *Jour. December 13, 1896.*

[10] Jean de Tinan, *Mercure de France,* XVII, 1896.   H. Fouquier, *Figaro.* February 12, 1896.

[11] *The Letters of Oscar Wilde.* Edited by Rupert Hart-Davis. Letter to Robert Ross, March 10, 1896 from Reading Gaol. p. 399.

[12] *Letters of Nikolai Gogol.* Edited by Carl R. Proffer. pp. 54-55.

[13] Henri Bauer, *L'Echo de Paris.* January 19, 1898.

[14] Gogol, pp. 54-55.

[15] *Le Cri de Paris.* January 16, 1898.

[16] Robichez, p. 458. Letter to Saint-Georges de Bouhélier, July 20, 1898.

[17] *L'Echo de Paris.* October 7, 1898.

Notes: Chapter 9

[1] Maurice Kurtz, *Jacques Copeau. Biographie d'un théâtre,* p. 62.

[2] Ibid., p. 20. From Jacques Copeau, *Critique d'un autre temps,* p. 227.

[3] André Boll, *Jacques Rouché,* p. 20.

[4] Ibid.

[5] Jacques Copeau, *Souvenirs du Vieux-Colombier,* p. 35. See Jean Schlumberger, "Le Théâtre," *Nouvelle Revue Française.* July 1, 1914.

[6] Francis Jourdain was asked to do the remodeling of the theatre.

[7] Henri Ghéon, "Le théâtre," *Nouvelle Revue Française,* December 1, 1913, p. 347.

[8] Toby Cole and Helen K. Chinoy, *Actors on Acting,* p. 223.   From *Nouvelle Revue Française,* September, 1913.   Translated by Joseph M. Bernstein.

Notes: Chapter 10

[1] Jacques Copeau, *Souvenirs du Vieux-Colombier*, p. 24.

[2] Bettina Knapp, *Louis Jouvet Man of the Theatre*, p. 28. From Copeau, *Souvenirs*, p. 25. Jacques Copeau, *Régistres du Vieux-Colombier*. III, p. 125.

[3] Lucien Aguettand told me this, 1952.

[4] "La Jalousie du Barbouillé," *Comoedia-Illustré*, February 20, 1914.

[5] Paul Claudel, *Mémoires improvisés*, p. 271.

[6] Jean Sarment, *Charles Dullin*, p. 93.

[7] Jacques Copeau, *Régistres*, III, p. 166.

[8] Jacques Copeau, *Nouvelle Revue Française*. May 1, 1913.

[9] Copeau, *Régistres*. III, p. 37.

[10] Henri de Régnier, *Le Journal des Débats*. April 10, 1911.

[11] Charles Dullin, "Je fus bien surpris d'entendre une voix," *Ce sont les dieux qu'il nous faut*.

[12] Ibid.

[13] Knapp, *Louis Jouvet*, p. 36. From Matei Roussou, *Choses de Théâtre*. I, 1922, p. 240.

[14] Harold Clurman, "More About Copeau of Paris," *Post*. January 8, 1927.

[15] Copeau, *Régistres*. IV. p. 204.

[16] Copeau, *Souvenirs*, p. 37.

[17] Ibid., p. 31

[18] Ibid., p. 45.

[19] Claude Roger-Marx, "La Nuit des Rois," *Comoedia-Illustré*. January 15, 1914.

[20] Copeau, *Souvenirs*, p. 33.

[21] Kurtz, p. 52.

[22] Ibid.

[23] Copeau, *Régistres*, III, pp. 200, 202. See also Jacques Copeau, *Notes sur le métier de comédien*, p. 18.

Notes: Chapter 11

[1] Toby Cole and Helen K. Chinoy, *Actors on Acting*. From "Un Essai de rénovation dramatique." Translated by Joseph Bernstein, p. 224.

[2] Ibid., p. 356

[3] Ibid., p. 360

[4] Lee Simonson, *The Stage is Set*, p. 353.

[5] Ibid, p. 358.

[6] Ibid., p. 367.

[7] Cole and Chinoy, *Actors on Acting*, p. 369.

[8] Jacques Copeau, *Oeuvres de Molière*, pp. 64-65.

[9] Jacques Copeau, *Notes sur le métier de comédien*, p. 25.

[10] Ibid., p. 29.

[11] Jacques Copeau, "Education de l'acteur," 1919. *Ecrits sur le théâtre.* From *Journal*, p. 49.

[12] Ibid., pp. 51-53.

[13] Louis Jouvet, Preface to *Les Fourberies de Scapin*, pp. 17-20.

[14] Jacques Copeau, *Régistres* IV, p. 178.

[15] Ibid., p. 181.

[16] Jouvet, pp. 44-46.

[17] Jacques Copeau, *Appel. Régistre.* I, p. 186.

[18] Ibid., p. 220. "Conférence prononcée par Copeau à Harvard," avril, 1917.

[19] Jacques Copeau, *Régistres.* III, p. 140.

[20] Charles Dullin, *Ce sont les dieux qu'il nous faut*, p. 215.

[21] Copeau, *Régistres.* III, p. 140.

[22] Copeau, *Régistres.* IV, p. 188.

Notes: Chapter 12

[1] Bettina Knapp, *Louis Jouvet Man of the Theatre*, p. 58.   From "Le Théâtre," *Nouvelle Revue Française*, March 1, 1920, p. 461.

[2] Maurice Kurtz, *Jacques Copeau*, p. 99.

[3] Ibid., p. 112.

[4] Ibid., p. 118. Letter to Jouvet. February 5, 1916.

[5] Ibid, p. 125.

[6] Ibid, p. 126.

[7] Ibid., p. 127. *Amis du Vieux-Colombier.* Published in Program Notes, 1920.

[8] Ibid.

[9] Ibid., p. 151.

Bibliography

Antoine, André, *André Antoine's "Memories of the Théâtre-Libre."* Translated by Marvin A. Carlson. Edited by H. D. Albright. Coral Gables, Florida: University of Miami Press, 1964.

Arnaud, Noel, *Alfred Jarry.* Paris: La Table Ronde, 1974.

Barrucand, Victor, Preface to *Le Chariot de Terre Cuite.* Paris: Payot, 1928.

Bauer, Henry, *L'Echo de Paris.* 1887-1899.

Becque, Henri, *Oeuvres complètes. Souvenirs d'un Auteur Dramatique.* VI. Paris: Crès, 1924-1926.

Boll, André, *Jacques Rouché.* Paris: Denoel, 1937.

Brandes, Georg. "Henrik Ibsen en France," *Cosmopolis.* V, 1897.

Brieux, Eugène, *Théâtre Complet.* I. Paris: Librairie Stock, 1921.

Brisson, Adolphe, *Le Théâtre et les Moeurs.* III. Paris: Flamarion, 1908.

—. *Estaphette.* October 8, 1893.

Claretie, Jules. *Profils de Théâtre.* Paris: Gaultier-Magnier, n.d.

Claudel, Paul, *Mémoires Improvisées.* Paris: Gallimard, 1969.

Clurman, Harold, *Post.* January 8, 1927.

Cole, Toby and Chinoy, Helen Krich, *Actors on Acting.* New York: Crown Publishers, 1949.

Collection Rondel, Dossier Théâtre-Libre. Bibliothèque de l'Arsenal, Paris.

Collection Rondel, Dossier de l'Oeuvre. Bibliothèque de l'Arsenal, Paris.

Comedia-Illustre. 1913-1918.

Copeau, Jacques, *Souvenirs du Vieux-Colombier.* Paris: Nouvelles Editions latines, 1931.

—. *Notes sur le métier de comédien.* Paris: Michel Brien, 1955.

—. Les Régistres du Vieux-Colombier. Appels. I. Paris: Gallimard, 1974.

—. Les Régistres du Vieux-Colombier. Oeuvres de Molière. Paris: Gallimard, 1979.

—. Les Régistres du Vieux-Colombier. III. Paris: Gallimard, 1979.

—. Les Régistres du Vieux-Colombier. IV. Paris: Gallimard, 1984.

Curel, François, de, Théâtre complet. I. Paris: Editions Georges Crès et Co., 1920.

—. Théâtre complet. II. Paris: Albin Michel, n.d.

Daudet, Léon, L'Entre Deux-Guerres. Paris: Nouvelle Librairie Nationale, 1905.

Doumic, René, De Scribe à Ibsen. Paris: Perrin, 1896.

Dullin, Charles, Ce sont les dieux qu'il nous faut. Paris: Gallimard, 1969.

Encyclopédie du Théâtre Contemporain. I. Paris: Collection de France, 1957. Edited by Gilles Queant, Frederic Towarnick, Aline Elmayan.

Fanger, Donald, The Creation of Nikolai Gogol. Cambridge, Mass.: Harvard University Press, 1979.

Fouquier, Henri, Figaro. 1887-1899.

Goncourt, Jules et Edmond, Journals. Edited and translated by Lewis Galantière. Garden City: Doubleday and Co., 1958.

Hauptmann, Gerhardt, The Weavers. New York: B. W. Huebsch, 1913. Translated by Mary Morison.

Henderson, John, A. The First Avant-Garde. 1887-1894.

Herold, Ferdinand, Le Mercure de France. XIII, 1895.

Hobson, Harold, French Theatre Since 1830. London: John Calder, 1979.

Hurt, James, Catiline's Dream. Urbana: University of Illinois Press, 1972.

Huret, J. "Conversation avec M. Maurice Maeterlinck," Figaro. May 17, 1892.

Huygue, René, Les Contemporains. Paris: Tisne, 1939.

Ibsen, Henrik, Four Major Plays. New York: New American Library, 1965.

Jarry, Alfred, Tout Ubu. Paris: Le Livre de Poche, 1962.

Jaspers, Gertrude, R. *Adventure in the Theatre.* New Brunswick: Rutgers University Press, 1947.

Journal, May 9, 1895.

Journal des Débats, 1893-1896.

Jouvet, Louis, Preface to *Les Fourberies de Scapin.*

—. "Le théâtre," *Nouvelle Revue Française,* March 1, 1920.

Jullien, Jean, *Feuilleton de Paris,* May 22, 1893.

—.   *Le Théâtre Vivant, Essai Théorique et Pratique.*   Paris: Charpentier-Fasquelle, 1892.

Knapp, Bettina, *Louis Jouvet Man of the Theatre.* New York: Columbia University Press, 1958.

—. *Maurice Maeterlinck.* Boston: Twayne Publishers, G. K. Hall, 1975.

—. *Theatre and Alchemy.* Detroit: Wayne State University Press, 1980.

Knowles, Dorothy, *La Réaction Idéaliste au Théâtre Depuis 1890.*   Paris: Droz, 1934.

Kurtz, Maurice, *Jacques Copeau. Biographie d'un Théâtre.* Paris: Nagel, 1950.

La Justice. May 31, 1892.

La Plume. 1889-1899.

La Revue d'Art Dramatique. 1886-1899.

La Revue Blanche. 1891-1899.

L'Eclair. 1896.

Lefranc, F. *Revue d'Art Dramatique.* XXII, 1891.

Lemaître, Jules, *Les Contemporains.* VI. Paris: Société Française d'imprimerie et de librairie, n.d.

—. *Impressions de Théâtre.* V. VI. VIII. IX. Paris: Société Française d'imprimerie et de librairie, 1891-1896.

Le Mercure de France. I-XXXII. 1890-1899.

Letters of Oscar Wilde. Edited and published by Rupert Hart-Davis. London, 1962.

Letters of Nikolai Gogol. Translated by Carl R. Proffer and Vera Krivoshein. Edited by Carl R. Proffer. Ann Arbor: The University of Michigan Press, 1967.

Lugné-Poë, Aurélien, "A Propos de l'inutilité du théâtre au théâtre," *Mercure de France,* October, 1896.

—. *La Parade.* I. Paris: Gallimard, 1931.

—. *Le Sot du tremplin,* II. Paris: Gallimard, 1930.

—. *Acrobaties,* III. Paris: Gallimard, 1931.

—. *Sous les étoiles,* IV. Paris: Gallimard, 1933.

—. *Ibsen.* Paris: Rieder, 1936.

—. "Souvenirs sur Henrik Ibsen," *Revue hebdomadaire.* 37 année. Numéro 3, 1928.

Nion, F. de, "Les Volontaires du Théâtre," *Théâtre.* December 16, 1892.

Noel, E. and Stoullig, Ed. *Les Annales du Théâtre et de la Musique.* Paris: Charpentier-Fasquelle, 1891.

Nouvelle Revue Française. 1913-1920.

Meyer, Michael, *Ibsen.* Garden City, N. Y.: Doubleday & Co., 1971.

Mendès, Catulle, *Journal.* November 16, 1896.

Méténier, Oscar, *L'Indépendence de l'Est.* May 20, 1887.

Mirbeau, Octave, *L'Echo de Paris.* May 9, 1893.

Prunier, Francis, *Le Théâtre Libre d'Antoine. Le Répertoire étranger.* Paris: Minard, 1958.

—. *Les Luttes d'Antoine.* Paris: Minard, 1964.

Renary, G., *La Réforme.* January 11, 1888.

Robichez, Jacques, *Lugné-Poë.* Paris: L'Arche, 1955.

—. *Le Symbolisme au Théâtre.* Paris: L'Arche, 1957.

Roussou, Matei, *André Antoine.* Paris: L'Arche, 1954.

Sarcey, Françisque, *Quarante Ans de Théâtre.* VIII. Paris: Bibliothequè des annales politiques et littéraires, 1902.

Sarment, Jean, *Charles Dullin*. Paris: Calman-Levy, 1950.

Shaw, George Bernard, *Dramatic Opinions and Essays*. I. New York: Brentano, 1909.

—. *"Peer Gynt* in Paris," *The Saturday Review*. LXXXII, 1896.

Sherard, R. H. *The Humanitarian*. January, 1897.

Simmons, Ernest, J. *Leo Tolstoy*. Boston: Little, Brown & Co., 1946.

Simonson, Lee, *The Stage is Set*. New York: Dover Pub., 1946.

Strindberg, August, *Seven Plays*. New York: Bantam Classic, 1960.

Thalasso, Adolphe, *Le Théâtre Libre*. Paris: Mercure de France, 1909.

Thomas, David, *Henrik Ibsen*. New York: Grove Press, 1983.

Touroude, H. *République*. January 21, 1895.

Vercourt, *Jour*. December 13, 1896.

Vitu, Auguste, *Figaro*. October 12, 1887.

Waxman, Samuel, M. *Antoine and the Théâtre Libre*. New York: Benjamin Bloom, 1926. Reissued, 1968.

Zola, Émile, *Le Roman Expérimental*. Paris: Charpentier, 1880.

—. *Le Naturalisme au Théâtre*. Paris: Charpentier, 1889.